PRIMARY PRODIGIES

CHAPTER 2 WORKBOOK

ProdigiesMusic.com

Level 2, Book 2

By Robert Young & Chris Hazewski

Edited By Samantha Young & Laura Green

Art & Illustrations By Aaron Poole & Rob Young

Videos By Jeff Sedwick & Rob Young

Music By Michael Lining & Rob Young

Published by: Young Music, LLC

ISBN: 978-1-7320173-4-4

2358 Dutch Neck Road
Smyrna, DE 19977

Table of Contents

Foreword

Parents! Teachers! Prodigies! Lend us your ears! Primary Prodigies Chapter 2 has FINALLY arrived and we're so very excited.

This is the 12th workbook from the Prodigies Team and I, and it's been an amazing adventure with you all so far. We hope the fun never stops.

As we move into Primary 2 though, please know that this is a more difficult chapter.

Students, in this book, you will focus on the nuances of the Treble Clef as we learn about the important concept of intervals. This book marks a significant point in your growth as young musicians and theorists. You, young prodigies, will be able to impress your friends while playing world famous songs & melodies that will level up your musical ears forever!

Many of us here at Prodigies have our degrees in music, and the concepts you'll learn in this book are what many of us learned in college. As advanced as it is, though, we've done our best to make these concepts approachable, colorful, and fun. We're confident that you'll come out on the other side understanding music on a whole new level.

Teachers, thank you so much for the hard work you put into educating our youth and providing them with the unique gift of musicality. As educators ourselves, we know how hard it can be and we will always strive to support your efforts to the best of our ability.

As always, we welcome all of your feedback. We know that there is more than one means to an end in music and we're open to ideas and edits for future editions.

Parents, last but certainly not least! There's a good chance you're playing the role of both parent and teacher, and for that, we give you a huge virtual hug! None of these young prodgies would exist without you, so thanks for bringing these bright stars into our musical universe!

We're over the moon with excitement for Primary Chapter 2. Let's begin!

- Mr. Rob and the Prodigies Team

PS - There's a good chance you're singing the Prodigies Theme Song in your head right now, turn to page 99 for the sheet music. Good luck, it can be tricky to play those 3rds **legato** (musician speak for smoothly and evenly).

Talking the Musical Talk

On your musical journey, it helps to be excited about both the progress you've made and the new challenges to come.

With greater musical knowledge, comes great musical power, but to effectively identify & communicate what you're hearing and playing, you'll need an expanded vocabulary to help you talk the musical talk.

Talking music theory is a bit like a secret language that only your fellow musos can understand. We've already learned some of the lingo like the Solfege names, the scale degrees, and the chords "one," "four," & "five." In this chapter, we'll pull back the curtain on some of this music theory biz and uncover what the pros know

Up until now, we've been simplifying a lot of bigger ideas. For example, we've talked about musical steps like C to D, and musical skips like C to E. What about bigger skips from C to F, or even smaller steps like from C to C#?

Here in Primary 2, we'll dive deeper into the relationship between the 7 C Major Notes that you know so well, and we'll even meet the 5 chromatic notes we haven't discussed much.

Not Just Steps and Skips

Like we were saying before, not all steps and skips are created equal.

E to F, a STEP, is not the same distance as G to A. These are both Intervals of a 2nd, but one is bigger (major) than the other (minor).

In this book, we'll learn about these subtle differences, we'll learn the lingo that describes them, and we'll observe how dramatically these subtle distinctions can affect the sound of our music.

In Primary Chapter 1 , we used SKIPS to build chords and play more powerful musical patterns called arpeggios (like C E G, D F A, F A C, etc).

These "SKIPS" however, are better identfied as THIRDS, and we'll learn exactly why in this book.

Now as we expand our vocabulary, we'll also start going outside of our C Major scale we've focused on so far. We'll meet other notes, work a bit above and a bit below our usual range, voice multiple octaves, and cover more musical terrain.

Up until now, we've been working almost entirely DIATONICALLY, i.e. within a key. In this Chapter, we will still do a lot of work diatonically in C Major, but we'll also run into the keys of F Major & G Major. Then toward the end of the chapter, we'll explore the entire alphabet of musical notes CHROMATICALLY.

Whole Steps and Half Steps

In Chapter 1, when we talked about STEPS, we were talking about moving from one note to the next note DIATONICALLY (within the key or scale).

But like we said, not all steps are created equal. In fact, there are 2 different types of steps to understand...the HALF STEP and the WHOLE STEP.

A half step is one semitone, and it's the smallest musical distance we can have (like from Ti to Do).

A whole step is two semitones, and is a more common musical distance (like Do to Re & Re to Mi).

Looking at the graphic below, the bells show us the scale DIATONICALLY (just the C Major notes).

Even though C to D is only a step away within the scale (no bells in between), there IS another note there (C#, which is not part of the C Major Scale). This is a WHOLE STEP (two semitones).

Like C to D, E to F is also a step, but it's only one space away. This step from E to F is a HALF STEP.

So, you might say, "D is a WHOLE STEP higher than C and F is a HALF STEP higher than E." Remember, not all steps are created equally.

We'll get into the subtle difference between a HALF STEP and a WHOLE STEP more in Section 2 of this book, but taking a quick look now will help you get a feel for what's ahead!

You can see it laid out on a piano as well below. Notice how the Whole Step from C to D has 2 red arrows where the Half Step from E to F is just the 1. This subtle difference has a BIG musical impact on the sounds and emotions that you get out of your music.

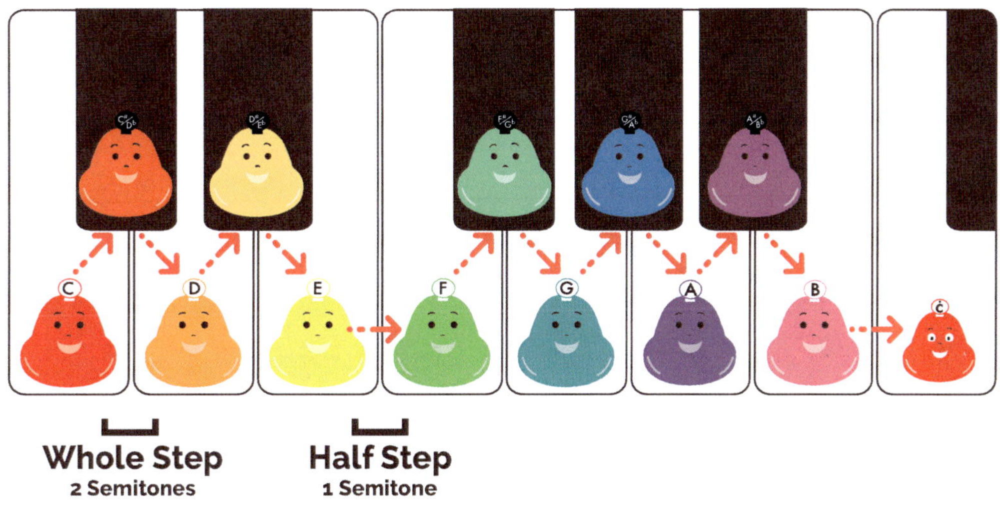

Building the Major Scale

Using what we now know about steps, we can explain the C Major Scale above a bit better!

C to D is a WHOLE step

D to E is a WHOLE step

E to F is a HALF step

F to G is a WHOLE step

G to A is a WHOLE step

A to B is a WHOLE step

B to C is a HALF step

Put it all together, and you have:

WHOLE - WHOLE - HALF - WHOLE - WHOLE - WHOLE - HALF

Which is often abbreviated as:

WWHWWWH

What's even cooler is that this is the pattern for all major scales!

If you're using a guitar or piano, you can start on any note and follow this pattern... you don't even need to know the note names!

If you have a chromatic instrument, give it a try! Does it sound like the major scale?

Not Just Color-Coded Music

It's preposterous, we know, but part of furthering our musical studies means moving away from color-coded music to more traditional black-and-white music. Like Primary Chapter 1, you'll play & work more and more without the colors in hopes of prepping you for the world of non-Prodigies sheet music!

We'll still have plenty of colorful sheet music in this book (and in future Primary books), because we believe that the colors serve as an important tool for developing your musical ear. They are another set of patterns for our brains to latch on to, and they'll help you draw connections between other musical concepts as we go.

Still, take the time to challenge yourself with the black-and-white music as it will become more and more necessary to complete the activities in this book.

Chapter 2 Warm-Up Duet: "Foamy"

Almost this entire chapter is going to be focused on the idea of INTERVALS, which is a way of talking about the relationship between two musical notes.

One way to experience those intervals in a very obvious fashion is to play a duet with a friend.

While Player 1 plays the top line, Player 2 plays the bottom line. As the notes ring out together, they create a harmony!

The harmony, or relationship, between the two notes is what intervals (and this book) is all about.

So to start, practice playing this with a friend and simply observe (with your ears) the sound of your two musical lines happening at the same time.

Take it slow -- like really slow at first! The famous Russian composer and virtuoso performer Rachmaninoff was known to practice his pieces incredibly slow (and by some accounts, only at this slower tempo). But when performance time came, he would play at blinding speeds and never miss a note!

Plus, taking it slow will allow you to focus on the sound of the harmonies you're creating together!

If you find yourself playing it alone, take it even slower and read both lines at once.

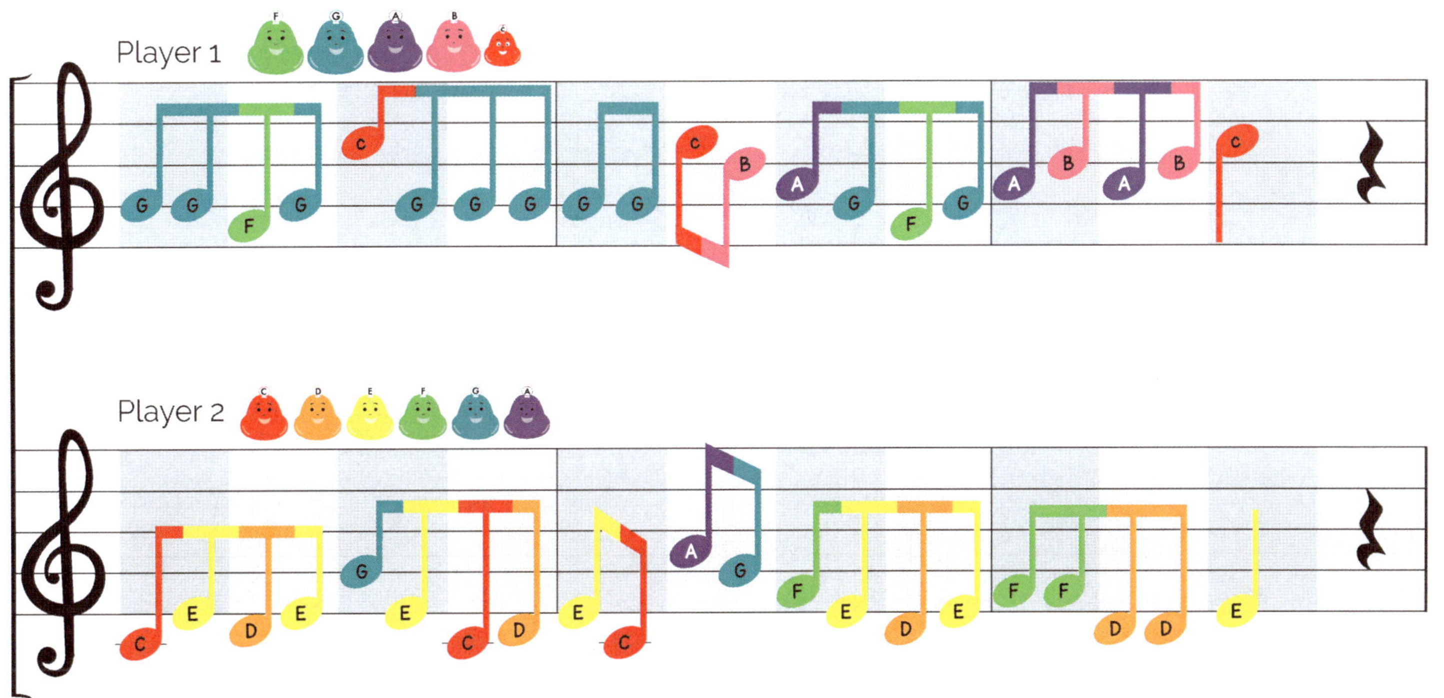

Chords, Chords, Chords

The desk bells' unique timbre make them an exceptional candidate for carrying a melody. In our conversation about intervals though, we'll end up implying chords **melodically** and **harmonically**.

We won't spend much time on chords in this chapter, but as a quick review, you should be familiar with the C Major (C E G), G Major (G B D), & F Major (F A C) chords.

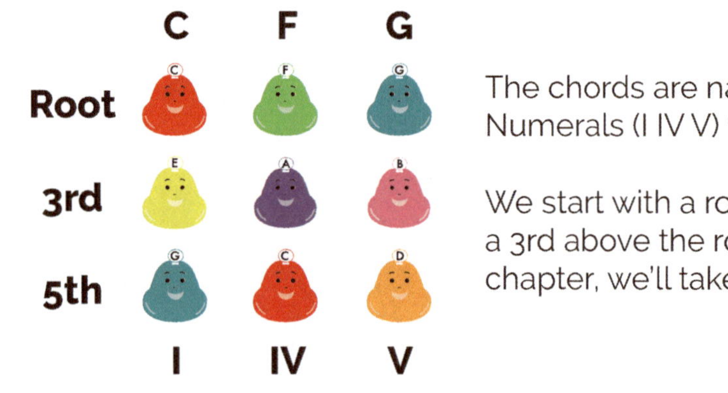

The chords are named from their root note and we use Roman Numerals (I IV V) to represent them.

We start with a root note, and then add two more notes -- one a 3rd above the root & a note a 5th above the root. In this chapter, we'll take a closer look at what that means!

There are also a handful of chords in C Major that we haven't really studied yet. You've probably run into these on your own just by playing around on the bells, so below we've listed out all the triads possible within C Major.

The ones we're less familiar with are the 3 minor chords (D minor, E minor, and A minor) and the 1 diminished chord (B diminished). We'll talk more about minor & diminished intervals in this book & more about similar chords in the next book.

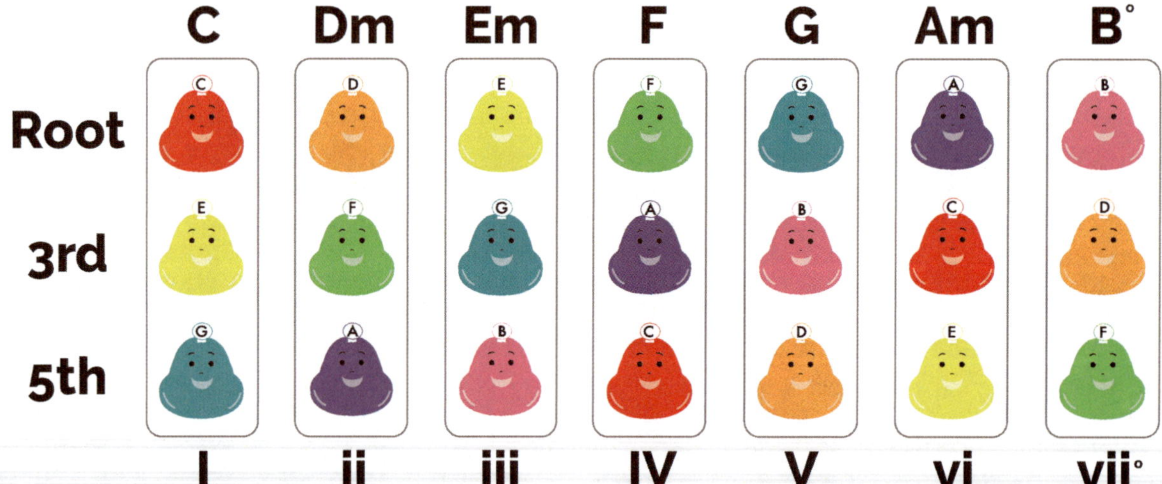

If this seems confusing or overwhelming, that's okay -- we'll work our way up to understanding all of this over the next two books!

If you feel comfortable with the above chart, take a moment to read the letter names within each chord box! Try playing them on your instrument and listen closely to the color of the chords!

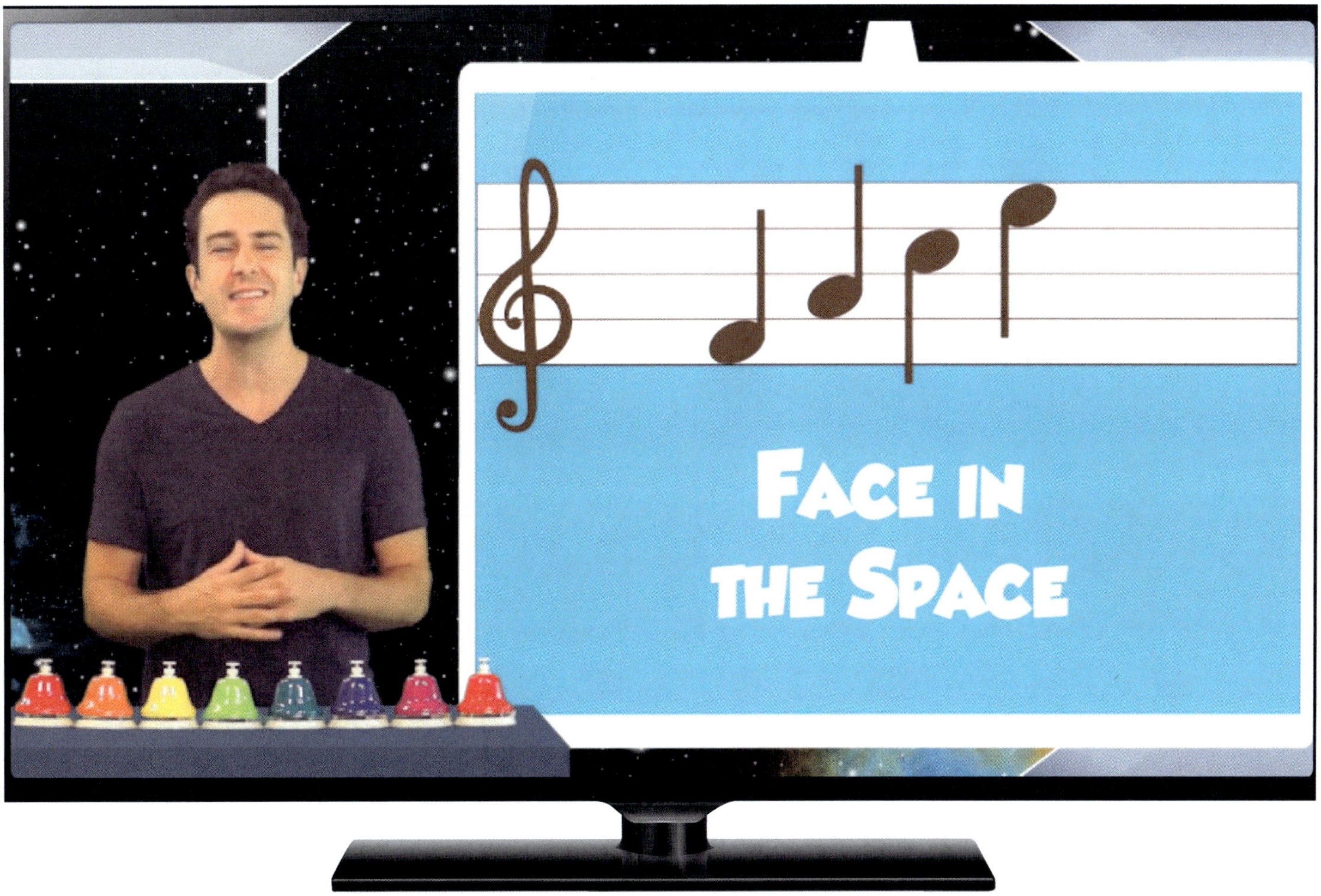

THE TREBLE CLEF

Section 2.1 (Part 1 of 2)

2.1 Intervals in C Major

Play the Piece Below to See & Hear the Sounds of Intervals in C Major

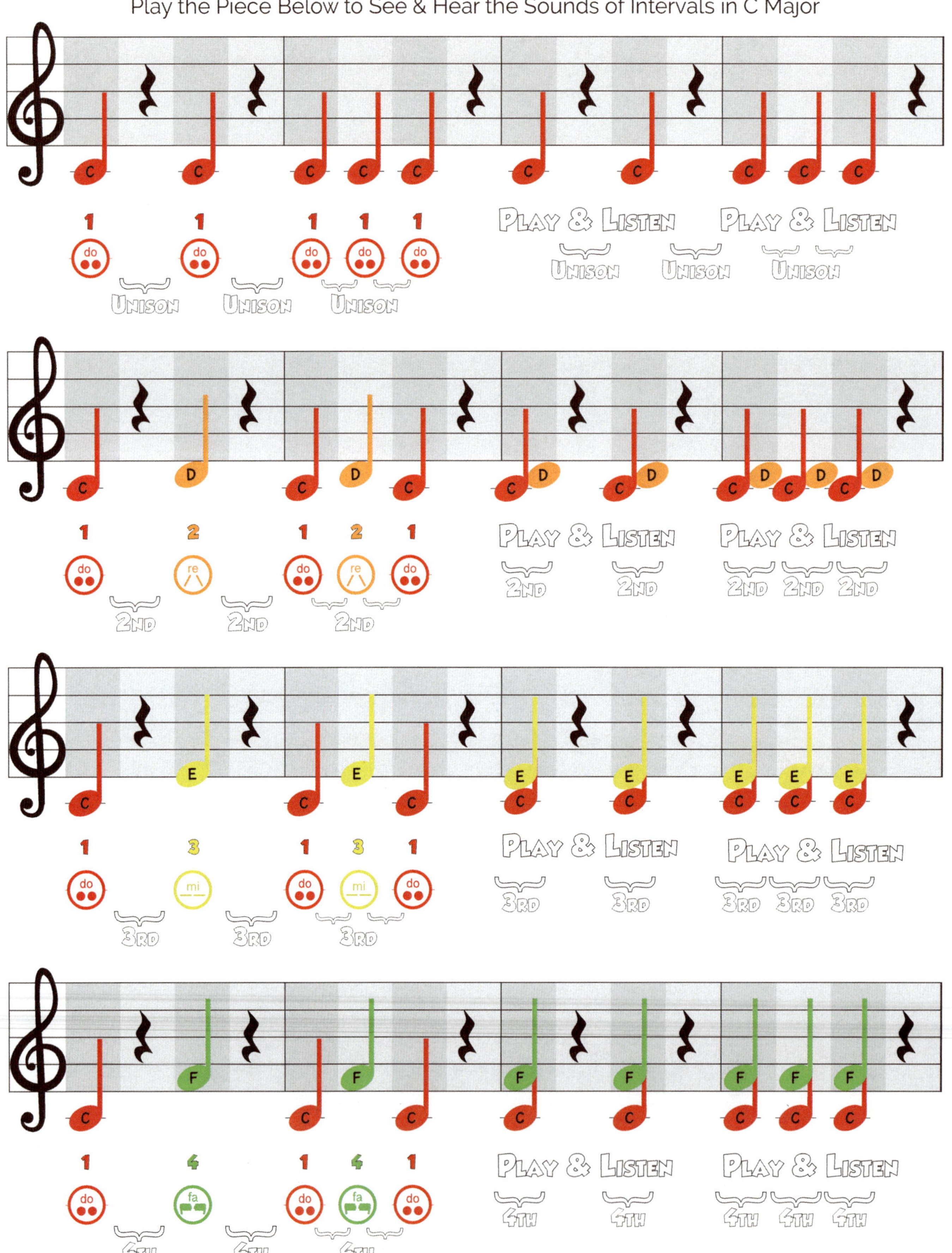

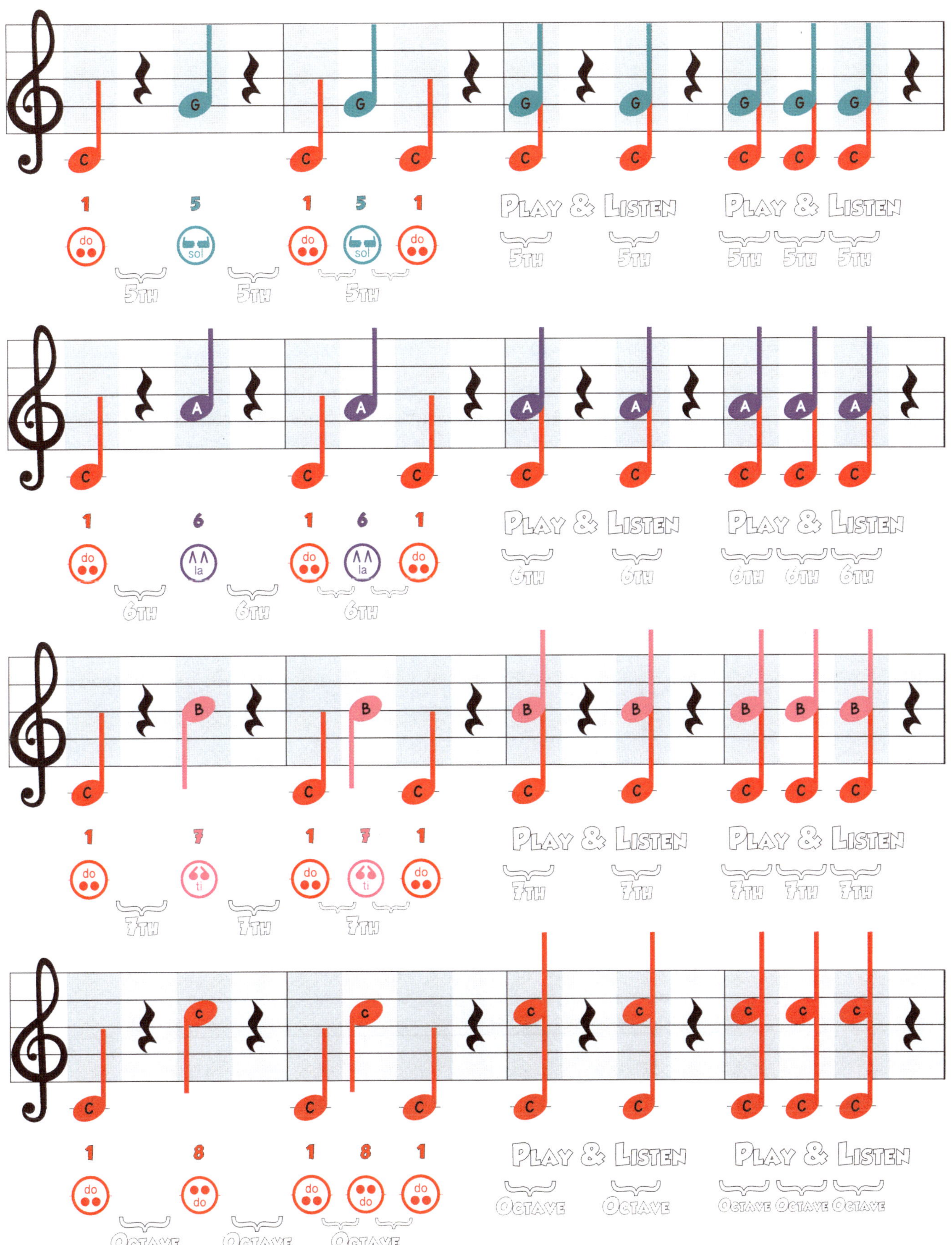
C G C G C G C G C G C G C G C
1 5 1 5 1
do sol do sol do
5th 5th 5th
Play & Listen
5th 5th
Play & Listen
5th 5th 5th
C A C A C A C A C A C A C A C
1 6 1 6 1
do la do la do
6th 6th 6th
Play & Listen
6th 6th
Play & Listen
6th 6th 6th
C B C B C B C B C B C B C B C
1 7 1 7 1
do ti do ti do
7th 7th 7th
Play & Listen
7th 7th
Play & Listen
7th 7th 7th
C C C C C C C C C C C C C C C
1 8 1 8 1
do do do do do
Octave Octave Octave
Play & Listen
Octave Octave
Play & Listen
Octave Octave Octave

Staff & Treble Clef Review

The Staff as Our Musical Map

You may recall that our STAFF is our Musical Map. Learning to read this map helps us understand which notes to play when we're not using color-coded music. Each of the notes lives on its own LINE or inside its own SPACE.

The STAFF is made up of FIVE LINES and FOUR SPACES. Build a STAFF below by tracing the lines and connecting the dots.

The Treble Clef

In music, we use symbols called CLEFS to show what kind of music we are reading. There are certain CLEFS for violin music, for piano music, for the bells, for the bass, and even for drums. The clef will reflect the range of our instrument, whether it's high or low.

The most popular clef, especially for reading bells, piano, and guitar is the TREBLE CLEF. The TREBLE CLEF is also called the G Clef because the clef itself (the swirl) circles around the note G.

Activity: Trace the Treble Clefs and Gs below.

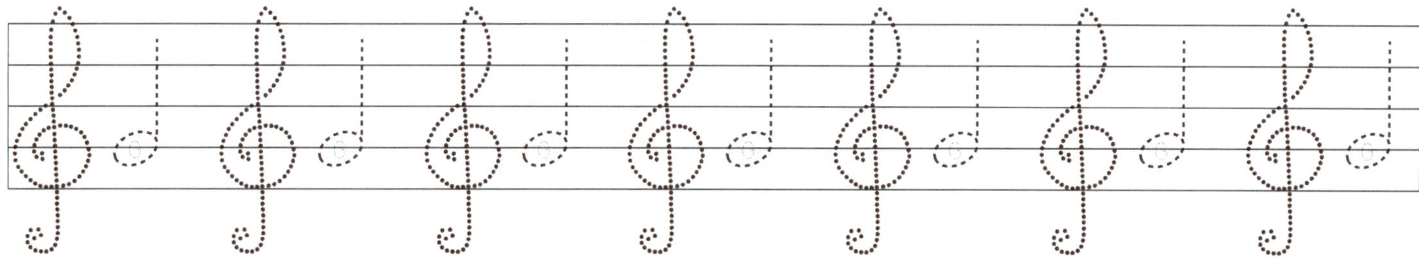

Our Music Alphabet on the Treble Clef

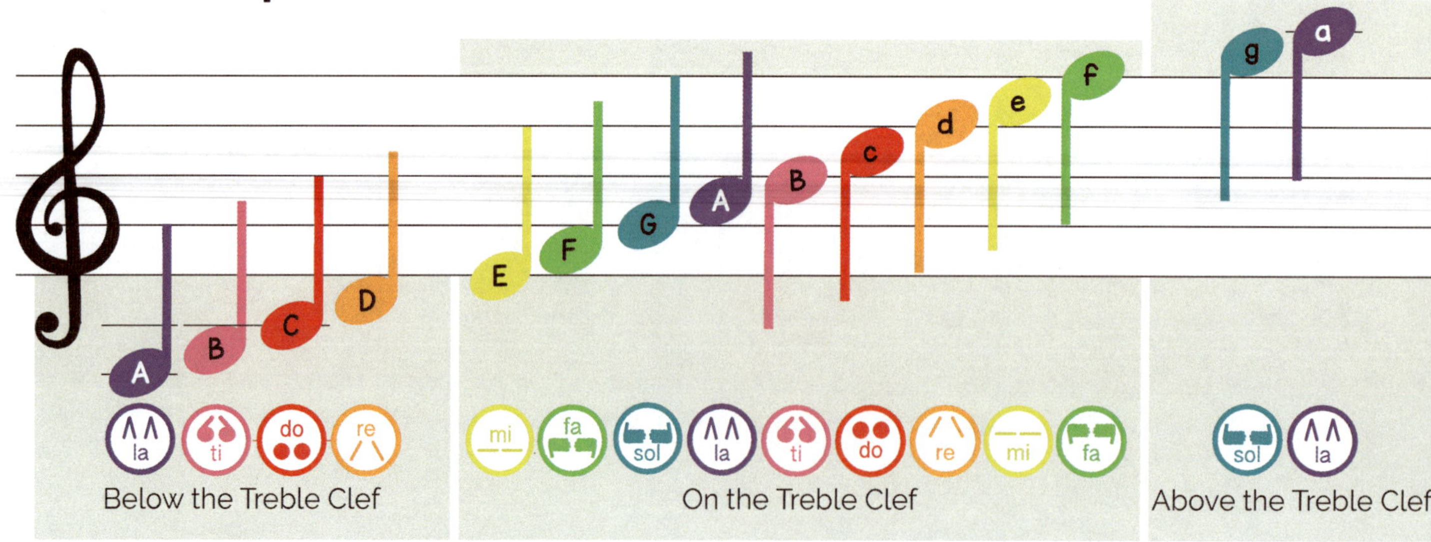

3 Ways to Read the Treble Clef

#1 Using the Treble Clef (G Clef) to Find the 2nd Line, G.

The treble clef shows us that the second line is a G. Use the swirl of the G clef like a treasure map where X marks the spot. This will help us place our G note.

Once you have placed the G note, you can continue down the clef, moving from line to space and space to line to find the notes F, E, D, & C.

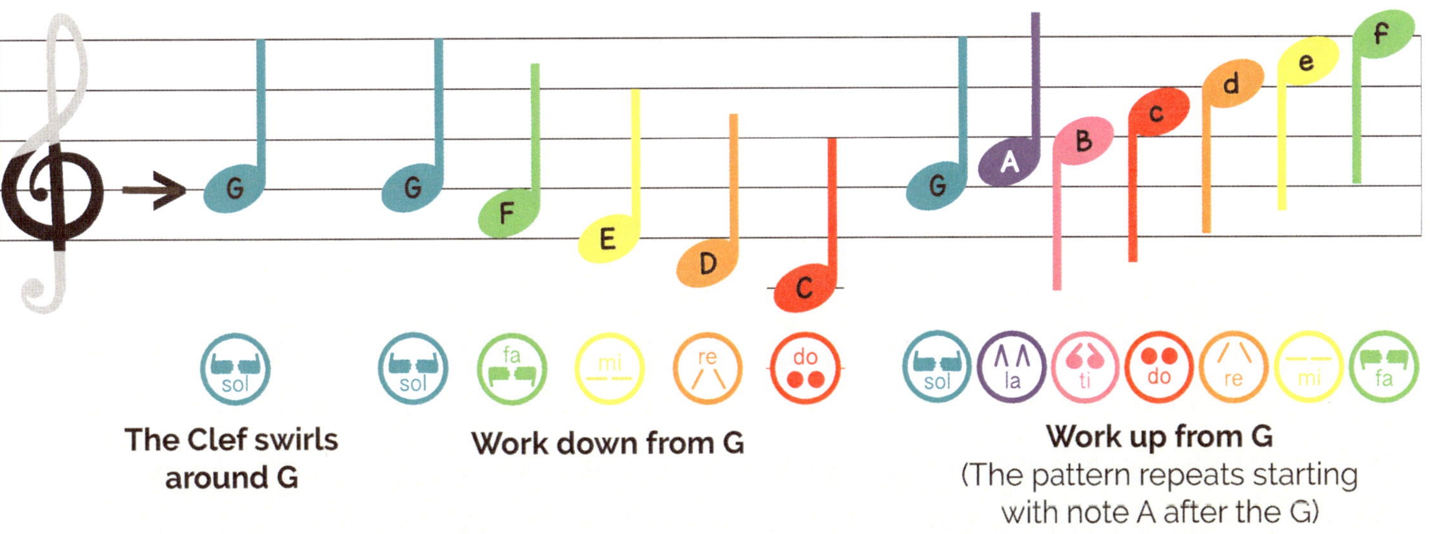

#2 Memorize the Space Notes with the Expression FACE IN THE SPACE

The expression FACE IN THE SPACE is an easy way to remember that the spaces in the TREBLE CLEF are F, A,C and E.

The SPACES are the blank areas in between the lines of the STAFF.

#3 Memorize the Line Notes with EVERY GOOD BOY DOES FINE.

The lines of the TREBLE CLEF, from the bottom to the top, are E, G, B, D, and F.

EGBDF doesn't spell a real word, so we use an expression like "Every Good Boy Does Fine" or "Every Girl Buys Dresses Friday," to help us memorize EGBDF.

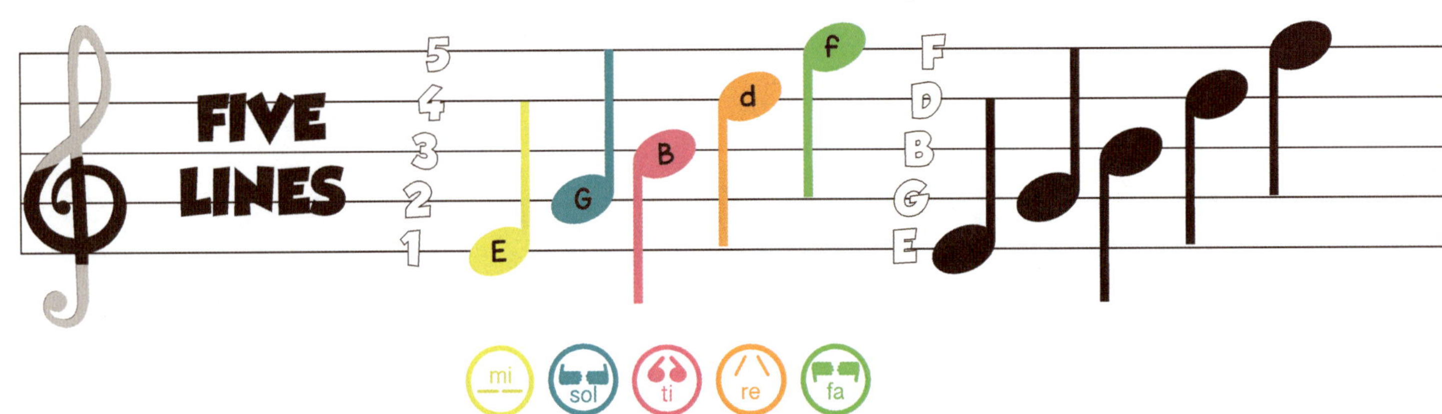

Notes on the Treble Clef

Putting It All Together

With these three different methods, you can easily find notes on the TREBLE CLEF.
If it's inside a SPACE, use the expression FACE IN THE SPACE.
If it's crossed by a LINE, use the first letters in the expression EVERY GOOD BOY DOES FINE, or you can use the SECOND LINE G as an anchor and work from there.

EGBDF on the Lines

FACE in the SPACE

"Name that Note" on the Treble Clef

We're going to practice labeling A LOT of notes and sheet music in this book. These excercises are really helpful for learning to read music quickly, so take some time to practice ALL of the pages in this book.

Part 1: The SPACES

Using the expression FACE IN THE SPACE, can you label the notes below?

Part 2: The LINES

Using the expression EVERY GOOD BOY DOES FINE, can you label the notes below?

Part 3: LINES & SPACES

Time to label LINE and SPACE notes! Good luck!!

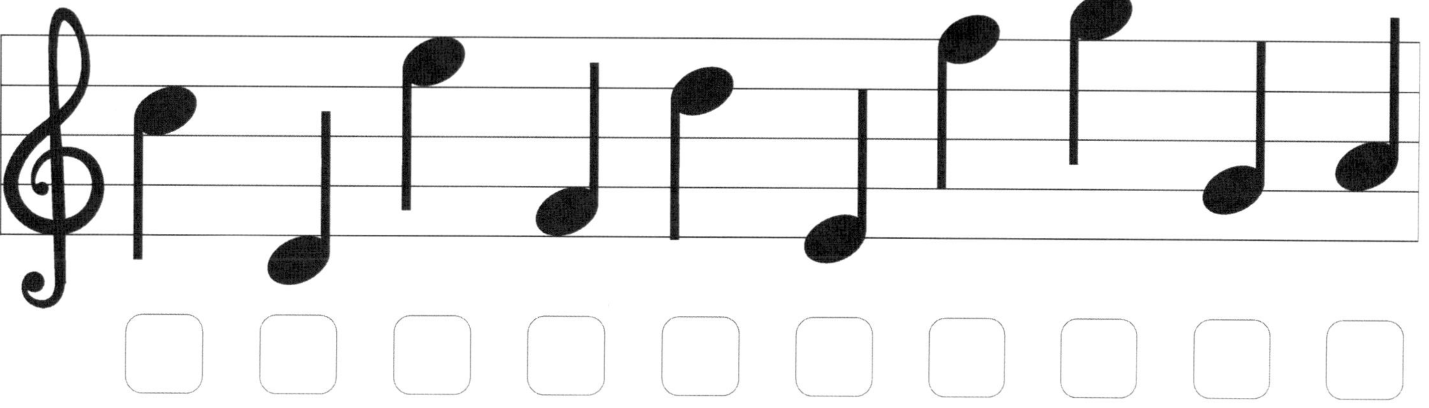

"Name that Tune" on the Treble Clef

Now for some more note labeling! This time, we'll use some famous Melodies.
Label the notes below and then Name that Tune! Try playing the melodies on your instrument to help you unlock the answer!

Tune #1: ______________________________

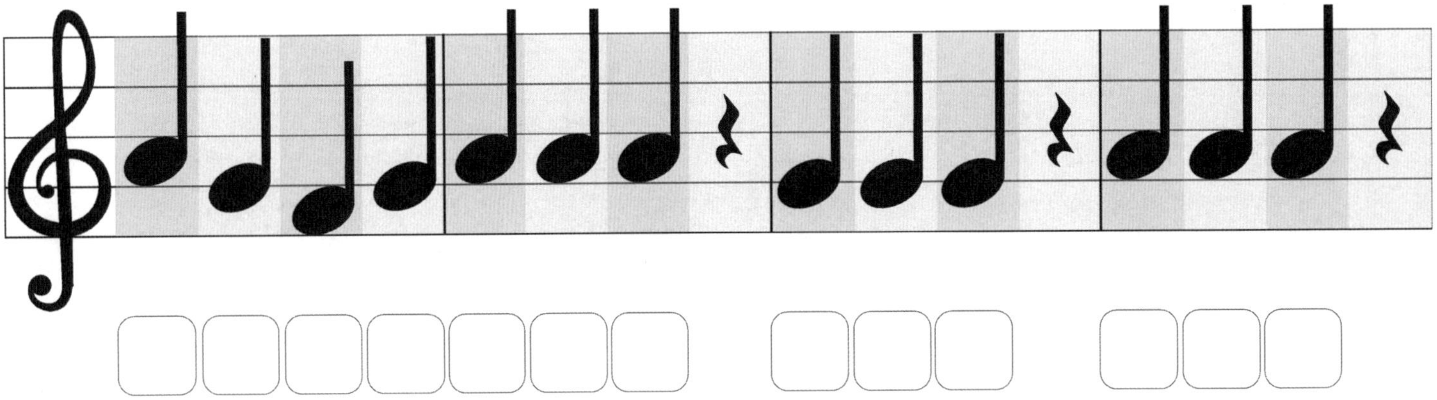

Tune #2: ______________________________

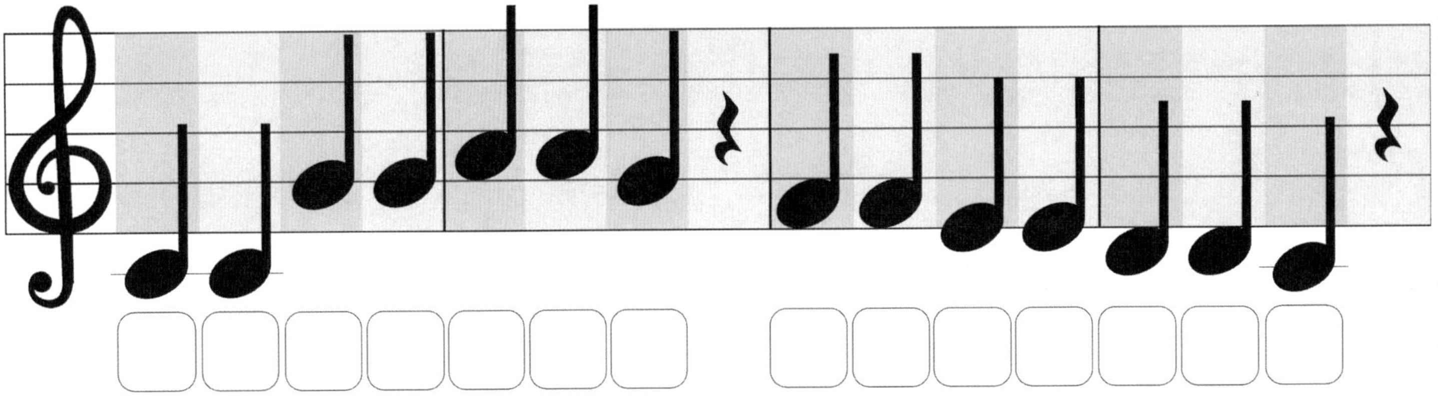

Tune #3: ______________________________

"Name that Tune" continued

Tune #4: ______________________________

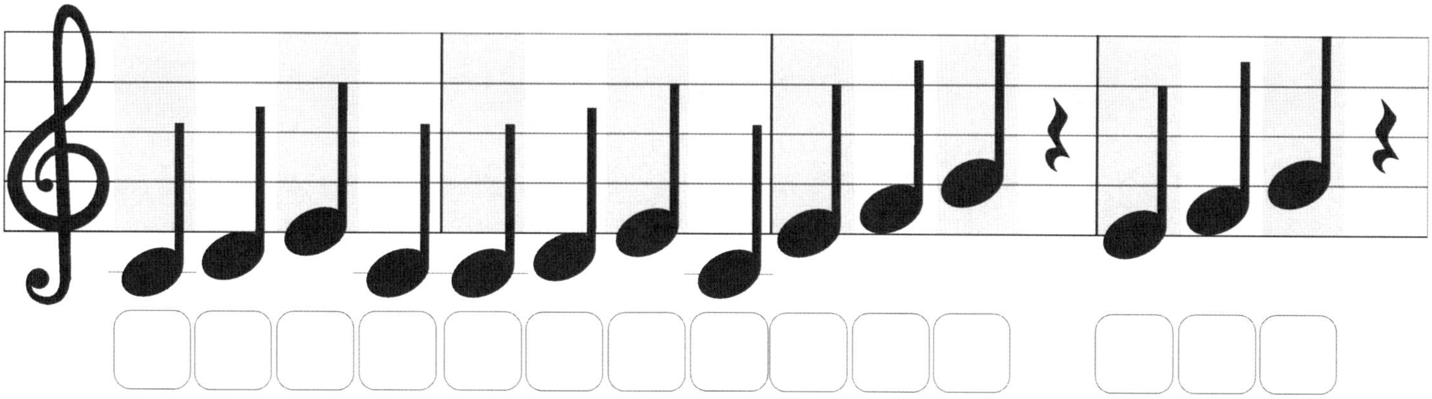

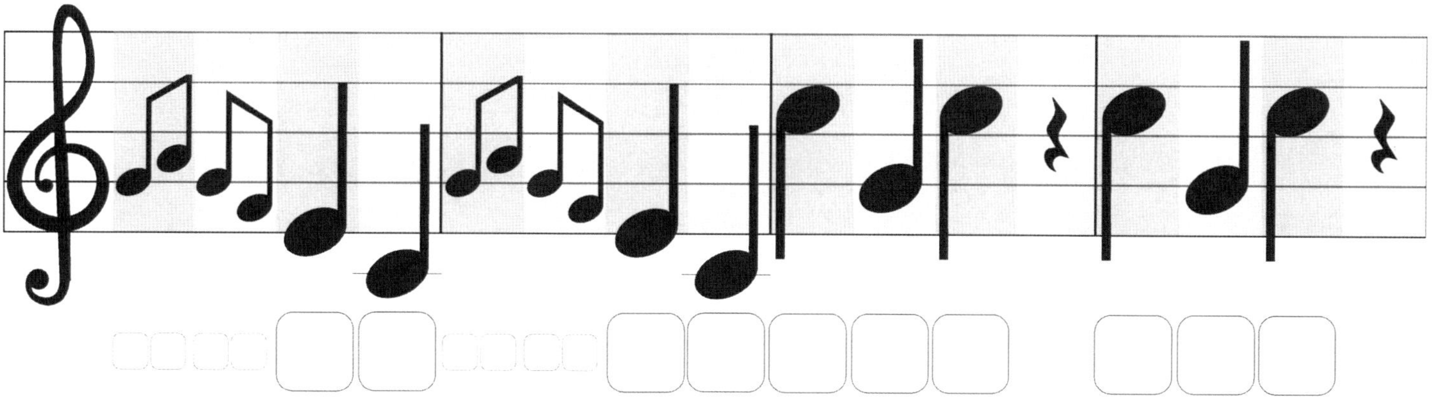

Tune #5: ______________________________

SILLY SENTENCES ON THE TREBLE CLEF

Below we have some Silly Sentences written using the letters in our musical alphabet. For each sentence, draw the notes of the letters above on the TREBLE CLEF. Some of the letters (like E, D, F, etc) have two possible answers, but you only need to draw one.

DAD FACED DECAF

D A D F A C E D D E C A F

DA FAB BAGGAGE

D A F A B B A G G A G E

CABBAGED EGG

C A B B A G E D E G G

Guided Composition on the Treble Clef

Here you'll write your own song on the treble clef. Some of the notes are already there to help guide you a little bit. The tonic (home base note) for this song is the note C (or Do).

Tip #1: If you remember the C, F, and G chords, you can use those to help you fill up each measure.
Tip #2: With a tonic (home base) of C, you can use the notes C, D, E, G, and A easily. The F and B, which we will learn more about later in this chapter, are a bit harder to use.

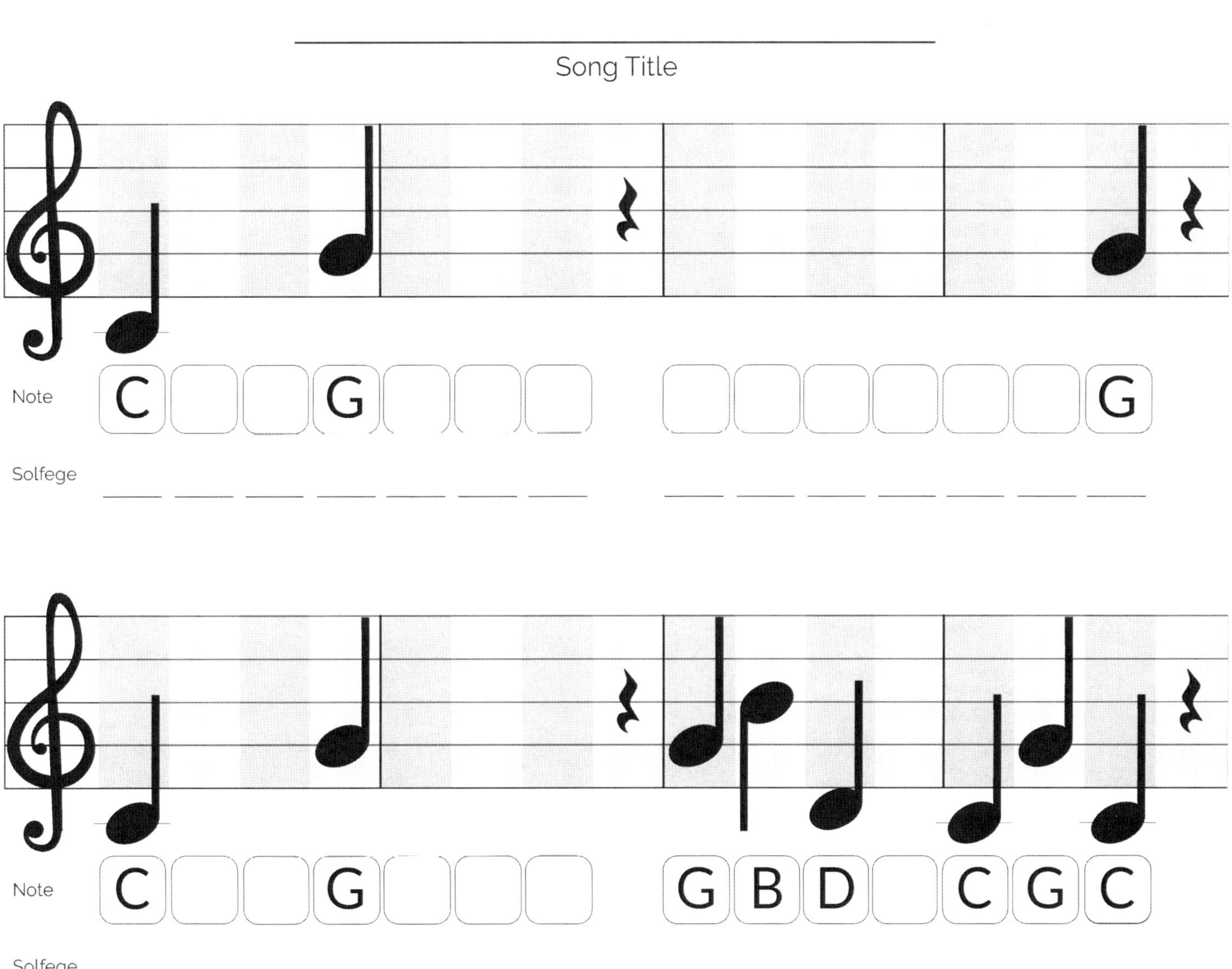

UNISON 2ND 3RD 4TH 5TH 6TH 7TH OCTAVE

INTERVALS
THE DISTANCE (UP & DOWN) BETWEEN TWO MUSICAL NOTES

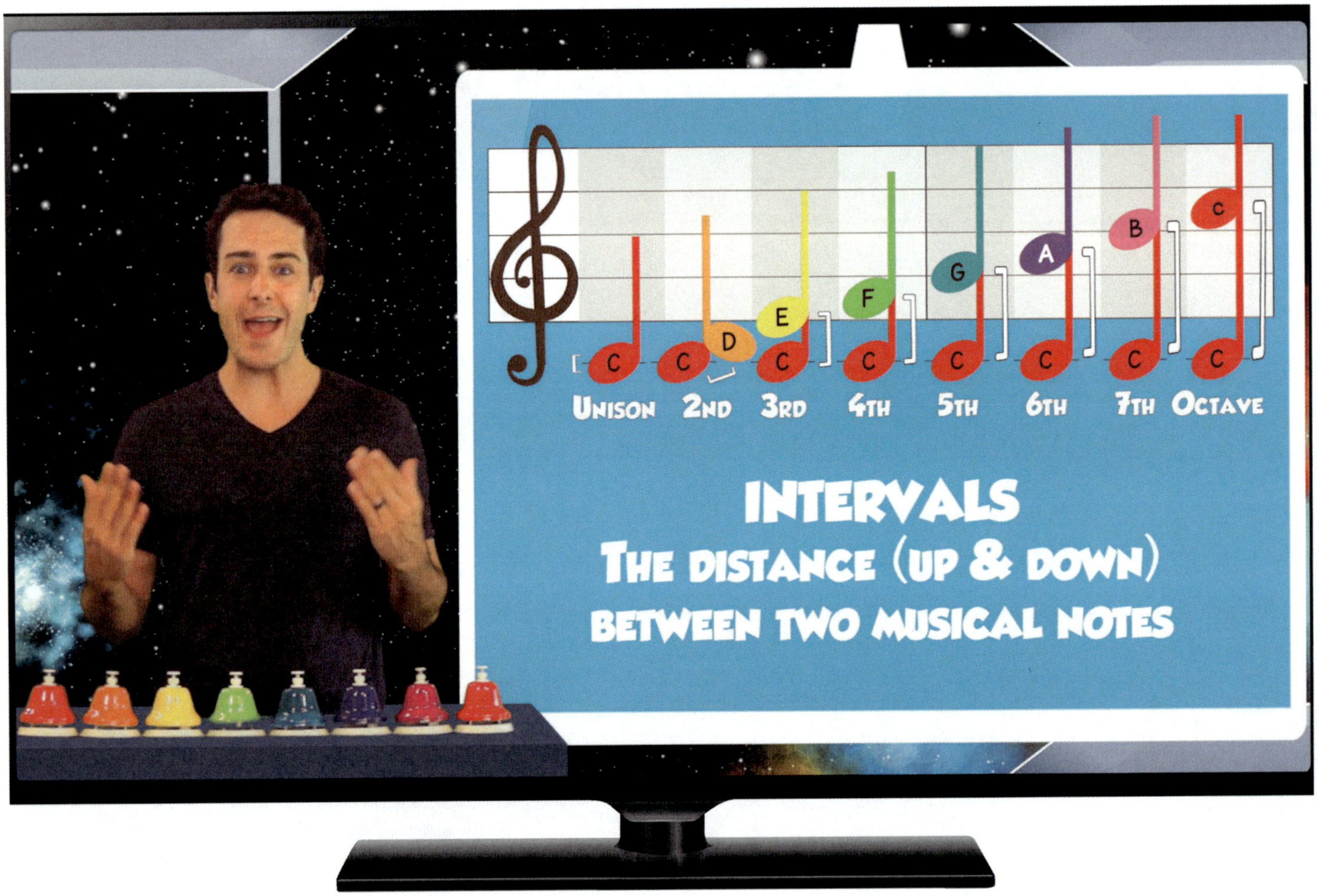

INTRO TO INTERVALS

Section 2.1 (Part 2 of 2)

2.1 Label the Black & White Music

Label the letter names (C, D, E) as well as the intervals between them

1 The note repeated in the passage above is _____ .

2 The interval between the repetitions is a _________.

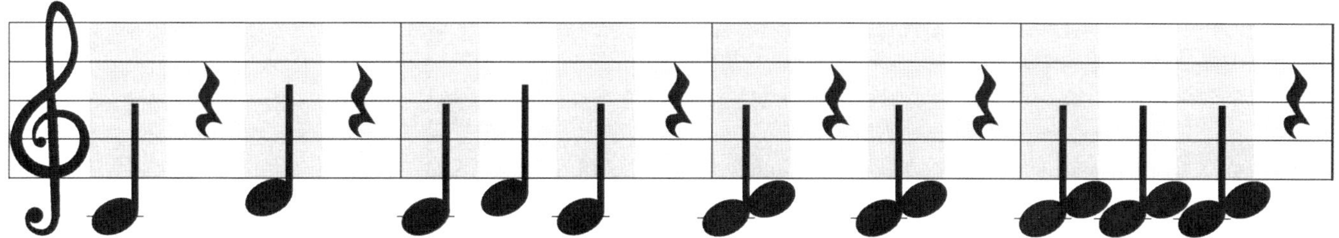

3 The two notes in the passage are _____ & _____.

4 The interval between them is a _________.

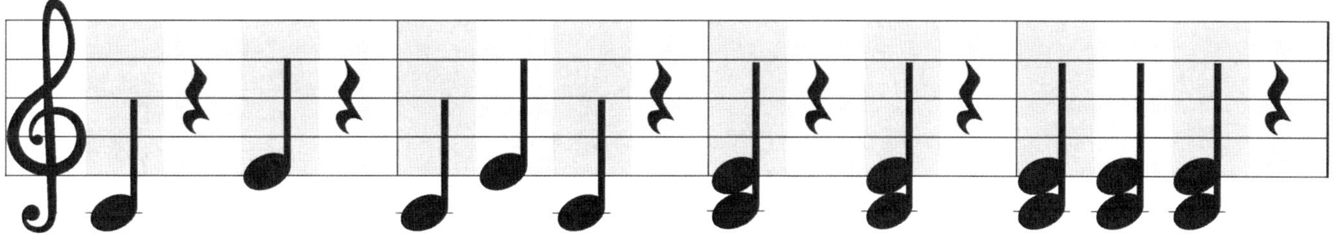

5 The two notes in the passage are _____ & _____.

6 The interval between them is a _________.

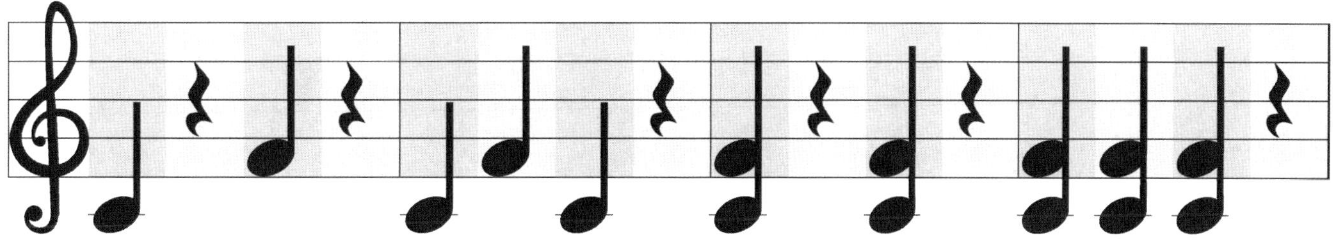

7 The two notes in the passage are _____ & _____.

8 The interval between them is a _________.

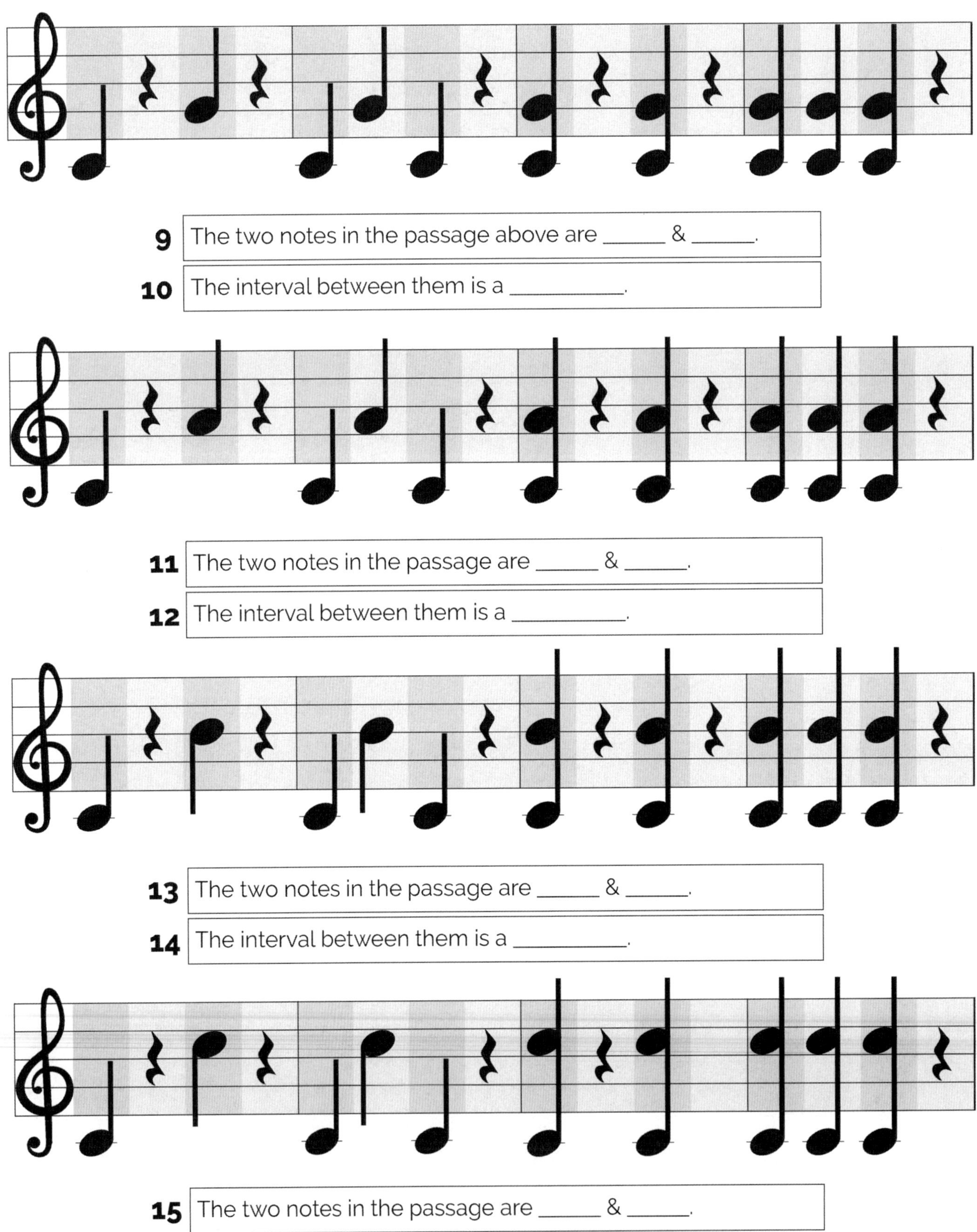

9 The two notes in the passage above are ______ & ______.

10 The interval between them is a __________.

11 The two notes in the passage are ______ & ______.

12 The interval between them is a __________.

13 The two notes in the passage are ______ & ______.

14 The interval between them is a __________.

15 The two notes in the passage are ______ & ______.

16 The interval between them is a __________.

2.1.2 What are INTERVALS?

Intervals - What Did One Note Say to the Other?

A **diatonic interval** is how one scale degree communicates with another note in the scale. Diatonic simply means, "within a key signature." **Intervals** provide us with the context necessary to discuss the aural qualities of chords, harmony, and melody. There are lots of tips for understanding that relationship.

Whenever you have more than one note happening, like in a melody or a chord, the **interval** is the harmonic distance between any two of those notes.

To find an interval, pick a starting note and count to the next note in the melody or chord. If you want to know the distance from C to E, you would count: C (1), D (2), E (3).

This interval is three scale degrees away, so we call it a 3rd.

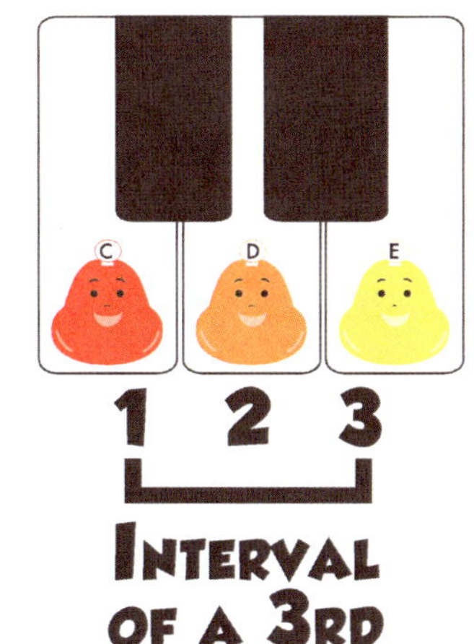

On bells or piano, the intervals are easy to find. Try counting for yourself like we did above!

Melodic & Harmonic Intervals

When we're looking at our sheet music, it's pretty easy to see if two notes are happening in unison or in a sequence.

When we have **one note followed by another,** the interval is **melodic.**

When we have both notes at the **same time,** the interval is **harmonic.**

Identifying Intervals within the Scale

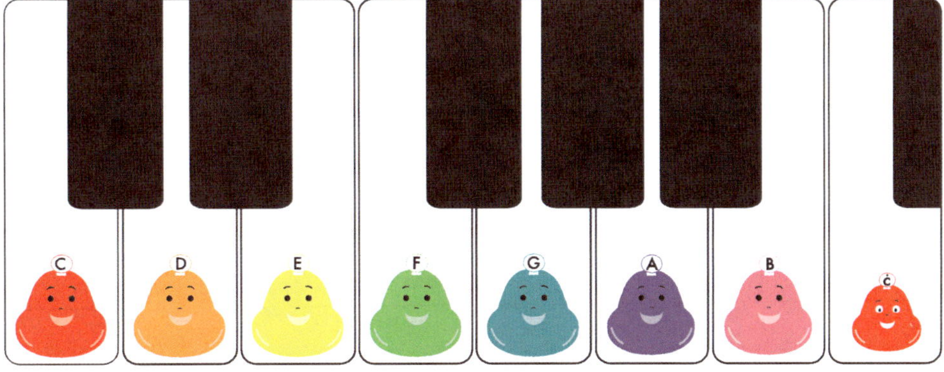

The best place to begin practicing is with **diatonic intervals** in the key of C Major. Using the major scale eliminates some "behind the scenes" music theory work for us and allows us to easier understand intervals.

Once we get the gist, we'll shift our focus to the chromatic notes, the black keys.

Practice Finding Interval Numbers in C Major

When talking about intervals, we're able to convey lots of valuable information with two essential parts, the interval **quality** and **number.**

First, let's focus on finding the **interval number**. If you wanted to answer the questions "How tall is that tree?" or "How deep is the ocean?" you'd reply some distance up or down. Similarly, interval numbers indicate how near or far it is to the next note UP or DOWN.

Just remember the musical alphabet, ABCDEFG, is cyclical. If you're on a full scale instrument, your next highest note after G is A. If you have an interval from D down to F, count backwards as you move through D(6) C(5) B(4) A(3) G(2) F(1).

To find the interval number:
- **count the lower note as 1**
- **count to 2, 3, 4, etc. until you reach the ending note.**
- **If you end at 2, that's a 2nd. If you end at 3, that's a 3rd. Read more ahead!**

1. Can you find a <u>2nd up</u> from C?

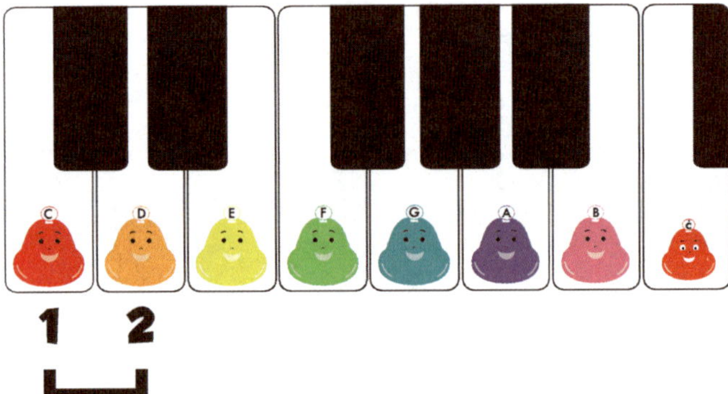

Start counting on C (1) and count up to 2. This lands you on a D. D is a 2nd up from C.

2. Can you find a <u>2nd up</u> from E?

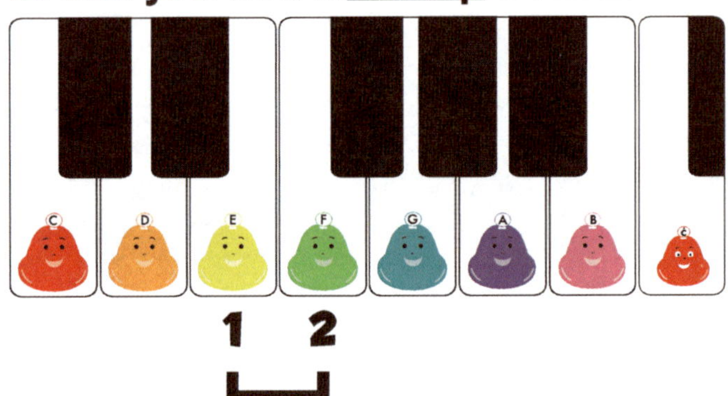

Start counting on E (1) and count up to 2. This lands you on an F. F is a 2nd up from E.

3. Can you find a <u>3rd ABOVE</u> G?

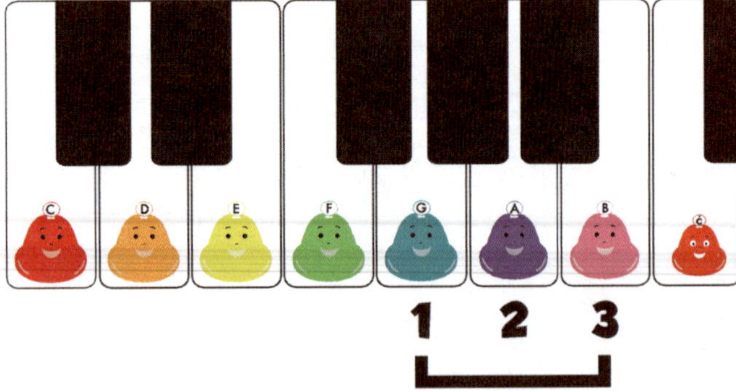

Start counting on G (1) and count up to 3. This lands you on a B. B is a 3rd up from G.

4. Can you find a <u>5th BELOW</u> A?

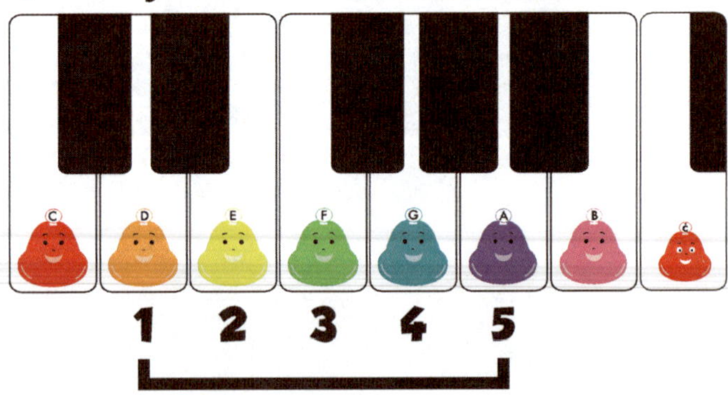

Start counting on D (1) and count up to 5. This lands you on an A. A is a 5th up from D.

Did you notice how we can start our intervals from ANY note (not just C)?
In our exercises, we'll often start on C and go up.

Diatonic Intervals in C Major

Find different intervals on the keyboards below, & circle the correct bell.

1. Find a 2nd UP from F

Hint: a 2nd is only 1 note away.

1

2. Find a 3rd UP from A

Hint: a 3rd is 2 notes away.

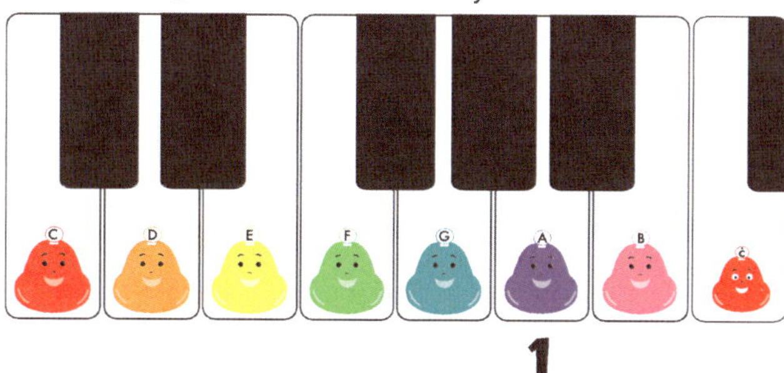

1

3. Find a 3rd DOWN from B

Hint: DOWN is to the LEFT

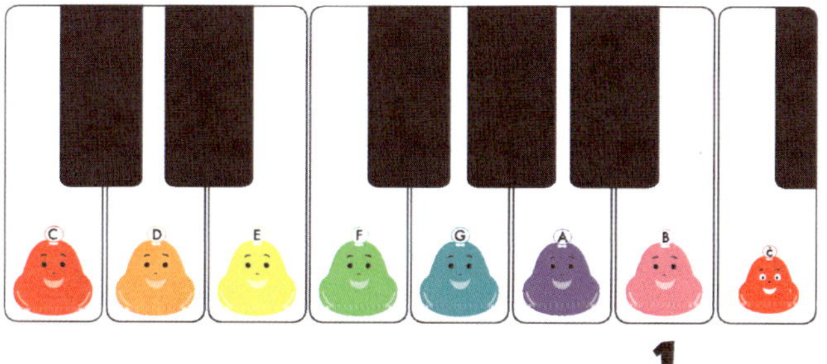

1

4. Find a 4th DOWN from F

Hint: DOWN is to the LEFT

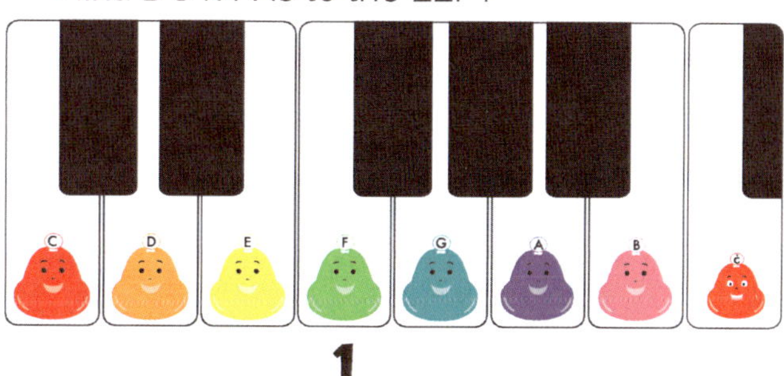

1

5. Find a 6th ABOVE D

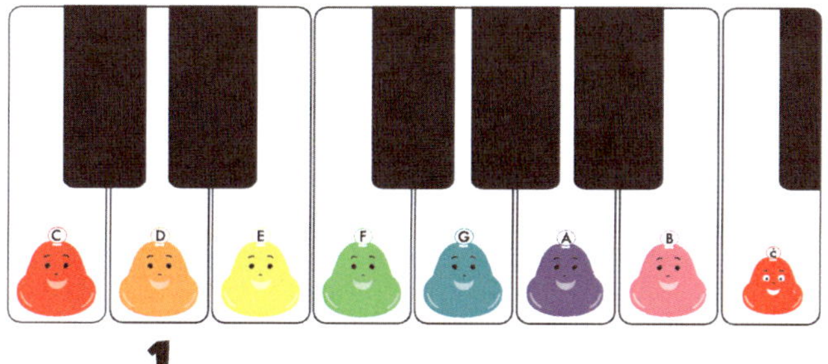

1

6. Find a 4th BELOW A

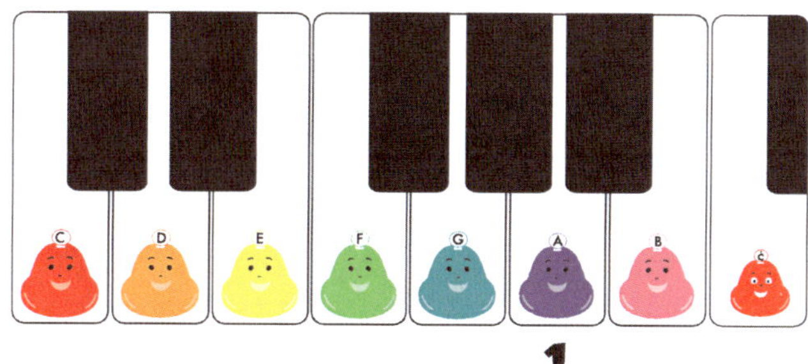

1

7. Find a 7th ABOVE C

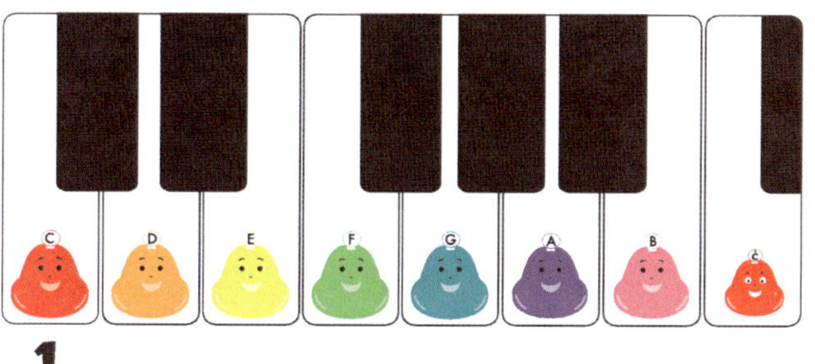

1

8. Find a 7th BELOW high C

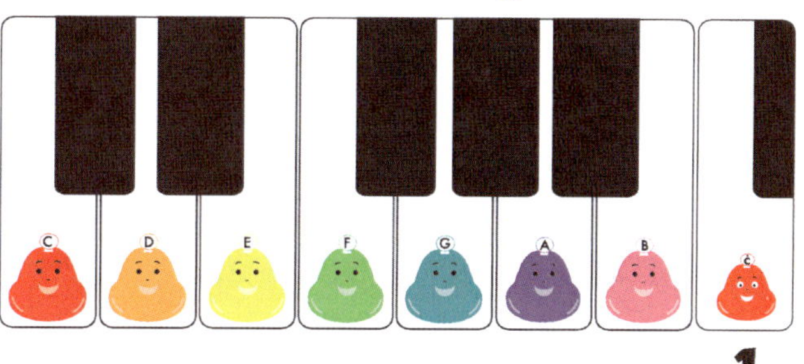

1

Intervals on the Keyboard & Staff

Now take the intervals from the keyboard and draw them on the staff.

Hint: Use Every Good Boy Does Fine & FACE in the SPACE
to remember where each note lives on the staff.

EGBDF on the Lines

FACE in the SPACE

Challenge: Cover up the hint above and try to work from memory.

1.

Circle a 2nd ABOVE F

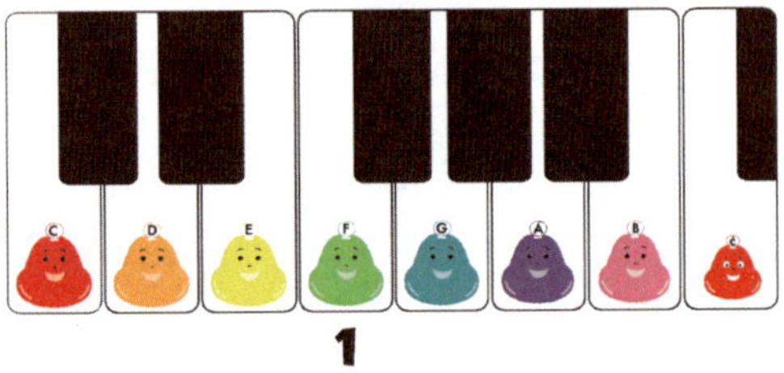

C D E F G A B C

1

Draw the notes melodically (apart)

F G

Draw the notes harmonically (together)

F G

2.

Circle a 5th ABOVE F

C D E F G A B C

Draw the notes melodically (apart)

Draw the notes harmonically (together)

3.

Circle a 4th ABOVE G

Draw the notes melodically (apart)

Draw the notes harmonically (together)

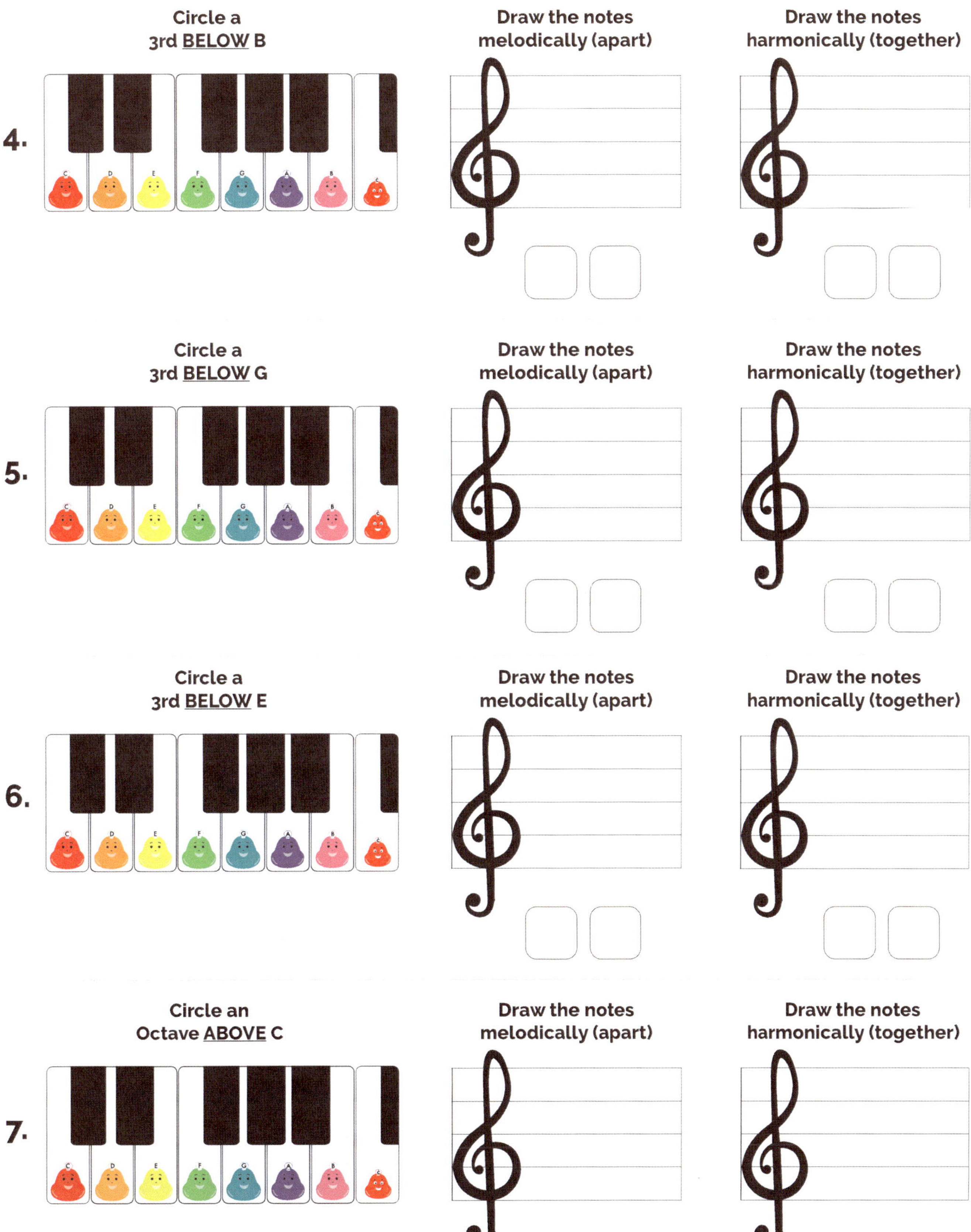
Circle a
3rd BELOW B
4.
Draw the notes
melodically (apart)
Draw the notes
harmonically (together)
Circle a
3rd BELOW G
5.
Draw the notes
melodically (apart)
Draw the notes
harmonically (together)
Circle a
3rd BELOW E
6.
Draw the notes
melodically (apart)
Draw the notes
harmonically (together)
Circle an
Octave ABOVE C
7.
Draw the notes
melodically (apart)
Draw the notes
harmonically (together)

Notating Intervals - Round 1

Let's try drawing intervals on just the staff.

Hint: Use Every Good Boy Does Fine & FACE in the SPACE
to remember where each note lives on the staff.

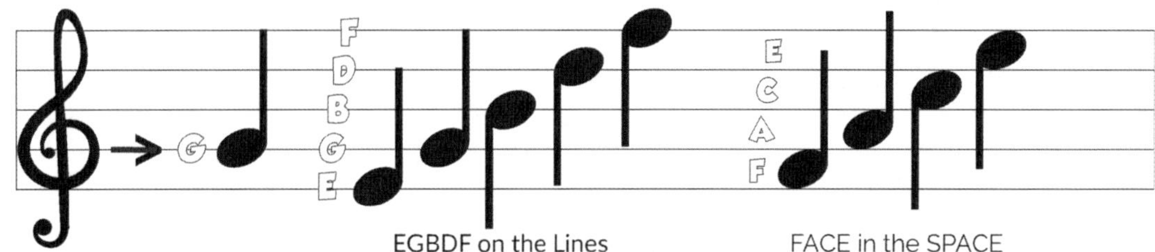

Challenge: Cover up the hint above and try to work from memory.

Draw a note a 3rd BELOW G

Ex 1

Hint: Count this line (G) as 1
Hint: Count this space (F) as 2
Hint: Count this line (E) as 3

G E

Draw a note a 4th ABOVE F

Ex 2

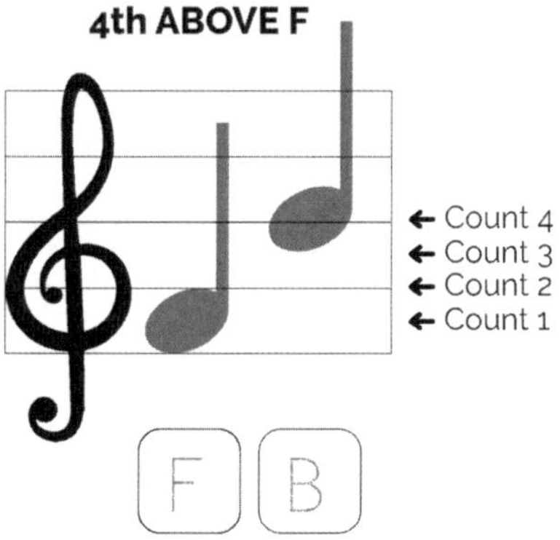

← Count 4
← Count 3
← Count 2
← Count 1

F B

1 **Draw a 3rd Below high E**

E

2 **Draw a 5th Below B**

B

3 **Draw a 2nd Above G**

G

4 **Draw a 3rd Below high F**

F

5 **Draw a 5th Below high C**

C

6 **Draw a 2nd Above A**

A

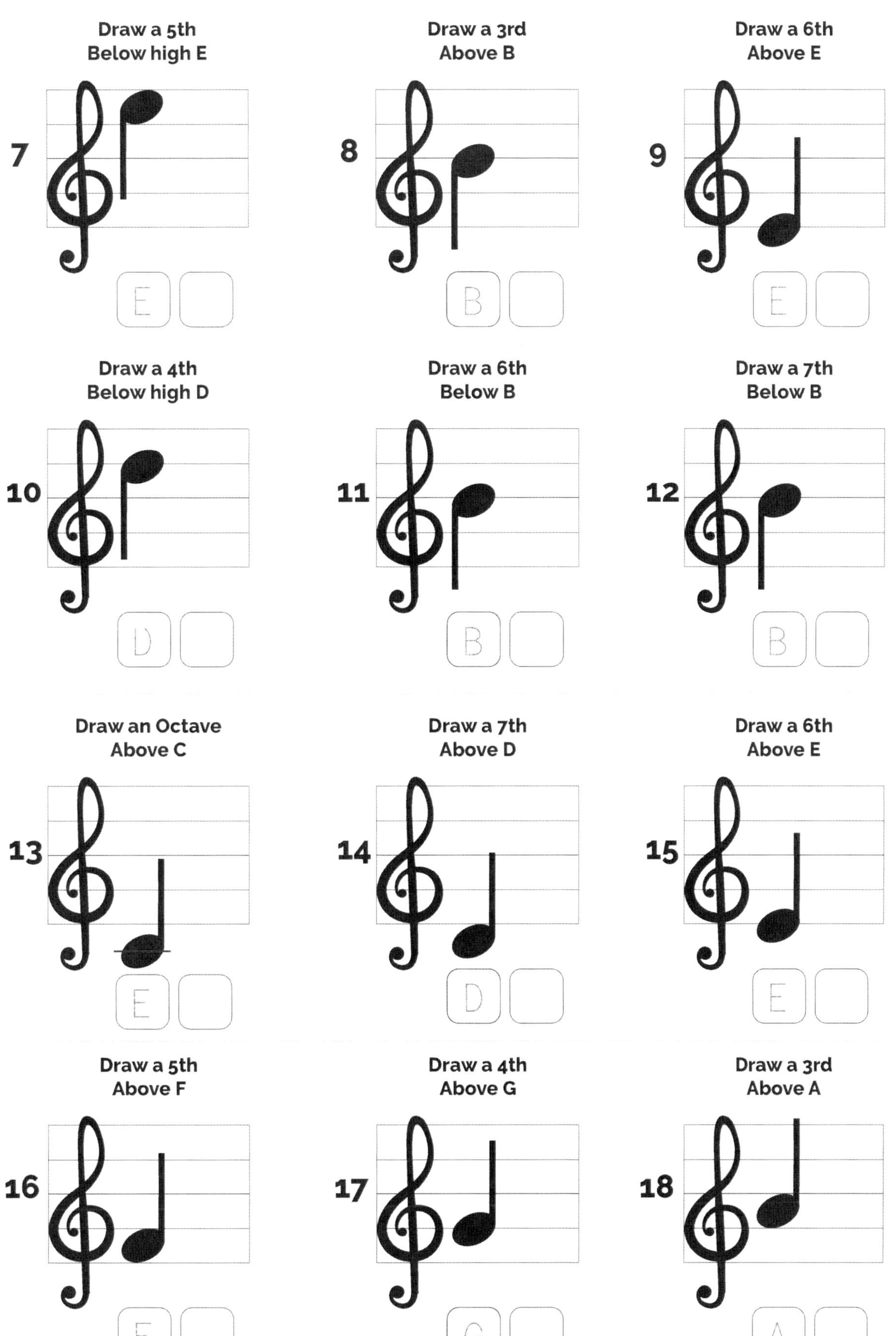
Draw a 5th
Below high E
7
E
Draw a 3rd
Above B
8
B
Draw a 6th
Above E
9
E
Draw a 4th
Below high D
10
D
Draw a 6th
Below B
11
B
Draw a 7th
Below B
12
B
Draw an Octave
Above C
13
E
Draw a 7th
Above D
14
D
Draw a 6th
Above E
15
E
Draw a 5th
Above F
16
F
Draw a 4th
Above G
17
G
Draw a 3rd
Above A
18
A

Interval Vocab

Match the interval on the left to the shorthand on the right.

Interval	Shorthand
Unison	3rd
Second	7th
Third	6th
Fourth	Uni
Fifth	2nd
Sixth	5th
Seventh	Oct
Octave	4th

Reverse Interval Vocab

Match the shorthand on the left to the interval on the right.

Shorthand	Interval
Uni	Fourth
2nd	Octave
3rd	Fifth
4th	Second
5th	Unison
6th	Sixth
7th	Seventh
Oct	Third

Primary Prodigies

2nds & Interval Quality with "Happy Birthday"

Section 2.2

Notes Used:

2.2 Happy Birthday

F Major

"Happy Birthday" starts with a **pickup measure.** This is a shortened first measure that allows the melody to begin before the harmony joins in. When you count in, you'll say "1, 2" then play the first 8th note on beat 3.

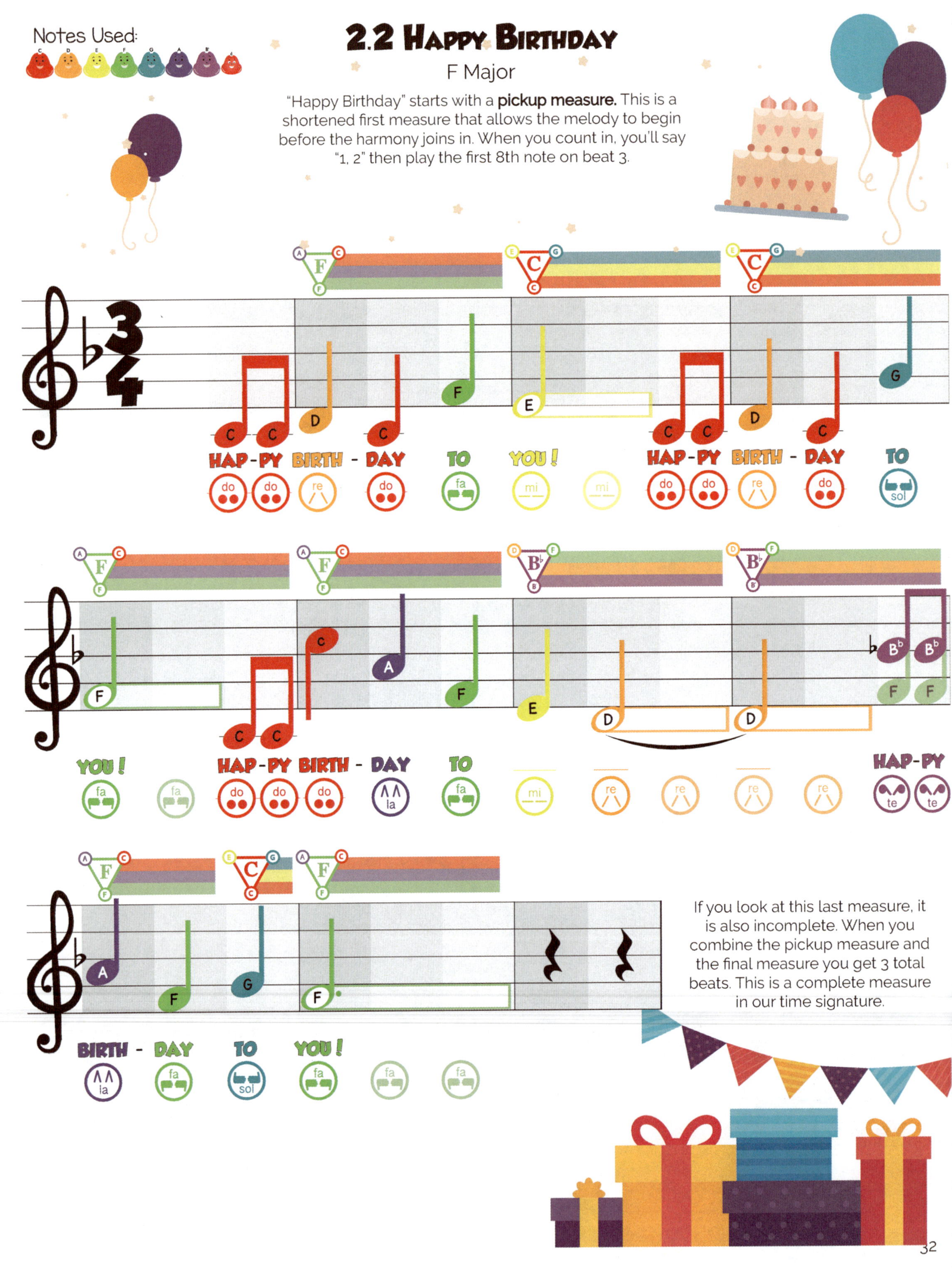

If you look at this last measure, it is also incomplete. When you combine the pickup measure and the final measure you get 3 total beats. This is a complete measure in our time signature.

Happy Birthday

Black & White Version

Practice "Happy Birthday" with black-and-white music!
Then take some time and label the intervals in the boxes below the lyrics.

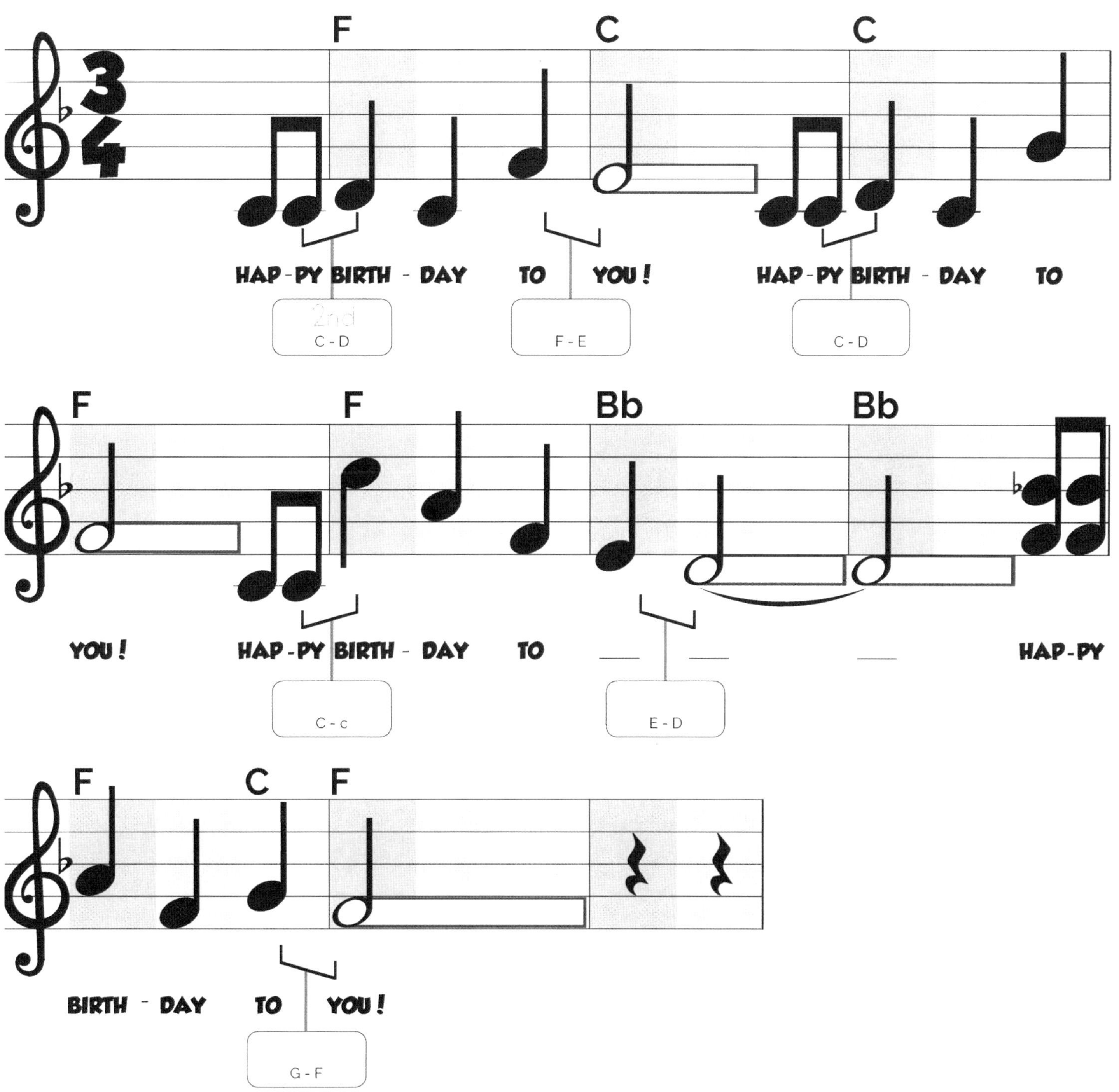

What are SEMITONES?

Before we can understand interval quality, we need to learn about what we'll measure it with, the **semitone**. The semitone is the smallest distance up or down we can move on our instruments.

To travel from one piano key to the next is to move one semitone. If we look at the piano below, we see the 7 unique notes in the C Major Scale, but what about the 5 black keys? Now we have ALL 12 musical notes,

When we're using the C Major bells, we can travel in 2nds from one scale degree to the next, each hand movement the same. However, when we practiced interval numbers, did you notice C to D was a 2nd but looked different than E to F, also a 2nd?

This is very important. Moving from C to D is TWO semitones however moving from E to F is only ONE semitone. This is the "behind the scenes" theory we referred to earlier. The movement is the same, but the distances are not equal.

Count the red arrows on the piano below as you move away from a note. How many semitones did you count? Did you get the same results we did?

Using Semitones

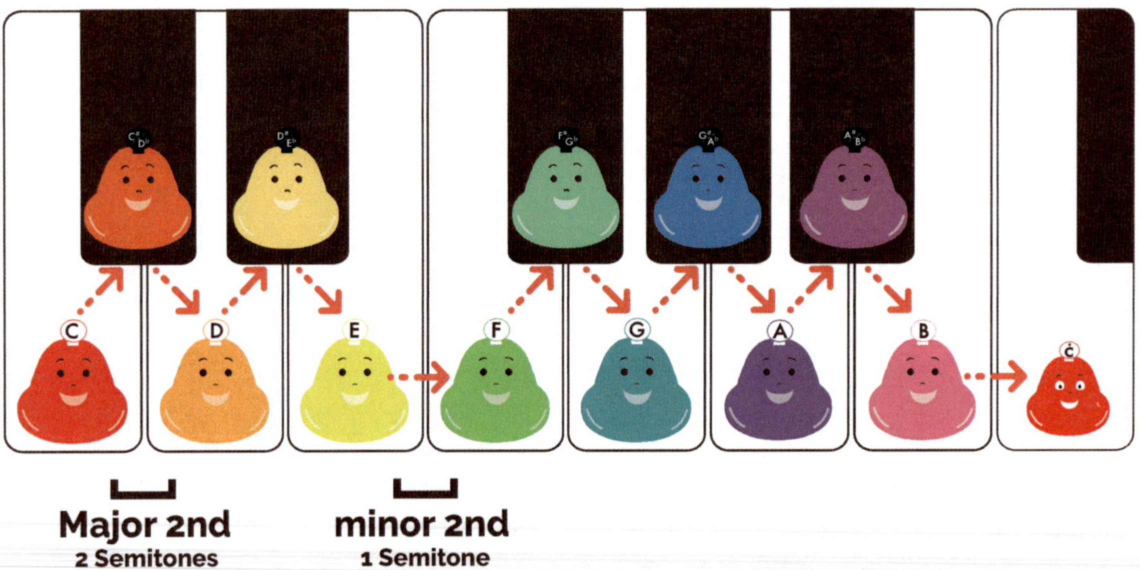

We haven't been using the black keys as much because they're outside of our C Major Scale, but they're going to become essential here in this Chapter.

2.2 Interval Quality

Now that we know how to measure with semitones, we can get back to intervals! We've discussed **interval number** (2nd, 3rd, etc); it's time to look at the other piece of the puzzle, **interval QUALITY.** Before we begin, we need to learn some important words used to describile quality: major, minor, perfect, augmented, and diminished. These are technical terms, but ultimately they help us to describe how the sounds make us feel.

To determine an interval's quality, use the piano as your guide. If we play the note D followed by F, what is the interval's number and quality? First, count the letters, D(1) E(2) F(3). It's a 3rd! Next, count the red arrows from D to F. 3 semitones. Can you find 3 semitones below? It's a MINOR 3rd!

In a major key, 2nds, 3rds, 6ths, & 7ths will be either be...

Major

Major 2nd (2 Semitones)
Major 3rd (4 Semitones)
Major 6th (9 Semitones)
Major 7th (11 Semitones)

Examples in C Major

M2: C-D, D-E, F-G, G-A, A-B
M3: C-E, F-A, G-B
M6: C-A, D-B, F-D, G-E
M7: C-B, F-E

OR

Minor

minor 2nd (1 Semitone)
minor 3rd (3 Semitones)
minor 6th (8 Semitones)
minor 7th (10 semitones)

Examples in C Major

m2: E-F, B-C
m3: D-F, E-G, A-C, B-D
m6: E-C, A-F, B-G
m7: D-C, E-D, G-F, A-G, B-A

In a major key, unisons, 4ths, 5ths & octaves are predominantly...

Perfect

Unison (0 Semitones)
Perfect 4th (5 Semitones)
Perfect 5th (7 Semitones)
Octave (12 Semitones)

Examples in C Major

P1: all scale degrees
P4: C-F, D-G, E-A, G-C, A-D, B-E
P5: C-G, D-A, E-B, F-C, G-D, A-E
P8: all scale degrees

Augmented

Augmented 4th (6 Semitones)

Diminished

Diminished 5th (6 Semitones)

Examples in C Major

A4: F-B **d5:** B-F

Unisons

Playing one note repetitively is a valuable skill. Hearing that a note is being played repetitively is a valuable skill. In learning intervals, you'll find unisons are valuable in your playing as well as your overall understanding of how music works.

If your band has a flautist and a guitar player, it would sound great to hear them play a melody in unison (meaning, not only at the same time, but also the same notes). You'd hear the same set of notes, but the **TIMBRE,** the personality of a sound, would be different.

All unisons in the major key are perfect.

In a major key, unisons will be...

Perfect Unison
0 Semitones

Melodically Sounds Like...	**Harmonically Sounds Like...**
First "twin-kle" of "Twinkle Twinkle" "Doos" of "Baby Shark" Same note repetition	Timbre or textural differences Groups singing in unison at a gathering or concert

Perfect Unisons in C Major

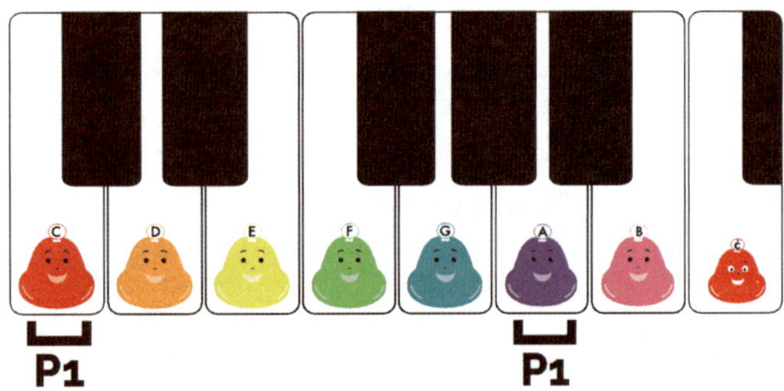

Perfect Unisons in C Major

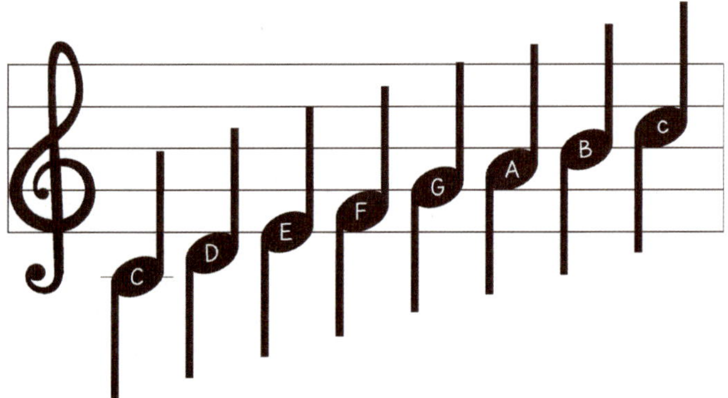

C to _____ is a Perfect Unison

A to _____ is a Perfect Unison

D to _____ is a Perfect Unison

G to _____ is a Perfect Unison

Augmented Unisons

Measured distances can become tricky with enharmonic note values. **Enharmonic** notes sound the same but are spelled differently.

C to Db is one semitone away. The letter ascends by one so the distance measured is a minor 2nd. However, C to C# (Db's **enharmonic equivalent**) is also one half-step away but the letter name doesn't change. Therefore it can't be measured as a 2nd. This is known as an **augmented unison**. Situations like this are less common, especially in a diatonic setting, but it is worth mentioning.

Seconds (2nds)

Seconds are the shortest distance you can travel within a scale or melody. If two notes are next to each other within a scale, they are 2nds. They're note neighbors!

There are a few synonyms for 2nds that we often use in music. The half steps and whole steps we discussed earlier can also be called minor and major 2nds respectively. Fun!

In a major key, 2nds will either be...

Minor 2nd 1 Semitone **<u>Melodically Sounds Like...</u>** Shark-like sound from "Jaws" theme Final two notes of "Baby Shark" (down a m2) The Pink Panther Theme **<u>Harmonically Sounds Like...</u>** Harsh rubbing An angry cat	**Major 2nd** 2 Semitones **<u>Melodically Sounds Like...</u>** Happy Birthday Intro (C to D) Do Re Mi (consecutive major 2nds) Frère Jacques **<u>Harmonically Sounds Like...</u>** Car Horns Hit Together "Duh" or "Er I dunno" The Chopsticks Waltz

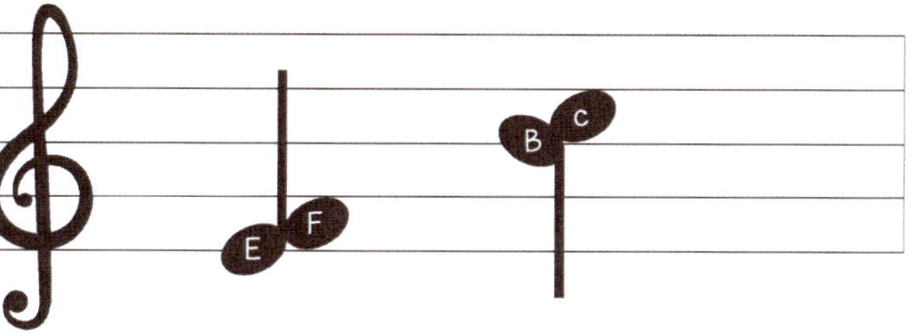

E to _____ is a minor 2nd

B to _____ is a minor 2nd

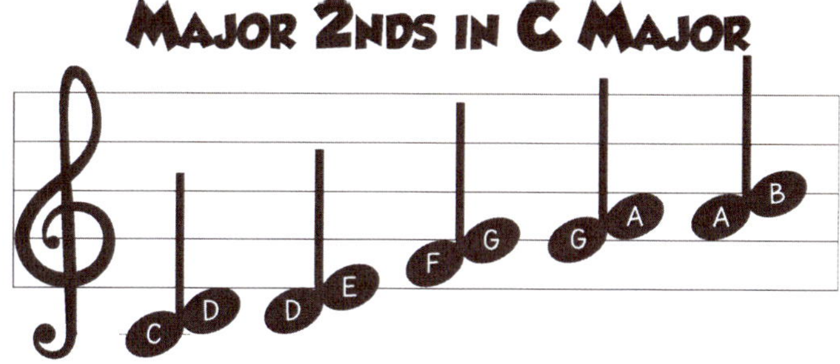

C to _____ is a Major 2nd

F to _____ is a Major 2nd

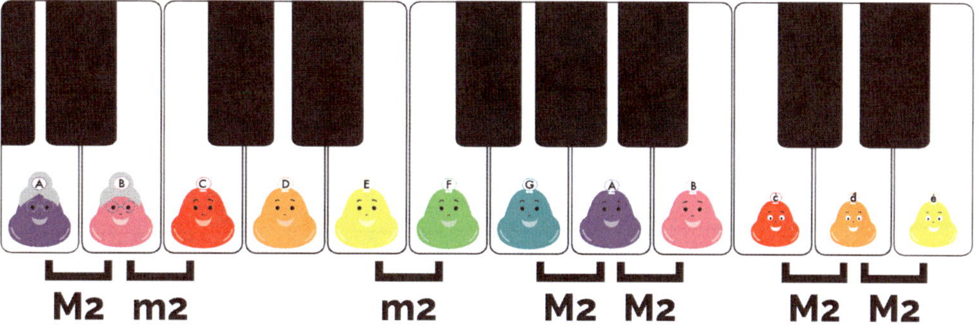

Did you notice???

ALL the Major 2nds above have a black key between the bells. For example, in between C and D there is a black key called C# (C Sharp). Then notice how ALL the Minor 2nds DO NOT have a black key between them. For example, in between E and F, there is NO black key.

Minor 2nd or Major 2nd?

On the keyboards below you'll see EITHER a
MINOR 2nd or a MAJOR 2nd. Circle the correct answer below each piano.
Hint: Minor 2nds will be 1 key away. Major 2nds will be 2 keys away.

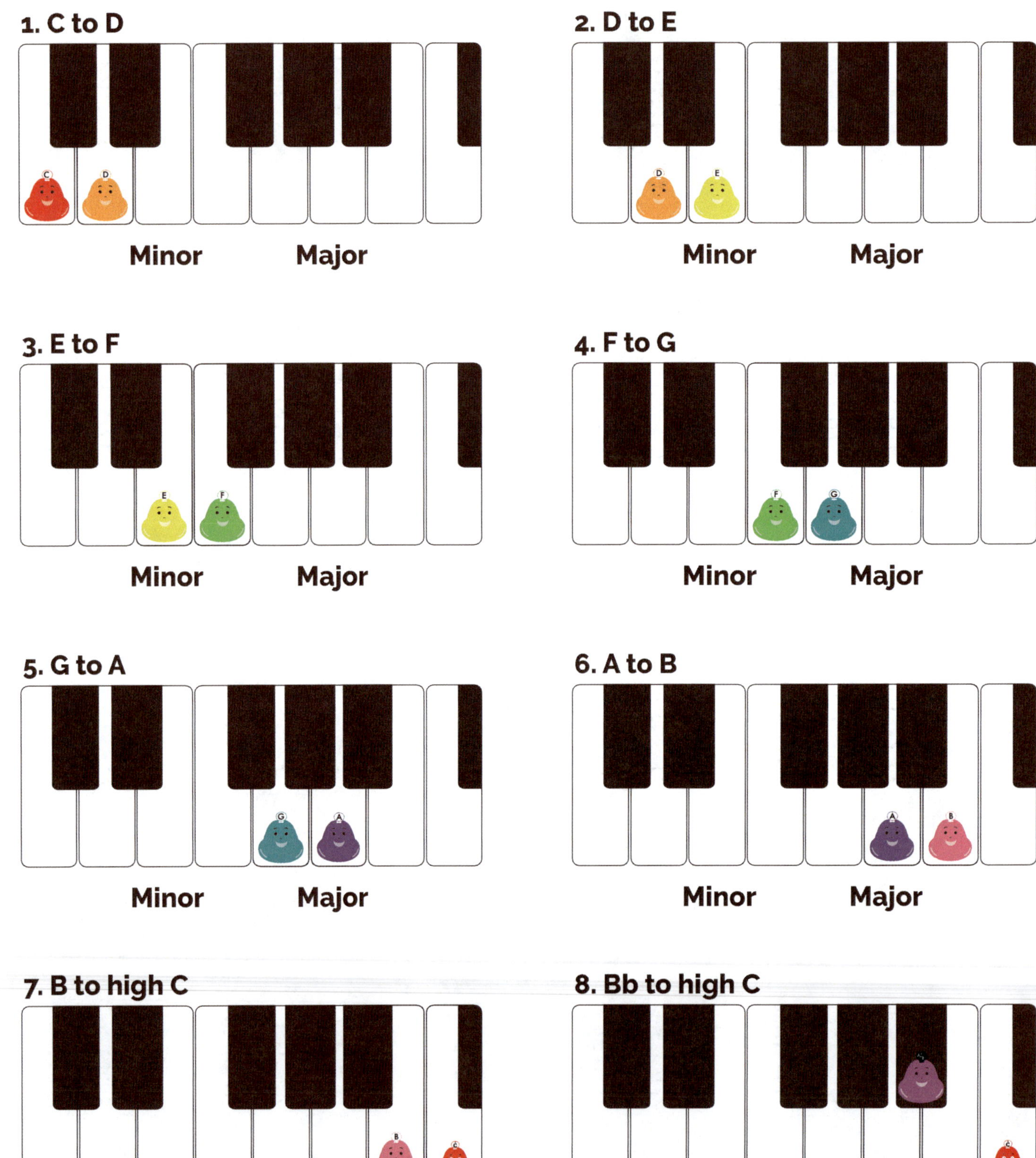

Minor **Major**

Minor **Major**

Notating Intervals - Round 2

Let's draw some more melodic intervals. This time though, you'll have to draw both the starting note AND the interval that follows.

Hint: Use Every Good Boy Does Fine & FACE in the SPACE
to remember where each note lives on the staff.

Challenge: Cover up the hint above and try to work from memory.

Ex 1 **Notate a G + a 2nd lower**

Hint: Count this line (G) as 1
Hint: Count this space (F) as 2

Ex 2 **Notate an A + a 3rd above**

← Count 3
← Count 2
← Count 1

1 **Notate B + a 2nd above**

2 **Notate Middle C + a 5th above**

3 **Notate F + a 6th above**

4 **Notate E + a 6th above**

5 **Notate G + a 4th below**

6 **Notate B + a 4th above**

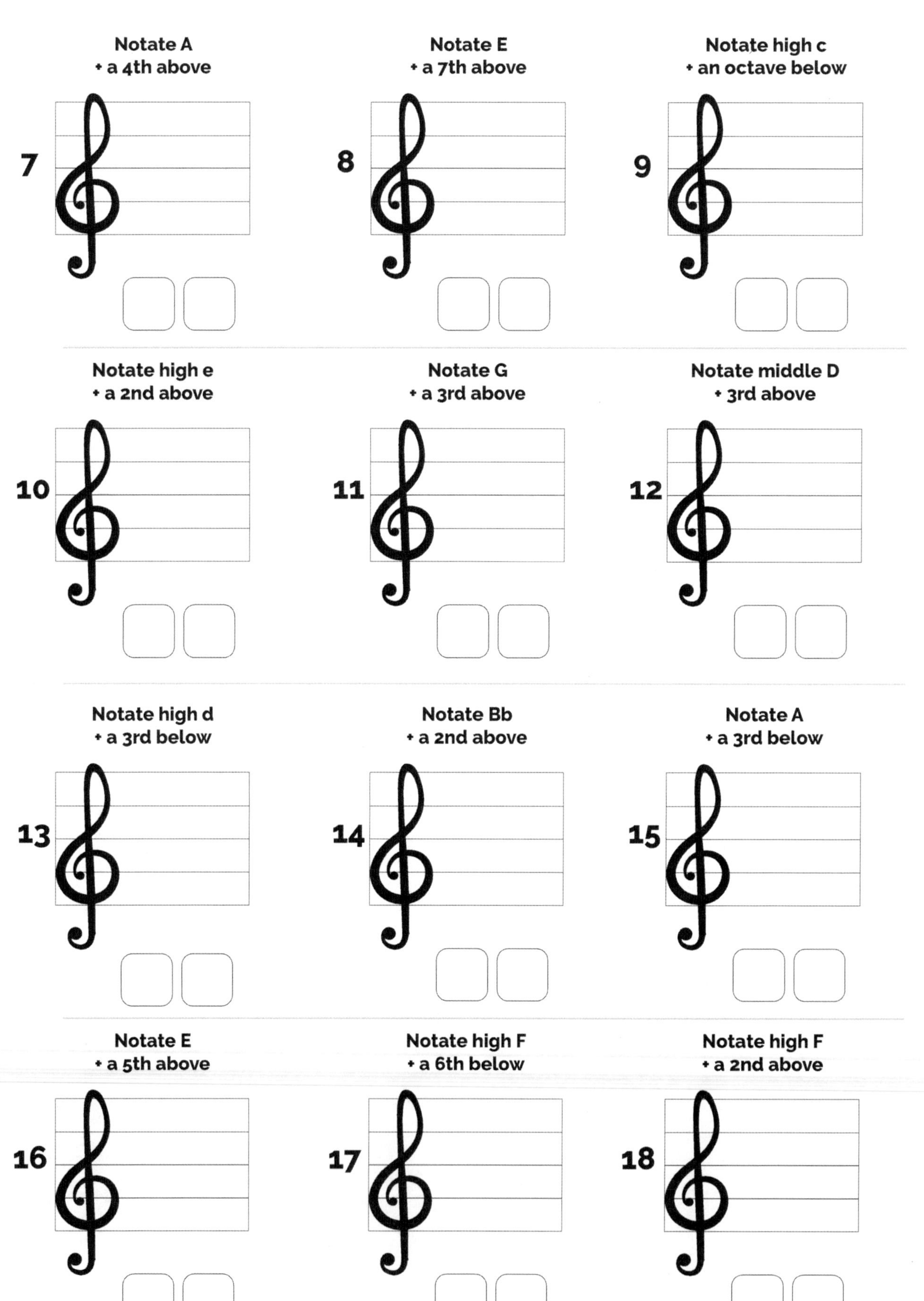
Notate A
+ a 4th above
7
Notate E
+ a 7th above
8
Notate high c
+ an octave below
9
Notate high e
+ a 2nd above
10
Notate G
+ a 3rd above
11
Notate middle D
+ 3rd above
12
Notate high d
+ a 3rd below
13
Notate Bb
+ a 2nd above
14
Notate A
+ a 3rd below
15
Notate E
+ a 5th above
16
Notate high F
+ a 6th below
17
Notate high F
+ a 2nd above
18

Semitone Challenge with 2nds

On the keyboards below we have ALL 12 of our notes.
When we have ALL 12 of our notes and we step from one note to the next, we are moving the distance of one SEMITONE.

Ex 1. Circle F and the note 1 semitone below

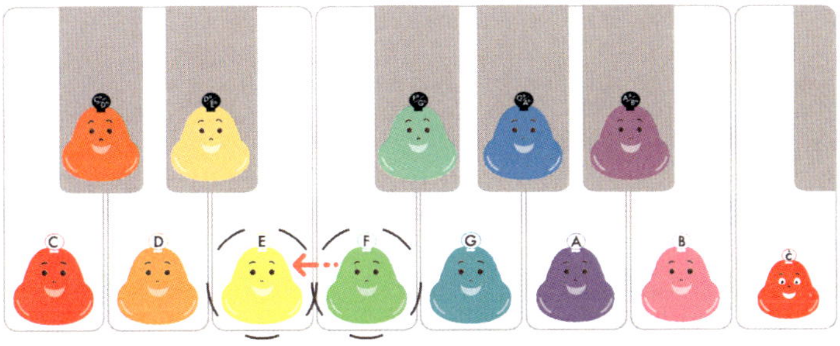

Hint: Start at F and count down (left) 1 note

Ex 2. Circle C and the note 1 semitone above

Hint: Start at C and count up (right) 1 note

1. Circle D and the note 1 semitone above

2. Circle D and the note 2 semitones above

3. Circle B and the note 1 semitone above

4. Circle E and the note 1 semitone below

5. Circle F and the note 2 semitones above

6. Circle D and the note 2 semitones below

PRIMARY PRODIGIES

3RDS WITH "WHEN THE SAINTS GO MARCHING IN"

Section 2.3

2.3 When the Saints Go Marching In

When the Saints Go Marching In

Black & White Verse

Practice "When the Saints" with black-and-white music!
Then take some time and label the intervals in the boxes below the lyrics.

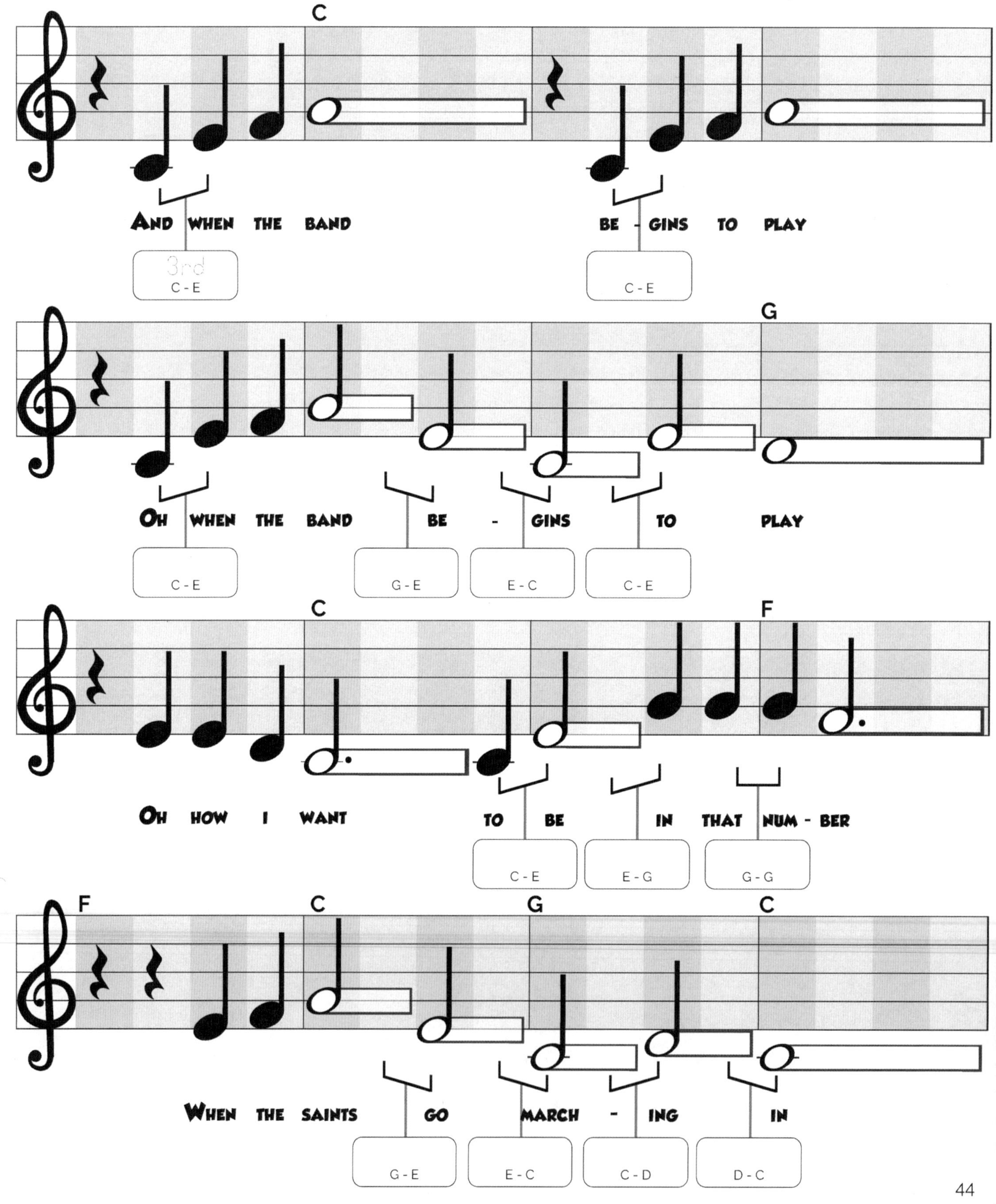

Page intentionally left blank for sheet music continuity

Player 1 Notes:

Au Clair De La Lune

Player 2 Notes:

This 19th century French folk song has been arranged as a duet. Player 1 will use notes that harmonize with Player 2's melody. The intervals created will be mostly 3rds with some variation.

Chords
D
G
Lyrics
MA CHAN - DELLE EST MOR - TE, JE N'AI PLUS DE FEU.
Solfege
la la la ti do do ti ti la do ti la sol sol sol sol
Lyrics
MA CHAN - DELLE EST MOR - TE, JE N'AI PLUS DE FEU.
Solfege
re re re re la la sol sol re la sol re re re re re

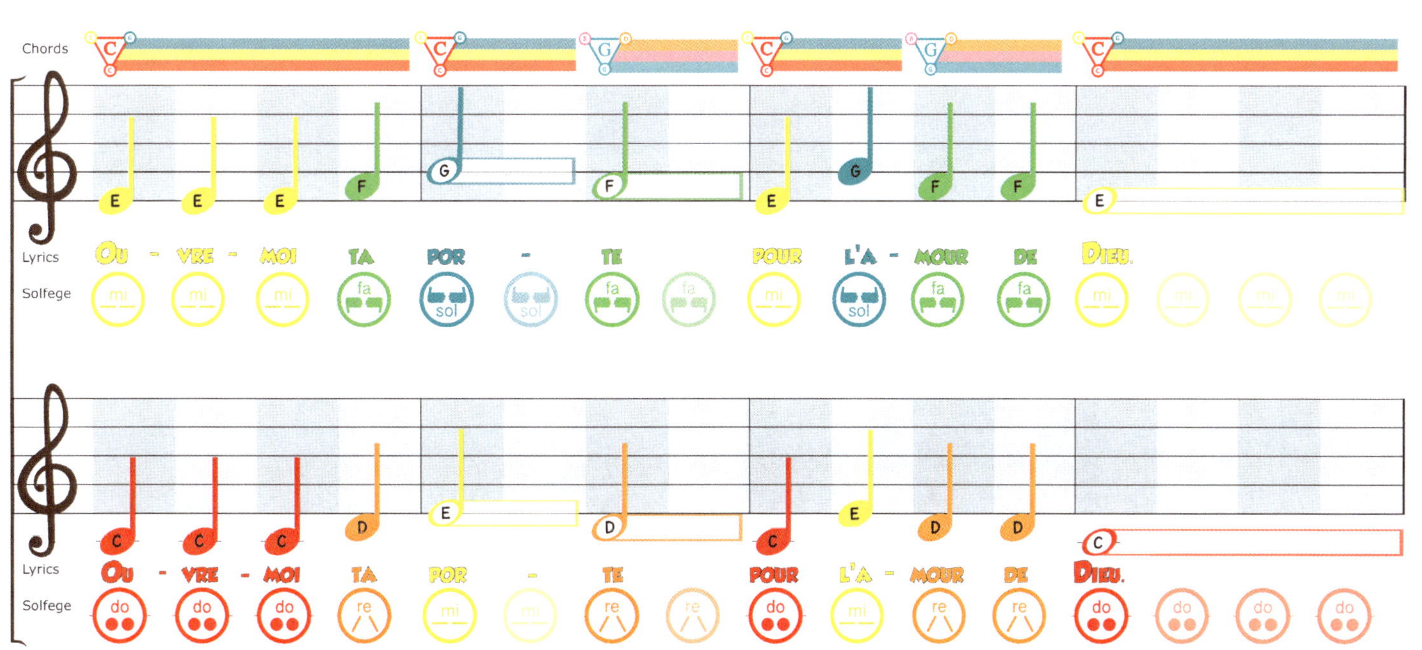
Chords
C
C
G
C
G
C
Lyrics
OU - VRE - MOI TA POR - TE POUR L'A - MOUR DE DIEU.
Solfege
mi mi mi fa sol sol fa fa mi sol fa fa mi mi mi mi
Lyrics
OU - VRE - MOI TA POR - TE POUR L'A - MOUR DE DIEU.
Solfege
do do do re mi mi re re do mi re re do do do do

Thirds (3rds)

Thirds are the essential building blocks that we use to build chords. Our simplest chords, triads, will be the result of what we call "stacking 3rds" on the staff. We'll see 3rds moving from line to line or space to space and, we'll hear 3rds making the sweetest sound.

Melodically, they create powerful music patterns, like Do Mi Sol, allowing us to skip around the scale.

In a major key, 3rds will either be...

Minor 3rd

3 Semitones

Melodically Sounds Like...

Start of "Greensleeves" (E-G)
Start of "Hey Jude" (c down to A)
Brahms' Lullaby

Harmonically Sounds Like...

"Nanny Nanny"
Consonant (pleasing)
"Sad" (when compared to M3)

Major 3rd

4 Semitones

Melodically Sounds Like...

Start of "When the Saints"
Start of "Kumbaya"
Do-Mi, Fa-La, Sol-Ti

Harmonically Sounds Like...

The beginning of a Major Chord
Consonant (pleasing)
"Happy" (when compared to m3)

Minor 3rds in C Major

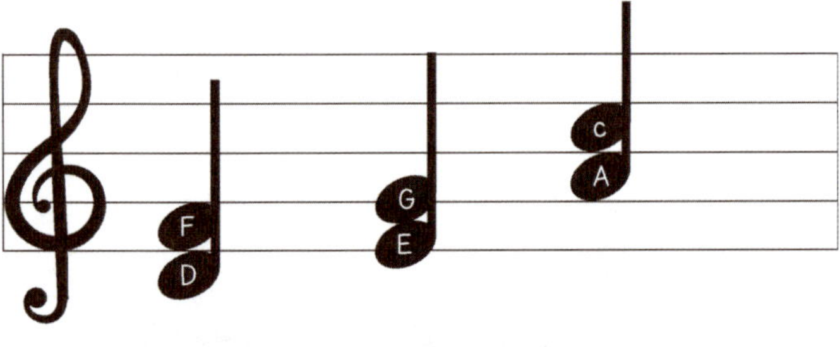

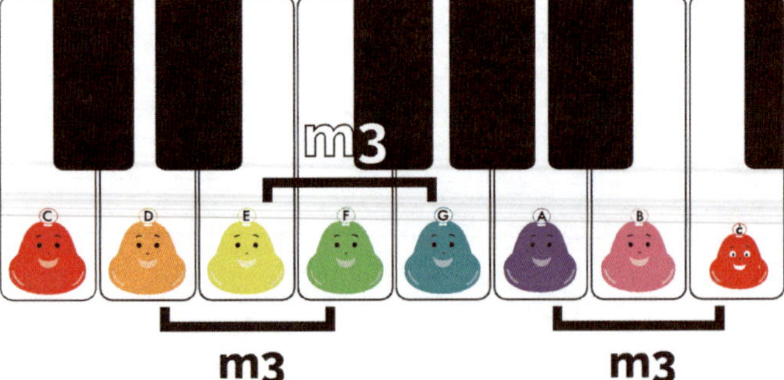

m3 m3

D to _____ is a minor 3rd

E to _____ is a minor 3rd

A to _____ is a minor 3rd

Major 3rds in C Major

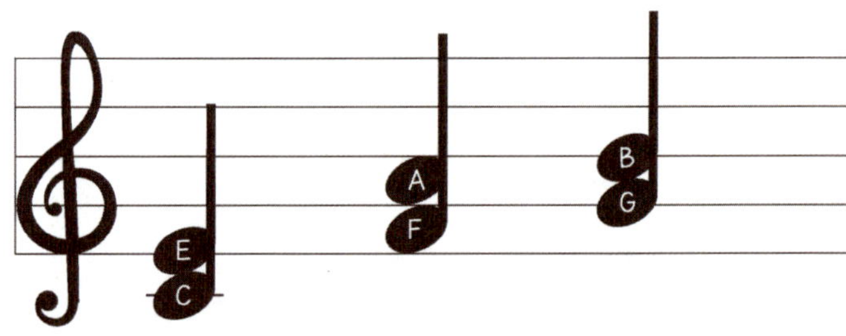

M3 M3

C to _____ is a Major 3rd

F to _____ is a Major 3rd

G to _____ is a Major 3rd

Flats

The flat is part of an important group of musical symbols used in notation known as **accidentals**. An accidental will change the note it is attached to by 1 semitone. Let's look at flats, natural symbols, and sharps.

On the staff, a **flat** before a note **lowers** it by 1 semitone. In the key of F, your melody will have more Bb (B flat) notes instead of B natural.

Using Flats to Make Minor 3rds

In the examples below, let's change some Major 3rds into minor 3rds. To do this, we'll add some flats (♭) to our notes! This means we'll turn E to Eb, A to Ab, and B to Bb.

This is a great example of math in music. C to E is 4 semitones, a major 3rd. Adding a flat to Eb shortens that distance to 3 semitones, a minor 3rd. One symbol affects the musical ratios as well as the aural qualities.

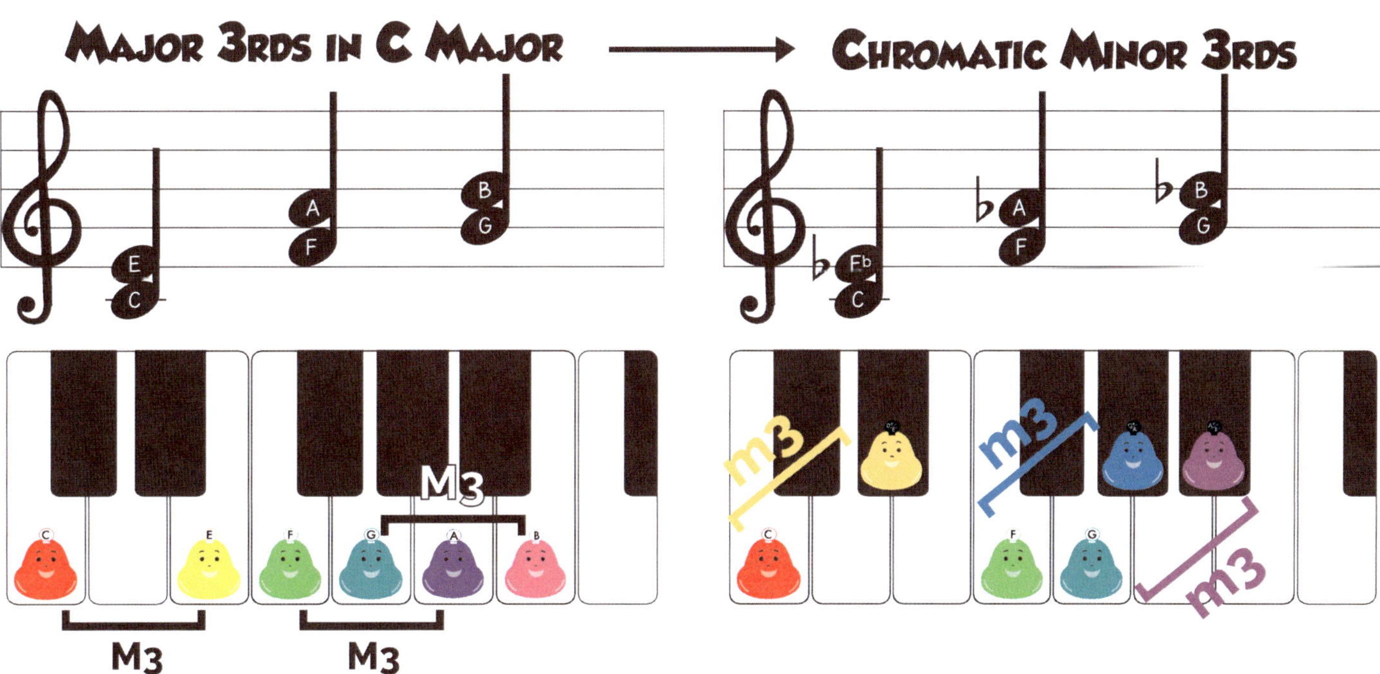

Take a minute to play a Major 3rd from above, and then play the corresponding minor 3rd. Observe the difference between C and E and C and Eb when played melodically & harmonically. Then do the same for the other two pairs of thirds above.

Natural

The natural symbol (♮) has the unique ability to change pitch up or down by 1 semitone. If a tune is in the key of G, there will be an F# in the key signature. Adding a natural before an F# note lowers it to F natural.

Similarly, a song in F major will have Bb in the key signature. Adding a natural before a Bb note raises it to B natural.

Sharps

We've got the flat, natural, and finally the sharp to complete our group of **accidentals**. On the staff, a **sharp** before a note **raises** it by 1 semitone. In the key of G, your melody will have more F# (F sharp) notes instead of F natural.

Using Sharps to Make Major 3rds

In the examples below, let's change some minor 3rds into Major 3rds. To do this, we'll add some sharps (♯) to our notes! This means we'll turn F to F#, G to G#, and high c to high c#.

Here we see the musical math being used again. E to G is 3 semitones, a minor 3rd. Adding a sharp to G# increases that distance to 4 semitones, a major 3rd. Another symbol affecting the look of the music and subtle changes in sound.

Minor 3rds in C Major → Chromatic Major 3rds

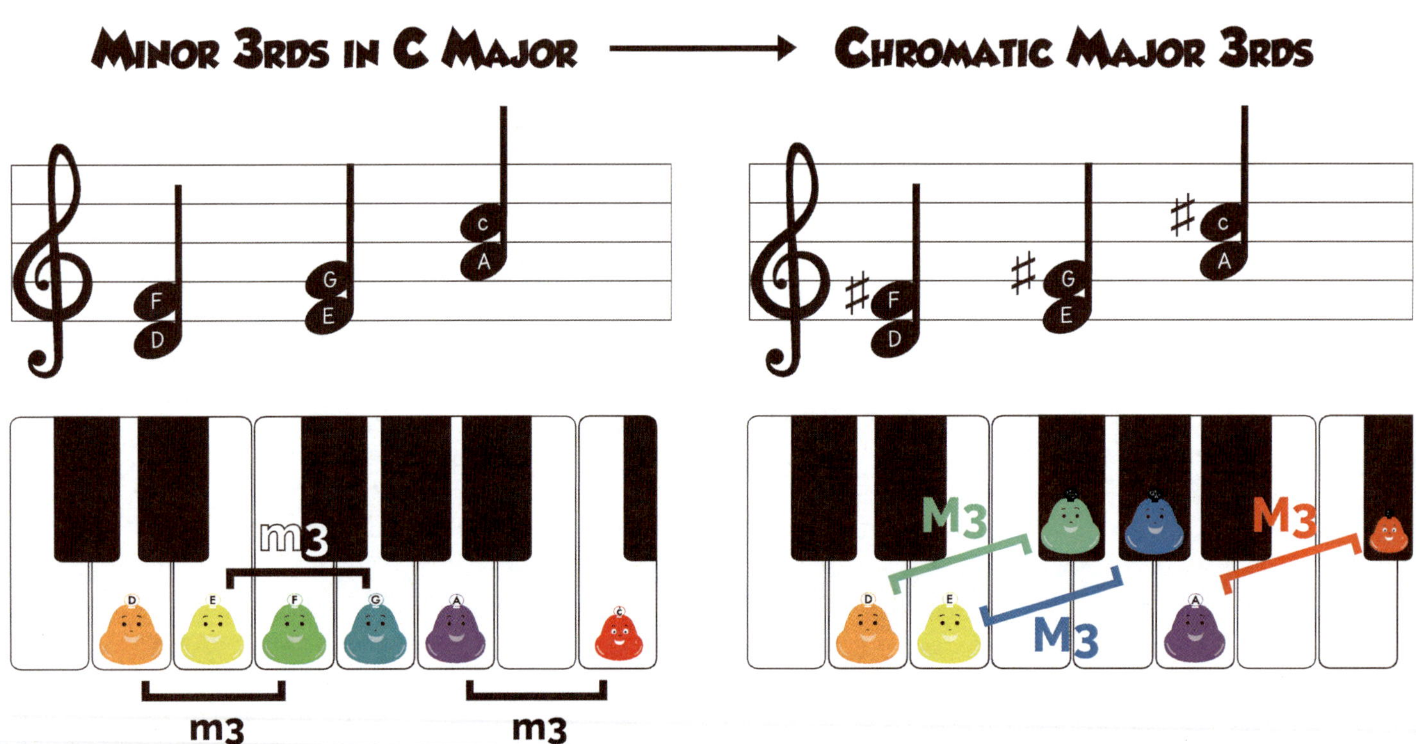

Take a minute to play a minor 3rd from above, and then play the corresponding Major 3rd. Observe the different between D and F and D and F# when played melodically & harmonically.

Then do the same for the other two pairs of thirds above.

2NDS OR 3RDS

On the keyboards below you'll see 2nds or 3rds.
Circle the correct answer below each piano.

Bonus: Play your instrument as you go to hear the sound of the interval

1. C to D

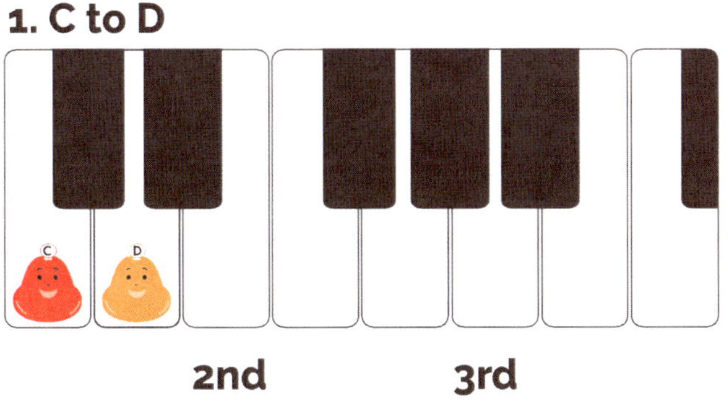

2nd **3rd**

2. D to E

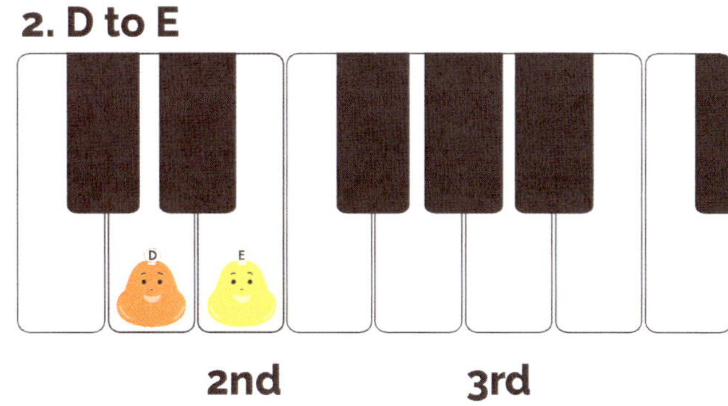

2nd **3rd**

3. E to F

2nd **3rd**

4. F# to G

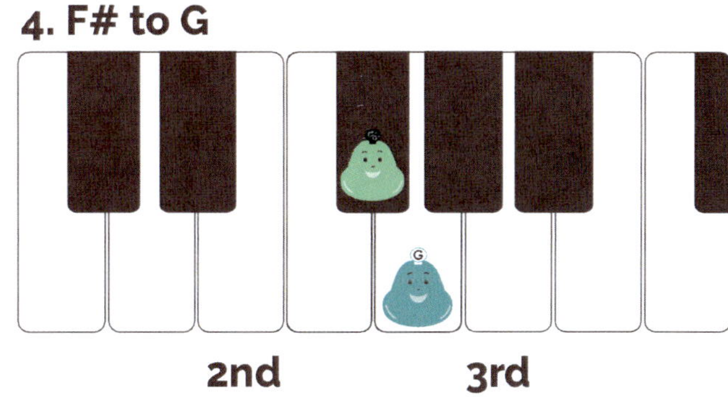

2nd **3rd**

5. G to Bb

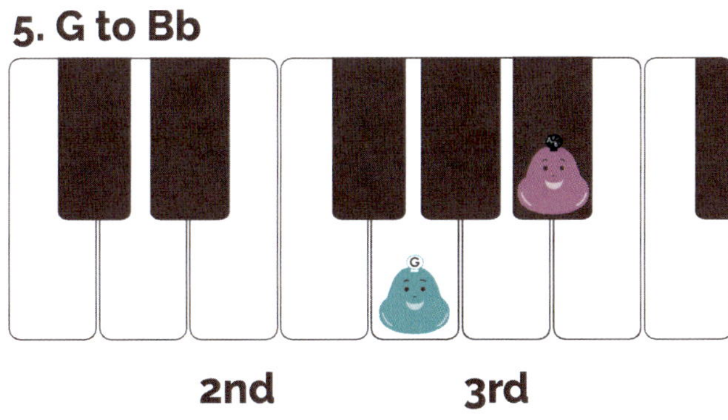

2nd **3rd**

6. F to A

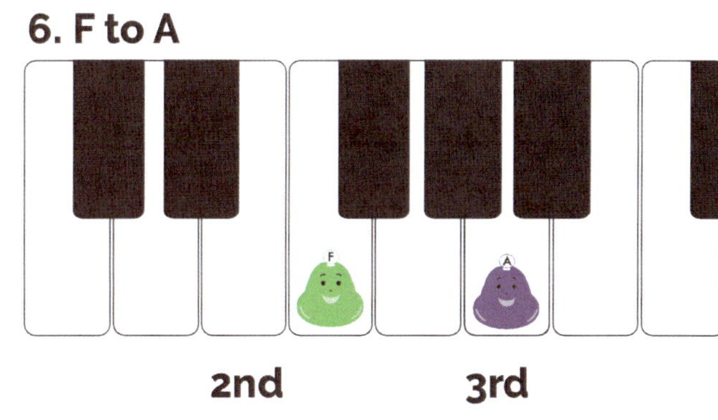

2nd **3rd**

7. B to high C

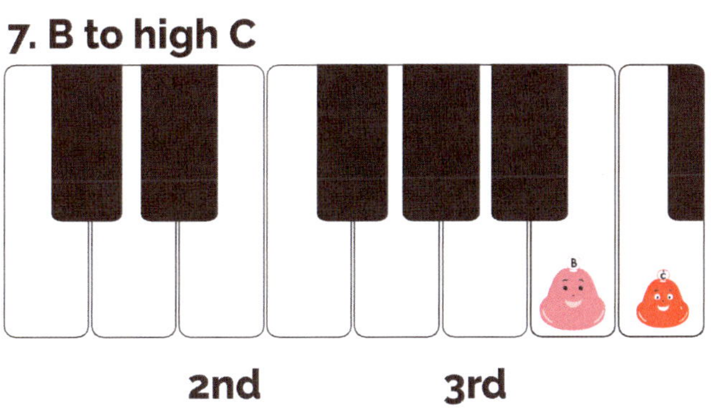

2nd **3rd**

8. Bb to high C

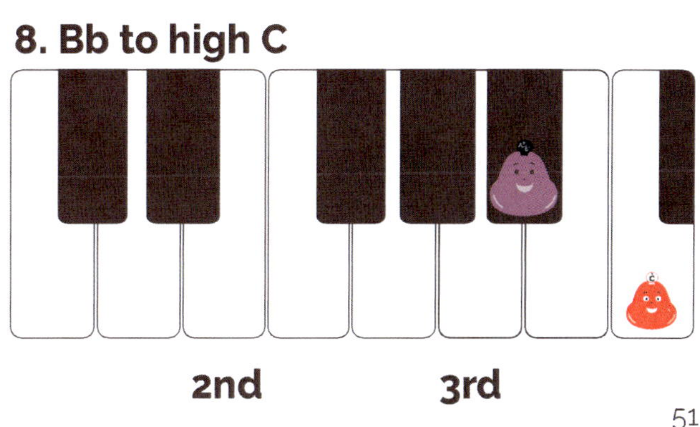

2nd **3rd**

Notating Intervals - Round 3

Let's draw some HARMONIC Intervals. These intervals happen at the same time.
Then, write the name of the interval below

Hint: Use Every Good Boy Does Fine & FACE in the SPACE
to remember where each note lives on the staff.

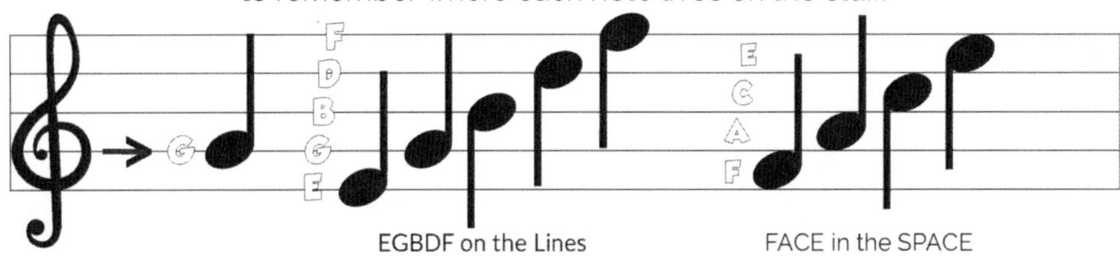

Challenge: Cover up the hint above and try to work from memory.

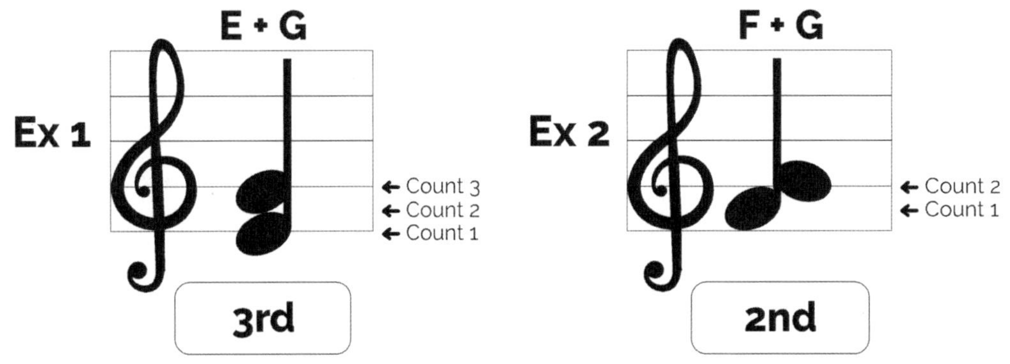

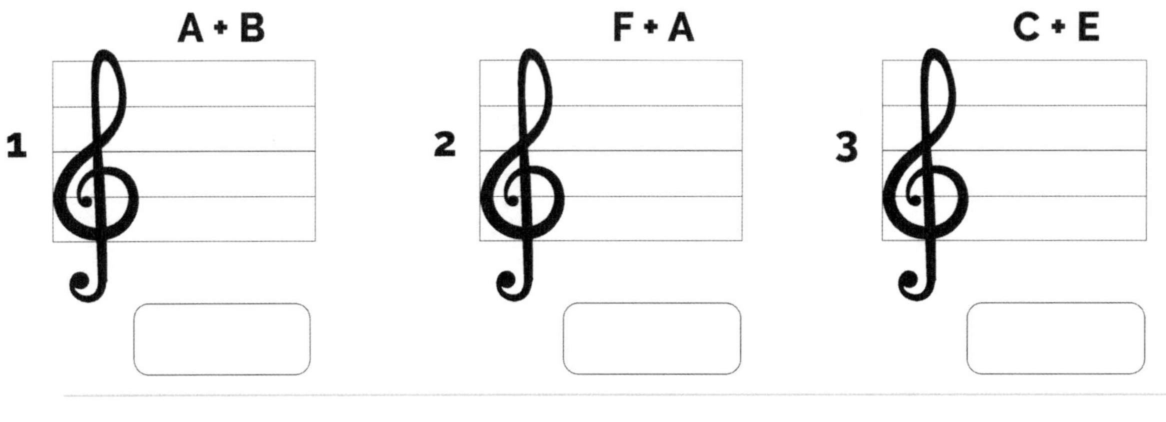

high c + D
7

A + high c
8

E + G
9

A + Bb
10

B + high c
11

F# + A#
12

G + Bb
13

D + F#
14

E + G#
15

C + E + G
16

F + A + high c
17

G + B + high d
18

Semitone Challenge with 3rds

Let's practice some more semitones. This time we'll use...

3 semitones (a minor 3rd) & 4 semitones (a Major 3rd)

Ex 1. Circle E and the note 3 semitones above

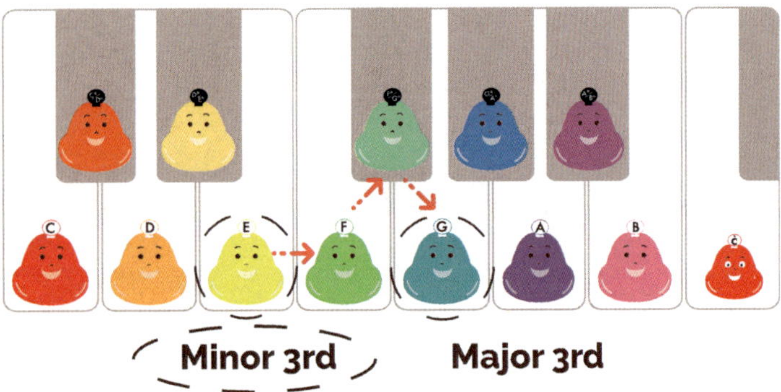

Minor 3rd **Major 3rd**

Ex 2. Circle C and the note 4 semitones above

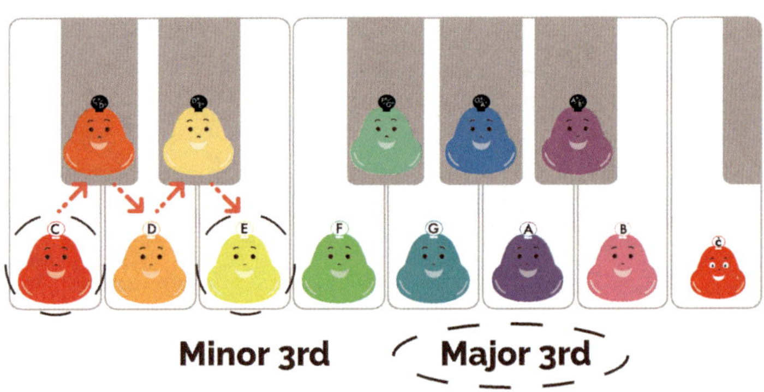

Minor 3rd **Major 3rd**

1. Circle D and the note 3 semitones above

Minor 3rd **Major 3rd**

2. Circle D and the note 4 semitones above

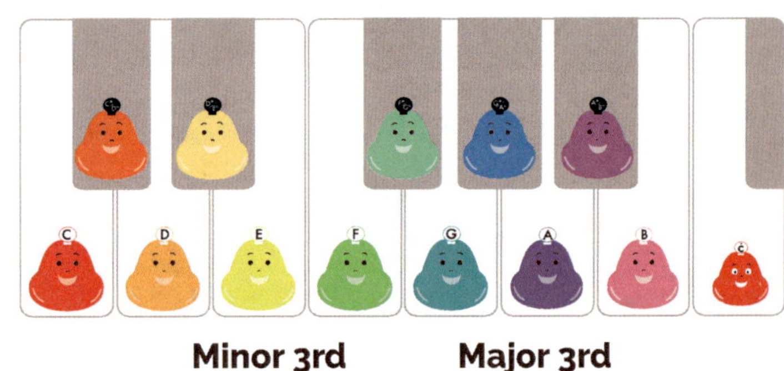

Minor 3rd **Major 3rd**

3. Circle F and the note 4 semitones above

Minor 3rd **Major 3rd**

4. Circle G and the note 4 semitones above

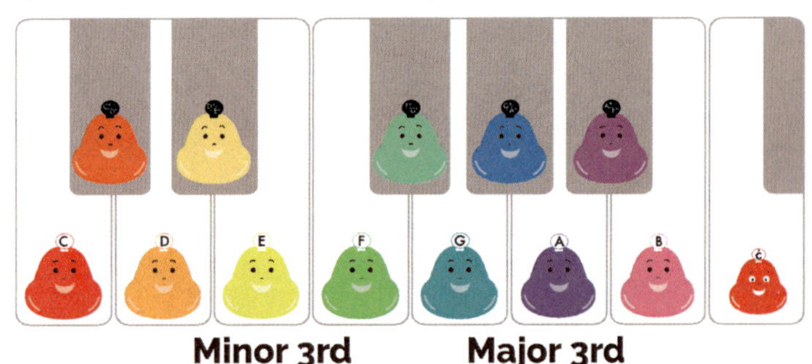

Minor 3rd **Major 3rd**

5. Circle A and the note 3 semitones below

Minor 3rd **Major 3rd**

6. Circle Bb and the note 3 semitones below

Minor 3rd **Major 3rd**

PRIMARY PRODIGIES

4THS WITH "BRIDAL CHORUS"

Section 2.4

Notes Used:

2.4 Bridal Chorus

F Major

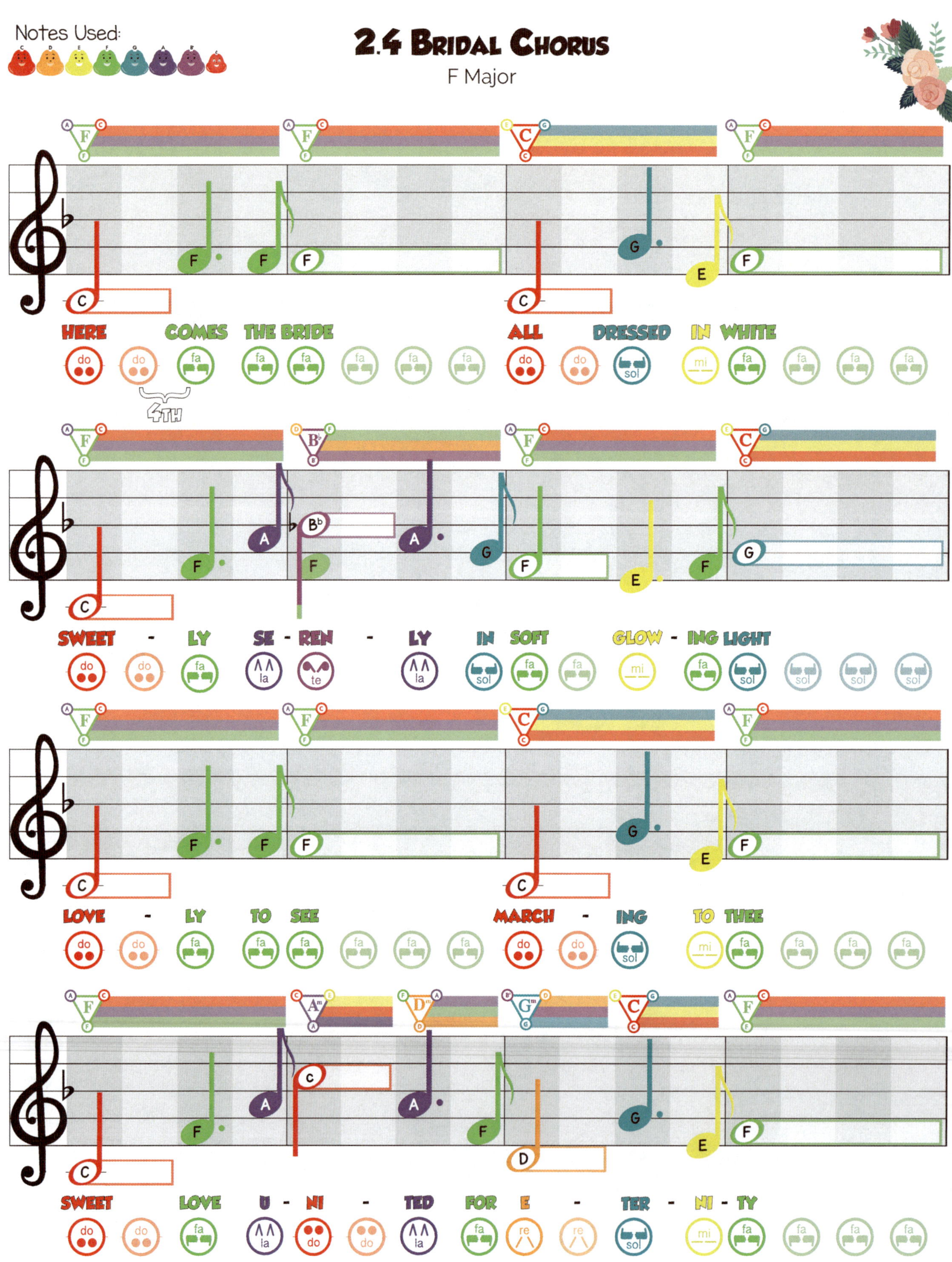

Bridal Chorus

Black & White Version

Practice the Bridal Chorus with black-and-white music!
Then take some time and label the intervals in the boxes below the lyrics.

Notes Used:

Gobble Gobble

BONUS SONG: Practice this Thanksgiving-themed song which also begins with the Perfect 4th from C up to F.

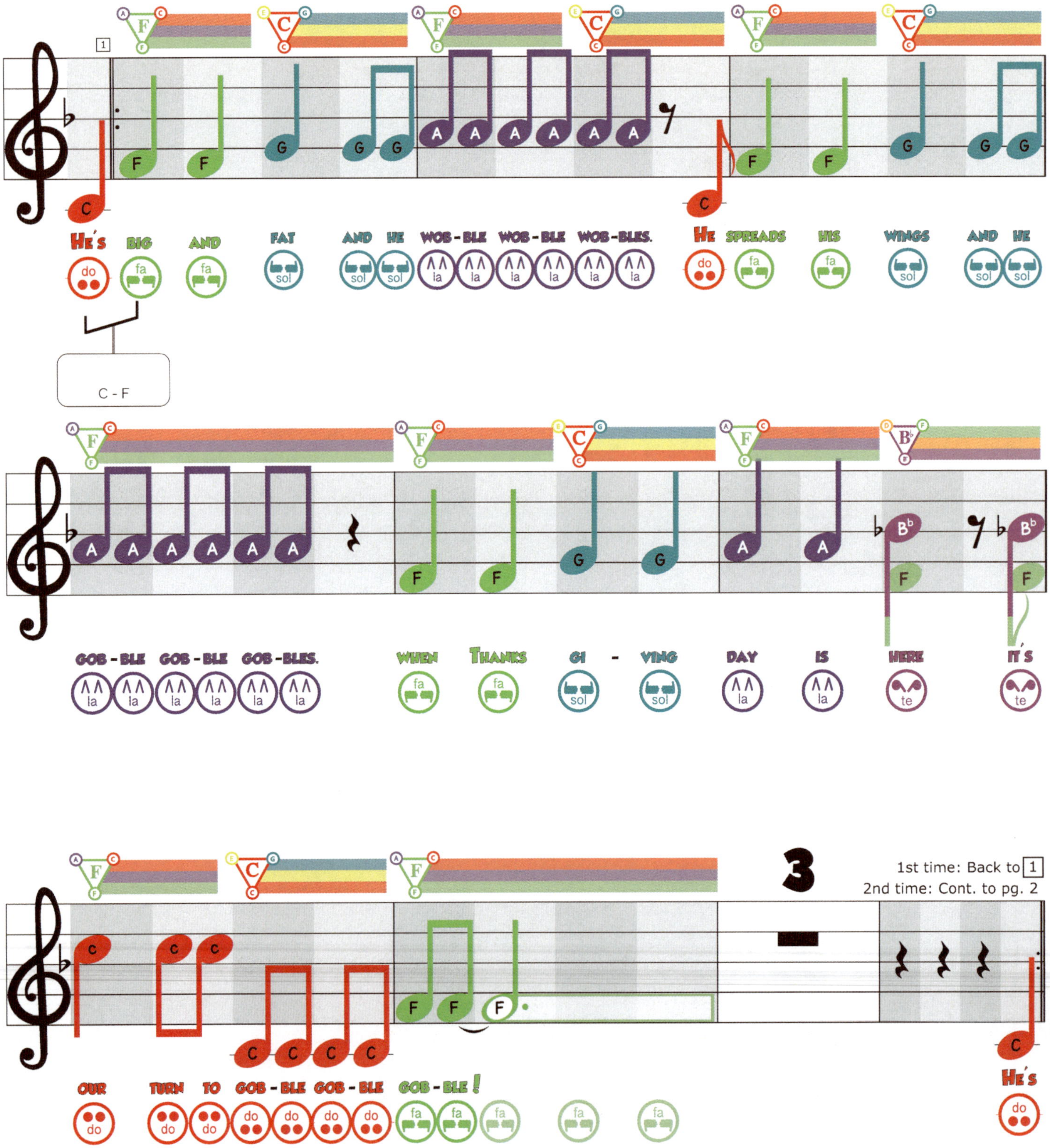

1

He's big and fat and he wob-ble wob-ble wob-bles. He spreads his wings and he

do fa fa sol sol sol la la la la la la do fa fa sol sol sol

C - F

gob-ble gob-ble gob-bles. When Thanks gi - ving day is here it's

la la la la la la fa fa sol sol la la te te

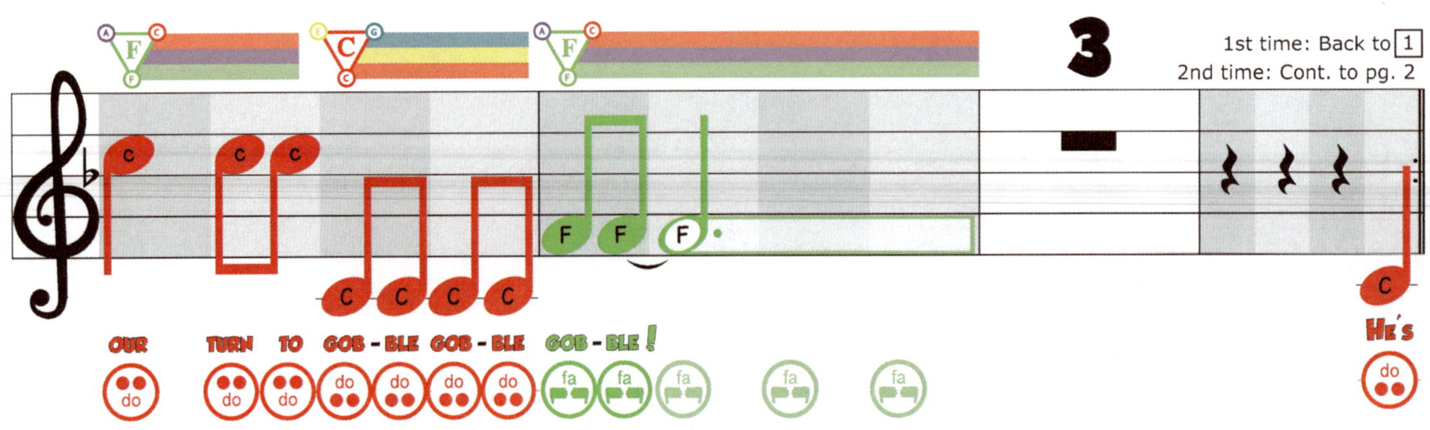

Gobble Gobble

Verse 3

Practice "Gobble Gobble" with black-and-white music!
Then take some time and label the intervals in the boxes below the lyrics.

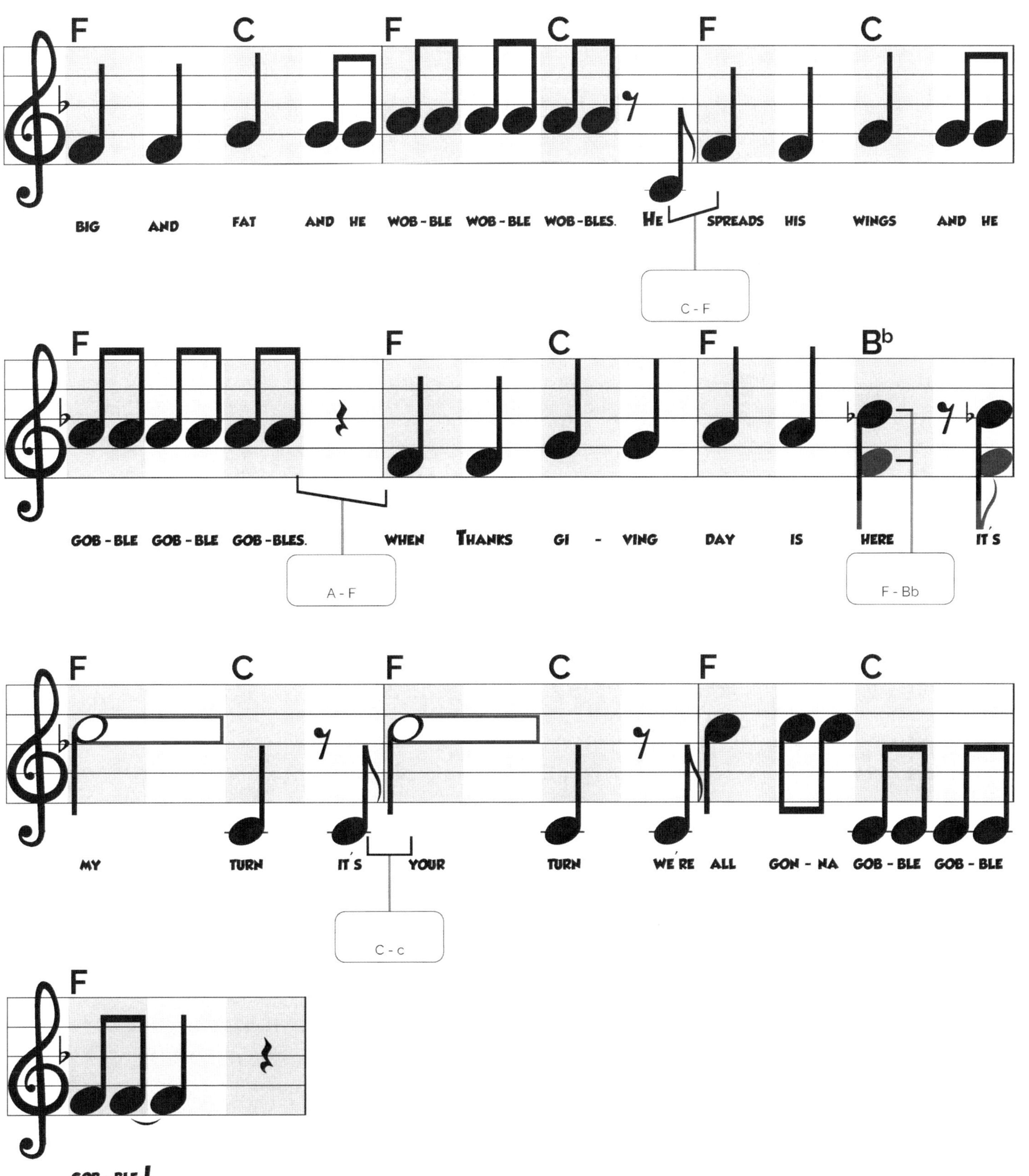

Fourths (4ths)

Fourths are a proud interval, sounding regal and important like the beginning notes of "Here Comes the Bride." In the major key, all 4ths will be perfect EXCEPT when the Fa pairs with Ti. This unusual pairing is called an **augmented 4th** or the **tritone**.

Harmonically, perfect 4ths occur when we build any major or minor triad inversion. In an F Major chord, spelled FAC, moving F above C creates a perfect 4th from C to F.

In a major key, 4ths will either be...

Perfect 4th
5 Semitones

Melodically Sounds Like...

Jeopardy Theme (up a P4)
"Shave and a Haircut" (down a P4)
Aura Lee

Harmonically Sounds Like...

Ambiguous, unlike major or minor
Strong
Hollow or square

Augmented 4th
6 Semitones

Melodically Sounds Like...

The Beatles "I'll Follow The Sun," on the lyrics "You'll look."
"Doggie in the Window" on "waggly"

Harmonically Sounds Like...

Ominous and dissonant
Demands resolution
(Fa to Re, Ti to Do)

Perfect 4ths in C Major

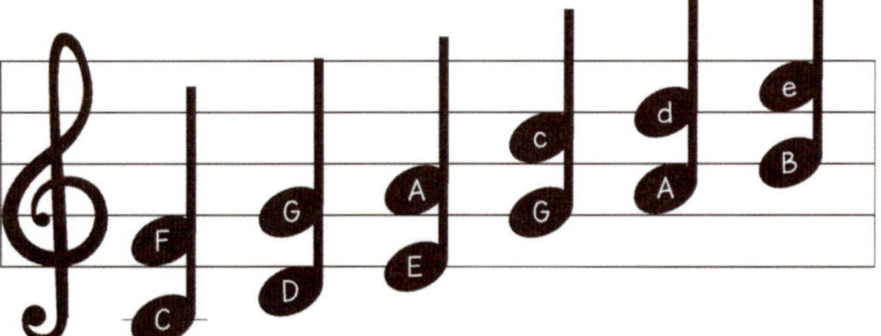

Here's 3 more examples:

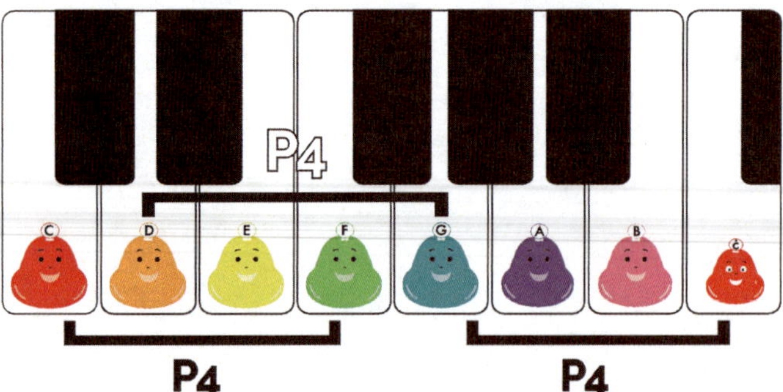

C to _____ is a Perfect 4th

D to _____ is a Perfect 4th

G to _____ is a Perfect 4th

Augmented 4th in C Major

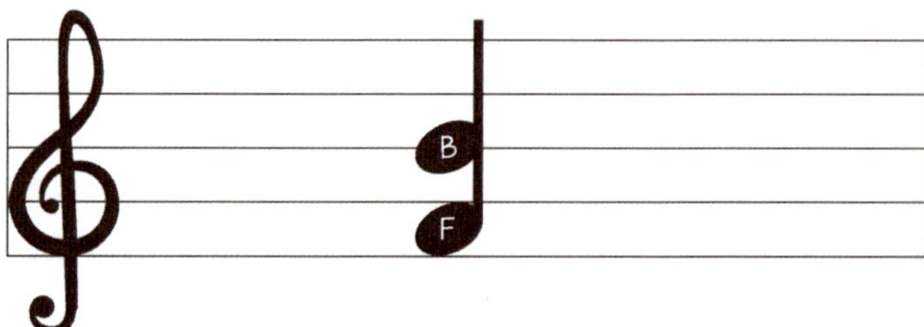

F to _____ is an augmented 4th

2nds, 3rds, & 4ths

On the keyboards below, you'll see 2nds, 3rds, & 4ths.
Circle the correct answer below each piano.

Bonus: Play your instrument as you go to hear the sound of the interval

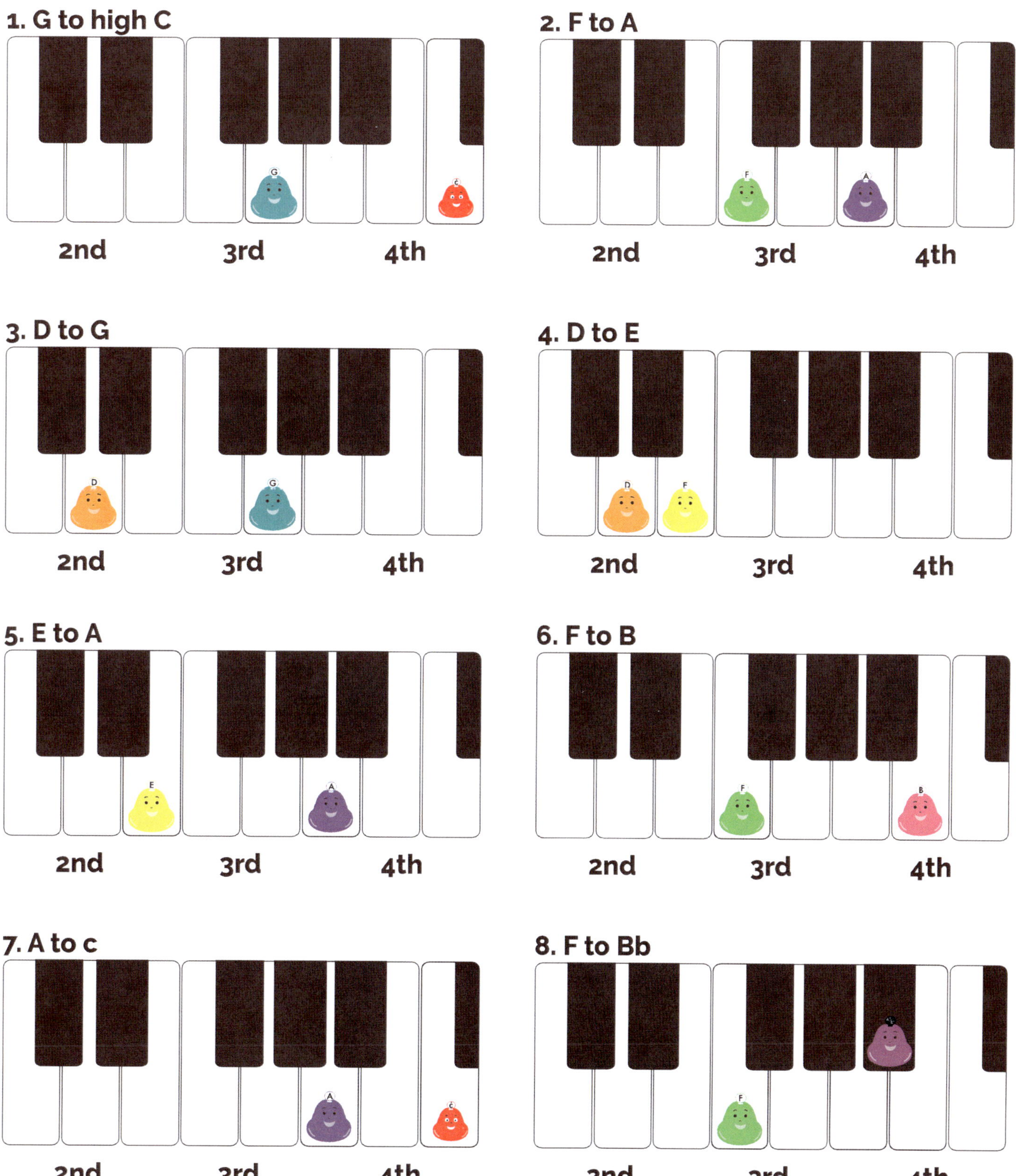

Notating Intervals - Round 4

Let's draw some HARMONIC Intervals. These intervals happen at the same time. Then, write the name of the interval below

Hint: Use Every Good Boy Does Fine & FACE in the SPACE to remember where each note lives on the staff.

Challenge: Cover up the hint above and try to work from memory.

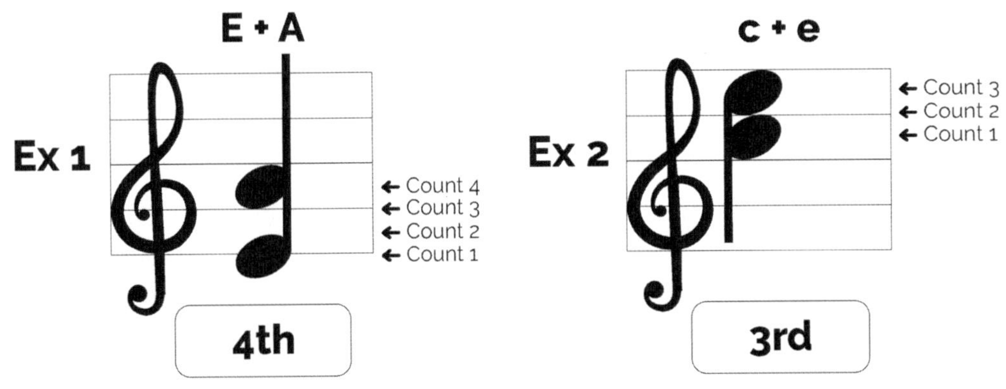

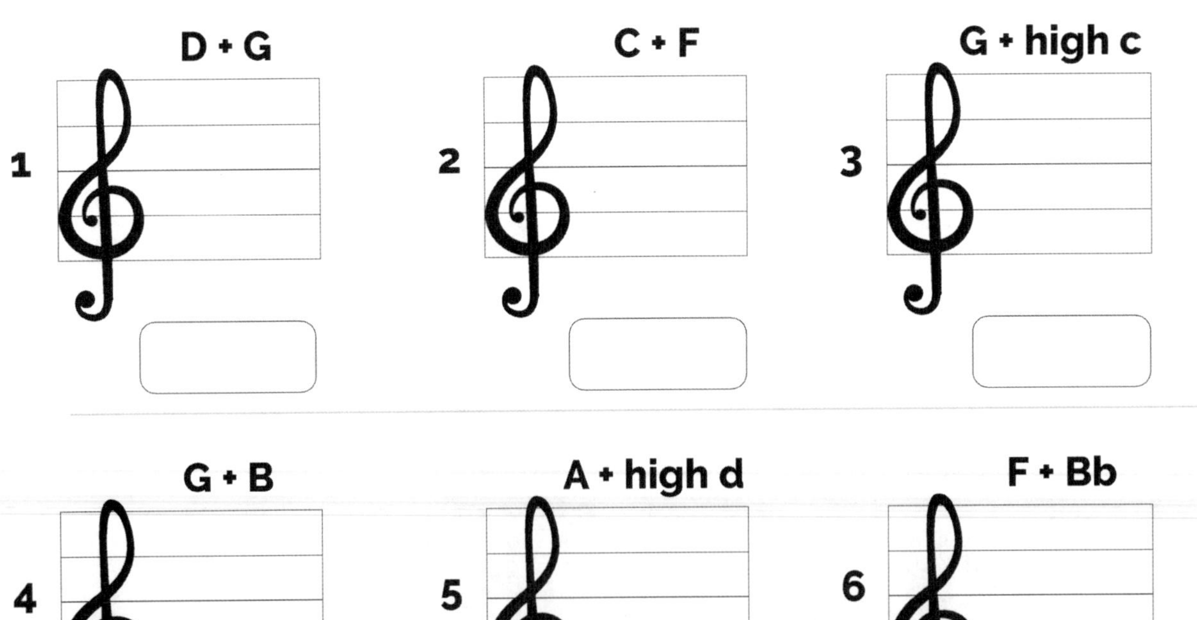

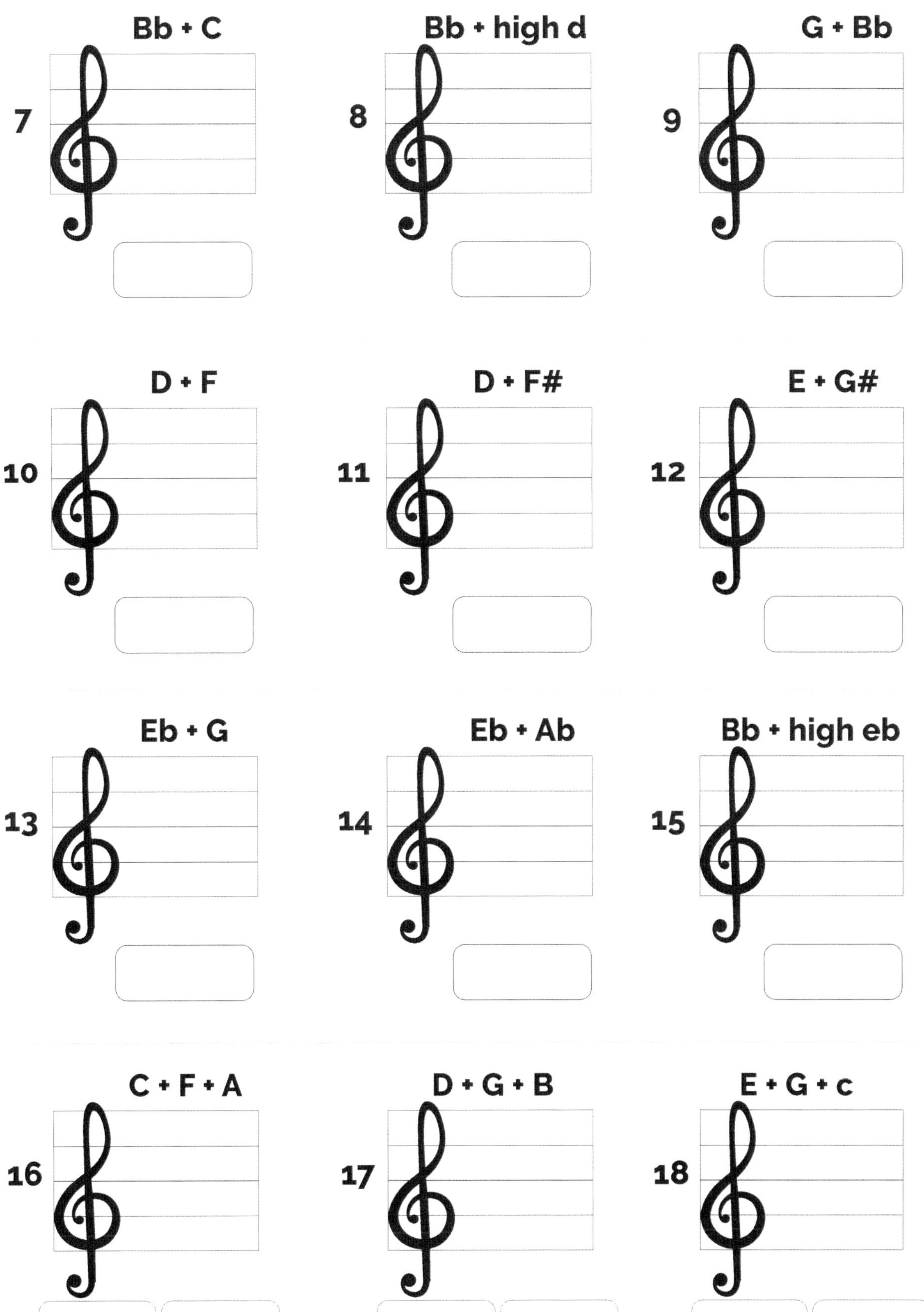
Bb + C
7
Bb + high d
8
G + Bb
9
D + F
10
D + F#
11
E + G#
12
Eb + G
13
Eb + Ab
14
Bb + high eb
15
C + F + A
16
C - F
F - A
D + G + B
17
D - G
G - B
E + G + c
18
E - G
G - c

Semitone Challenge with 4ths

Let's practice some more semitones. This time we'll use...

5 semitones (a Perfect 4th) & 6 semitones (an Augmented 4th or Tritone)

Ex 1. Circle C and the note 5 Semitones above

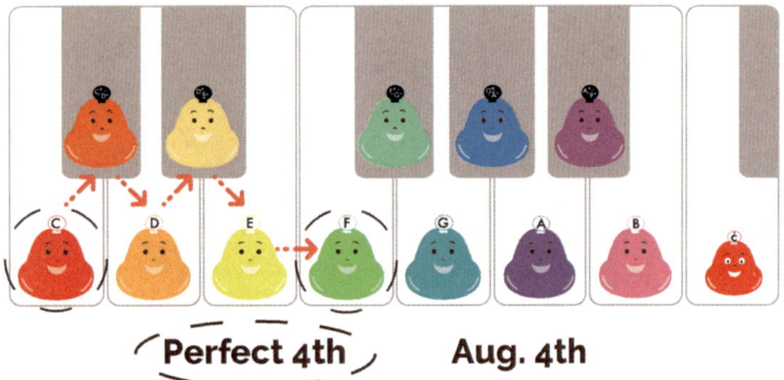

Perfect 4th **Aug. 4th**

Ex 2. Circle C and the note 6 Semitones above

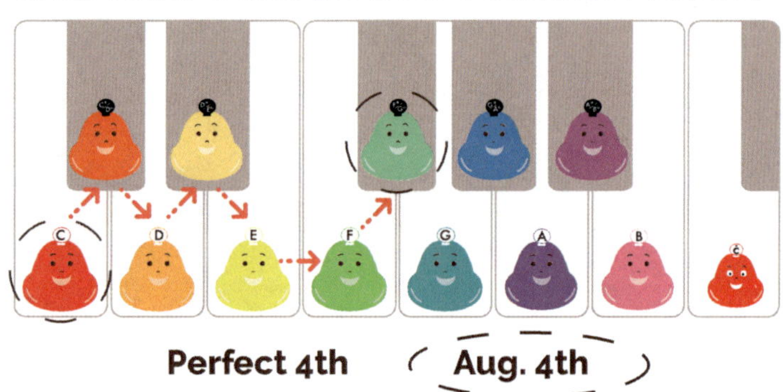

Perfect 4th **Aug. 4th**

1. Circle G and the note 5 semitones above

Perfect 4th **Aug. 4th**

2. Circle F and the note 5 semitones above

Perfect 4th **Aug. 4th**

3. Circle F# and the note 5 semitones below

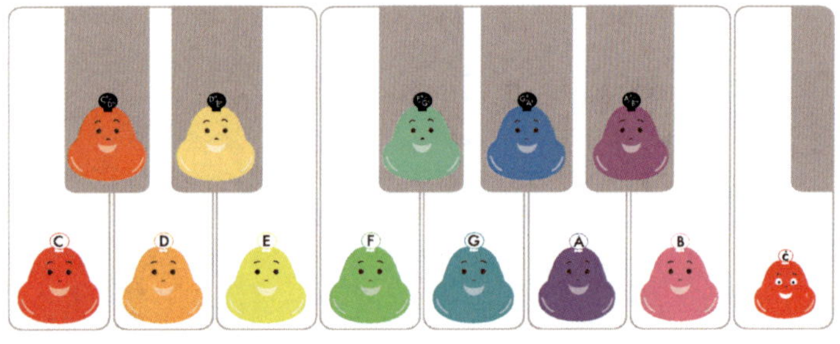

Perfect 4th **Aug. 4th**

4. Circle G and the note 5 semitones above

Perfect 4th **Aug. 4th**

5. Circle A and the note 5 semitones below

Perfect 4th **Aug. 4th**

6. Circle G# and the note 6 semitones below

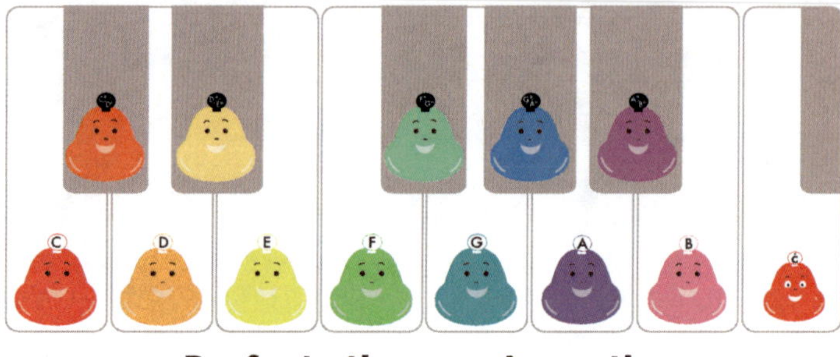

Perfect 4th **Aug. 4th**

5THS WITH "BAA BAA BLACK SHEEP"

Section 2.5

Notes Used:

Baa Baa Black Sheep

C Major

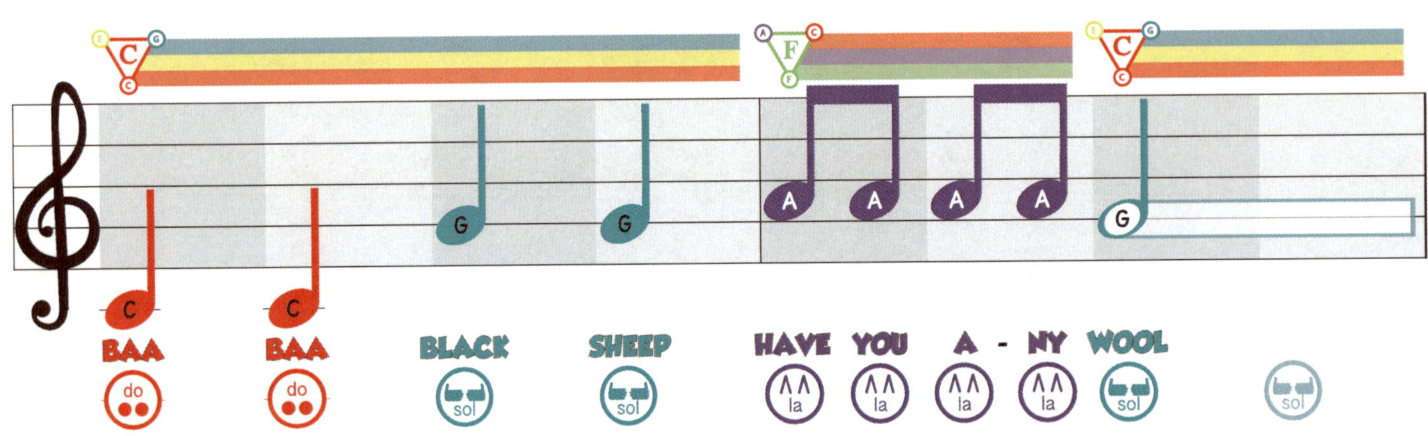

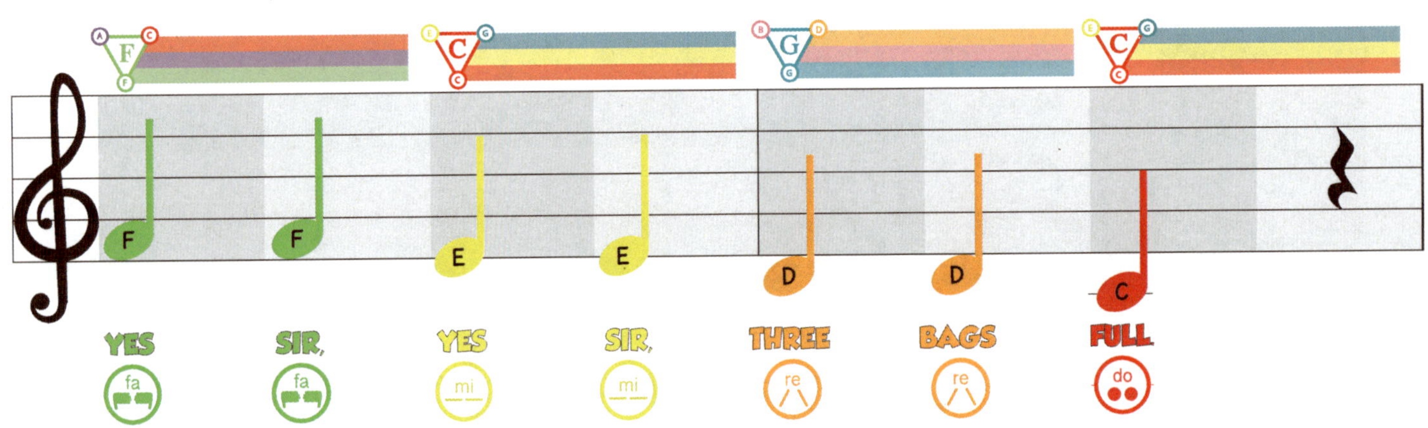

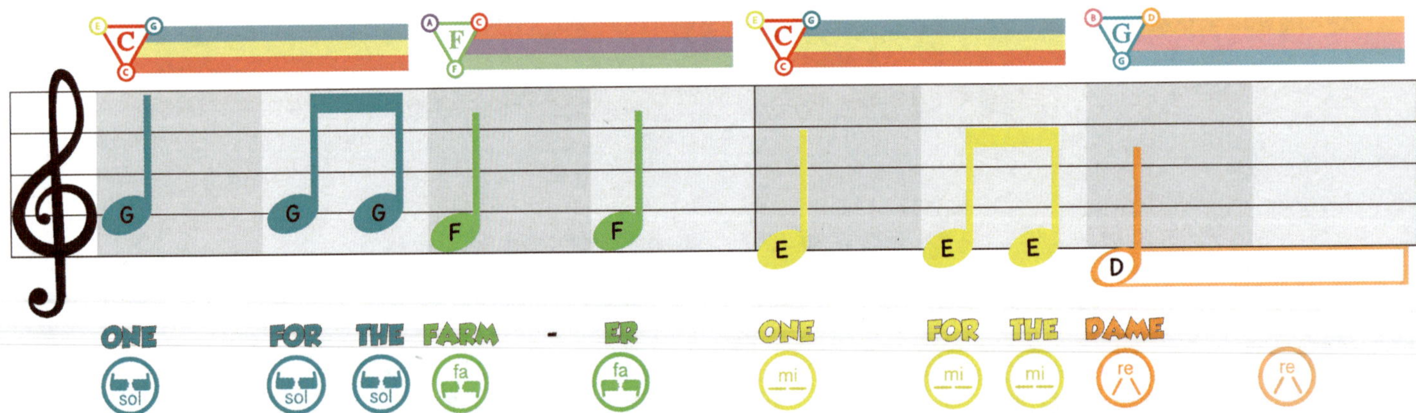

C F C G
G G G F F F F E E E D
ONE FOR THE LIT - TLE BOY WHO LIVES DOWN THE LANE
sol sol sol fa fa fa fa mi mi mi re re
C F C
C C G G A A A A G
BAA BAA BLACK SHEEP HAVE YOU A - NY WOOL
do do sol sol la la la la sol sol
F C G C
F F E E D D C
YES SIR, YES SIR, THREE BAGS FULL
fa fa mi mi re re do do

Scale Degrees with Baa Baa Black Sheep

Let's review some Scale Degrees with Baa Baa Black Sheep in C Major.
With C as our Tonic (Scale Degree 1), label the rest of the notes with their relative degrees.

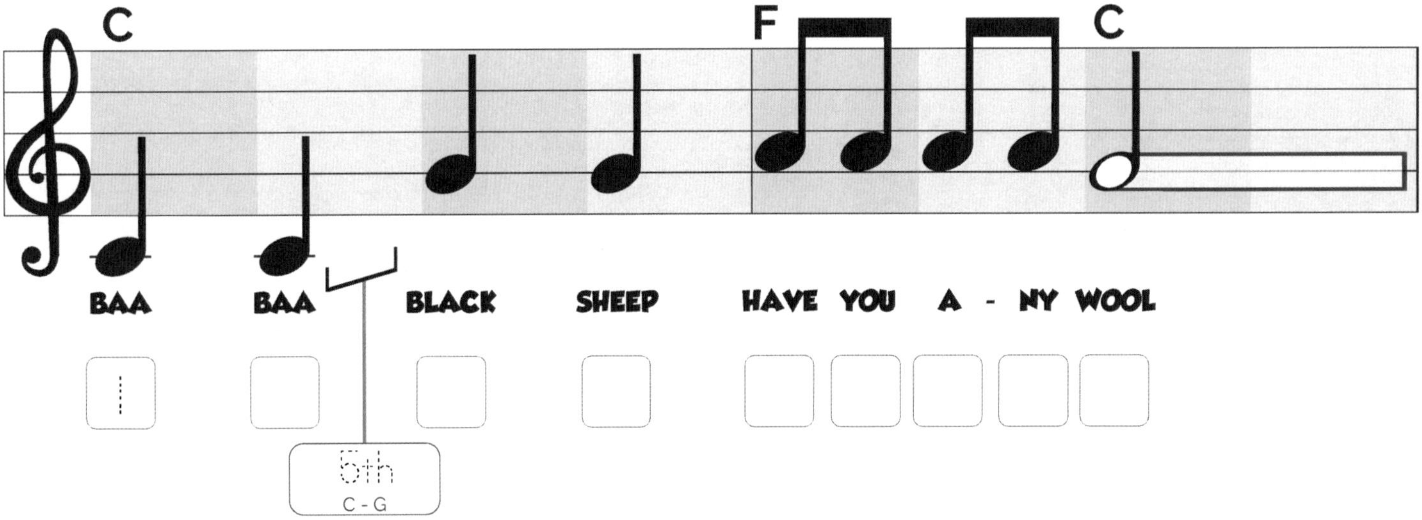

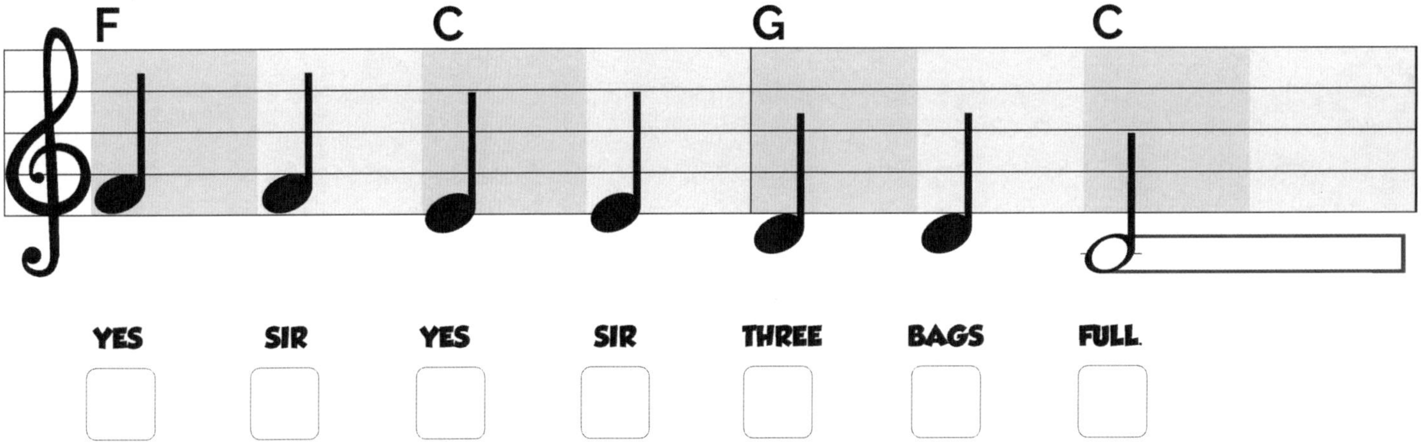

C F C

BAA BAA BLACK SHEEP HAVE YOU A - NY WOOL

1

5th
C - G

F C G C

YES SIR YES SIR THREE BAGS FULL.

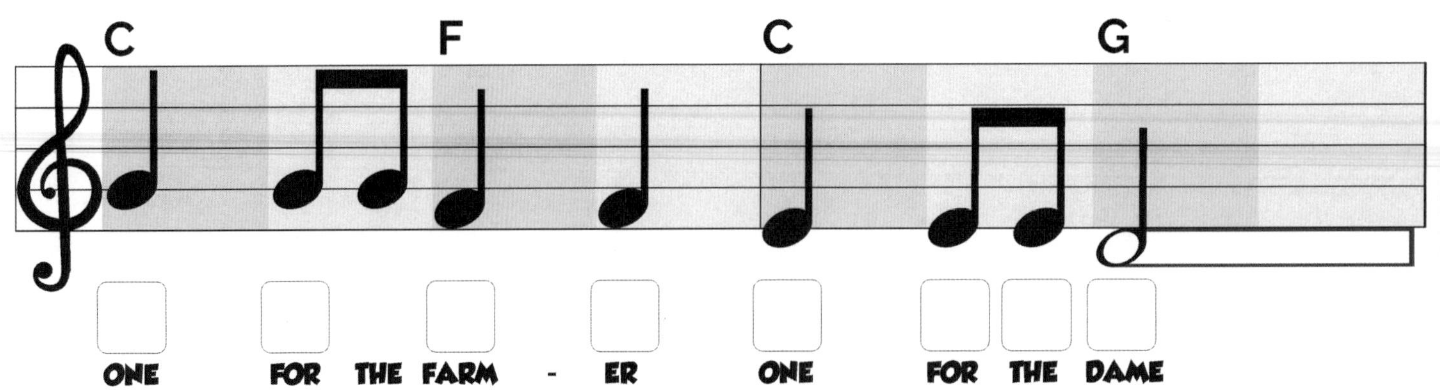

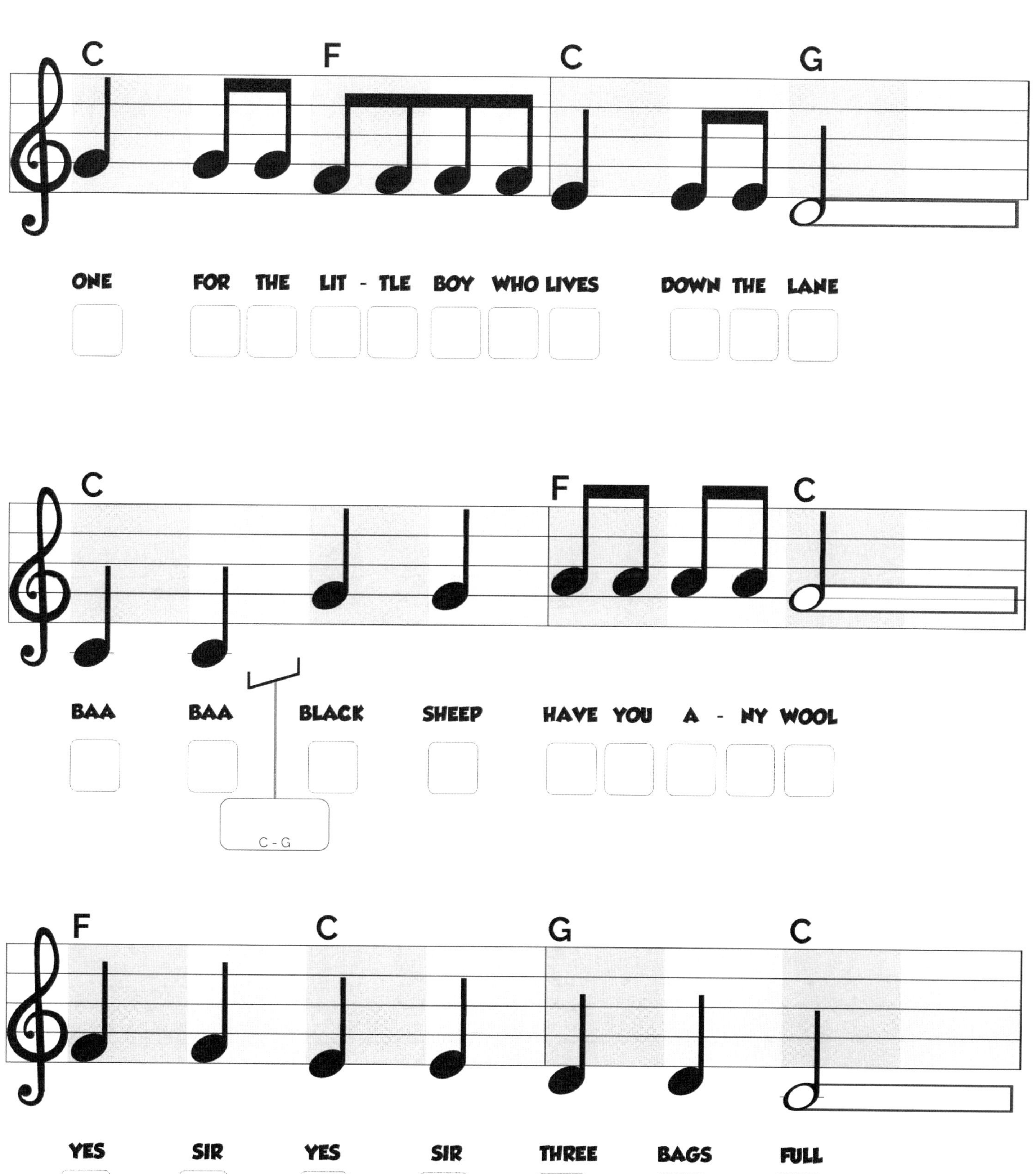
C
F
C
G
ONE
FOR
THE
LIT - TLE
BOY
WHO
LIVES
DOWN
THE
LANE
C
F
C
BAA
BAA
BLACK
SHEEP
HAVE
YOU
A - NY
WOOL
C - G
F
C
G
C
YES
SIR
YES
SIR
THREE
BAGS
FULL

Fifths (5ths)

Fifths are the kings of rock'n'roll. Typically used by guitarists, perfect 5ths are also known as power chords, an essential sound in rock music. Similiar to 4ths, in the major key, all 5ths will be perfect EXCEPT when the Ti pairs with Fa. This time the pairing is called a diminished 5th but still considered the tritone.

Harmonically, 5ths occur when we build any root position major or minor triad. In a C Major chord, spelled CEG, the distance from C to G is a perfect 5th.

In a major key, 5ths will either be...

Diminished 5th	**Perfect 5th**
6 Semitones	7 Semitones
Melodically Sounds Like...	**Melodically Sounds Like...**
"Purple Haze" by Jimi Hendrix - guitar and bass intro "The Simp" from "The Simpsons Theme"	Start of "Twinkle Twinkle" (up a P5) Star Wars - Main Theme Also sprach Zarathustra - "Sunrise"
Harmonically Sounds Like...	**Harmonically Sounds Like...**
Ominous and dissonant Demands resolution (Fa to Re, Ti to Do)	Rock'n'roll music Ambiguous, unlike major or minor Gregorian Chant

Diminished 5th in C Major

Perfect 5ths in C Major

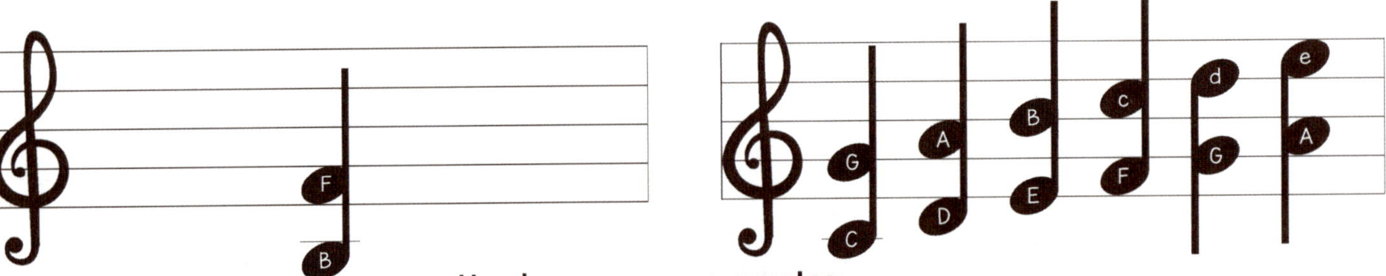

Here's some more examples:

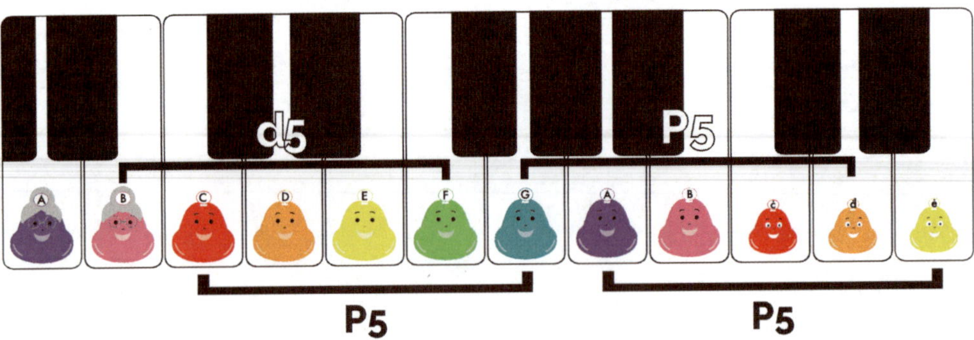

B to _____ is a Diminished 5th

C to _____ is a Perfect 5th

D to _____ is a Perfect 5th

E to _____ is a Perfect 5th

Piano Intervals - 2nds, 3rds, 4ths, 5ths

On the keyboards below you'll see 2nds, 3rds, 4ths & 5ths.
Circle the correct answer below each piano.

Bonus: Play your instrument as you go to hear the sound of the interval

Notating Intervals - 2nds, 3rds, 4ths, 5ths

Let's draw some HARMONIC Intervals. These intervals happen at the same time. Then, write the name of the interval below.

Hint: Use Every Good Boy Does Fine & FACE in the SPACE to remember where each note lives on the staff.

Challenge: Cover up the hint above and try to work from memory.

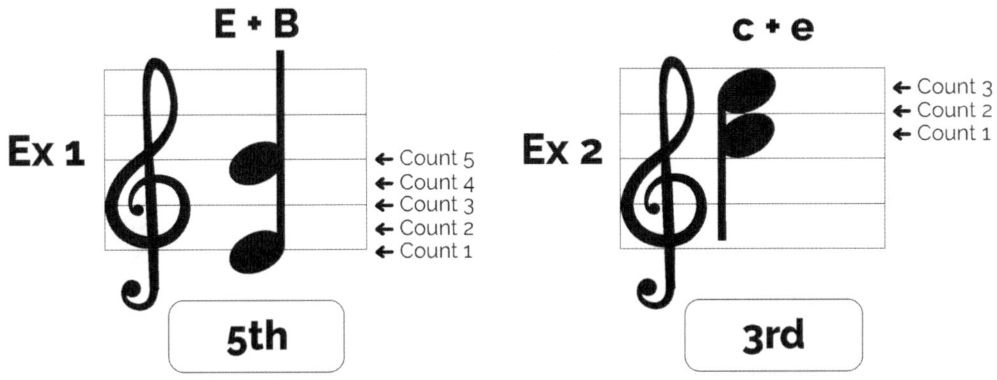

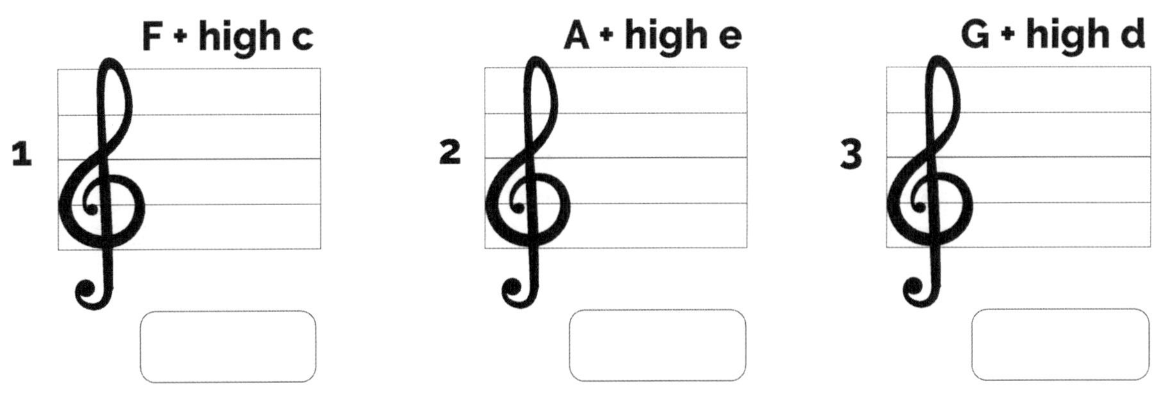

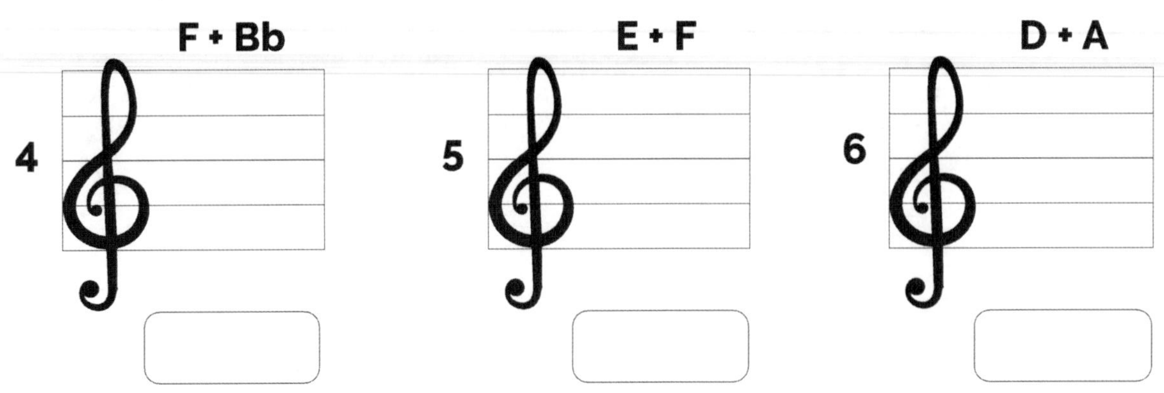

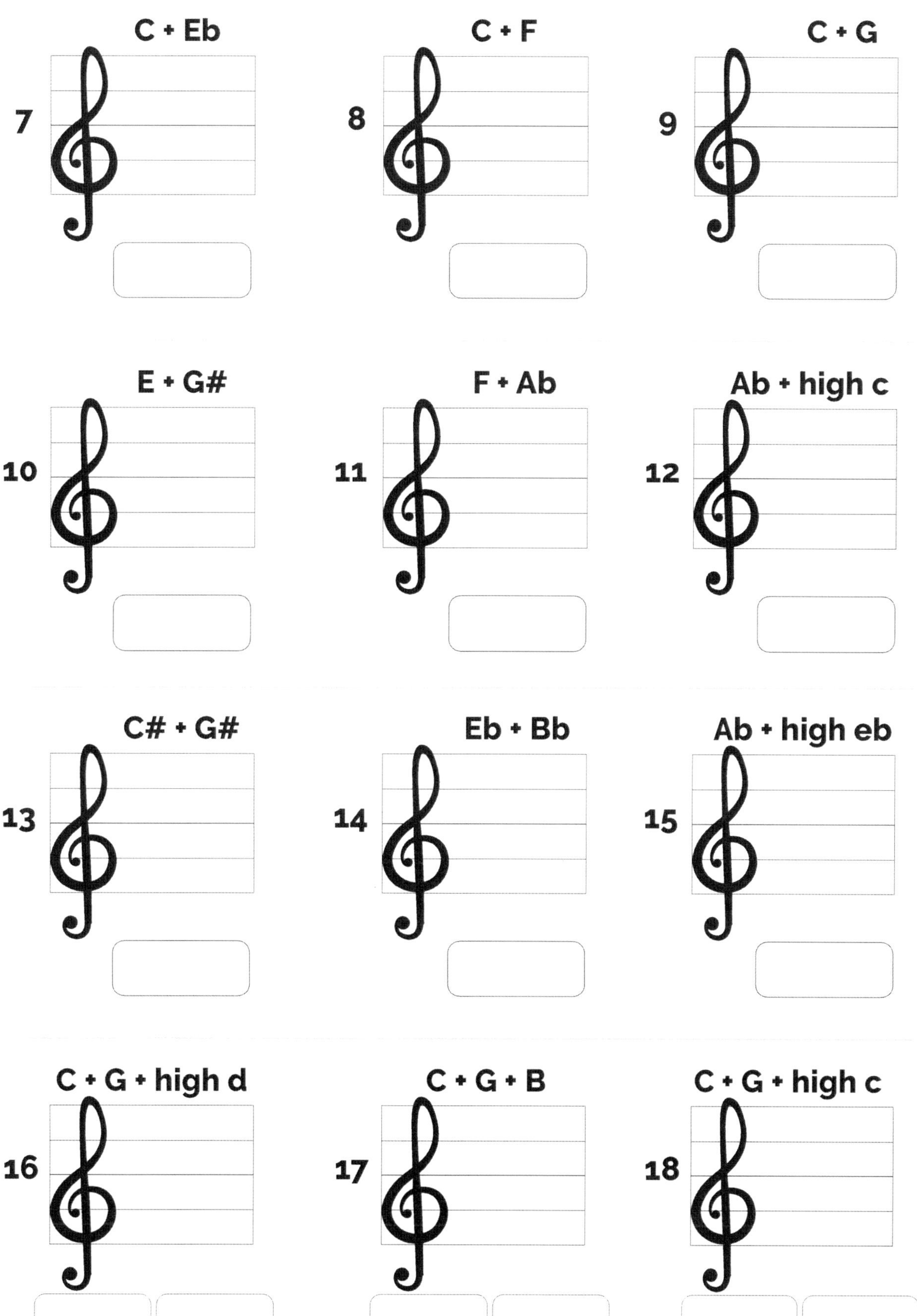

C + Eb
7
C + F
8
C + G
9
E + G#
10
F + Ab
11
Ab + high c
12
C# + G#
13
Eb + Bb
14
Ab + high eb
15
C + G + high d
16
C - G
G - D
C + G + B
17
C - G
G - B
C + G + high c
18
C - G
G - c

Semitone Challenge with 5ths

Let's practice some more semitones. This time, we'll use...

6 semitones (a diminished 5th or Tritone) & 7 semitones (a Perfect 5th)

1. Circle C and the note 7 semitones above

dim. 5th **Perfect 5th**

2. Circle C and the note 6 semitones above

dim. 5th **Perfect 5th**

3. Circle A and the note 7 semitones below

dim. 5th **Perfect 5th**

4. Circle high c and the note 6 semitones below

dim. 5th **Perfect 5th**

5. Circle C# and the note 7 semitones above

dim. 5th **Perfect 5th**

6. Circle B and the note 7 semitones below

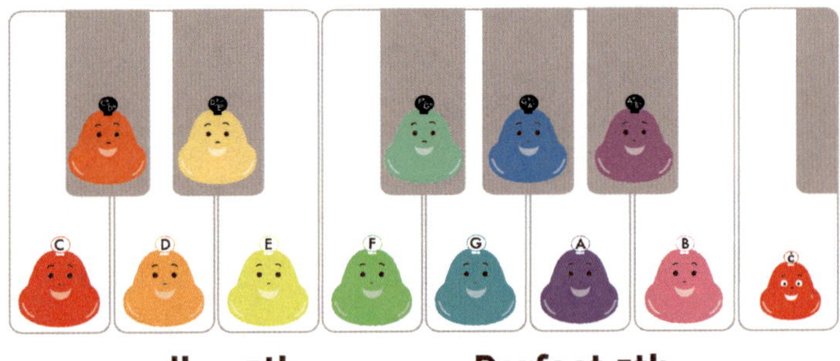

dim. 5th **Perfect 5th**

7. Circle G and the note 7 semitones below

dim. 5th **Perfect 5th**

8. Circle Bb and the note 6 semitones below

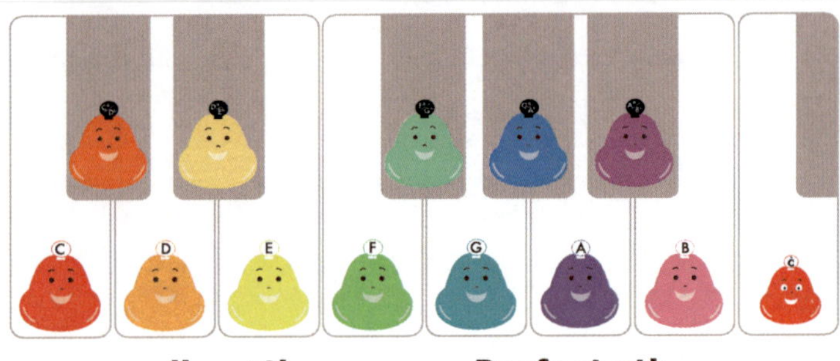

dim. 5th **Perfect 5th**

THE 6TH (SIXTH)

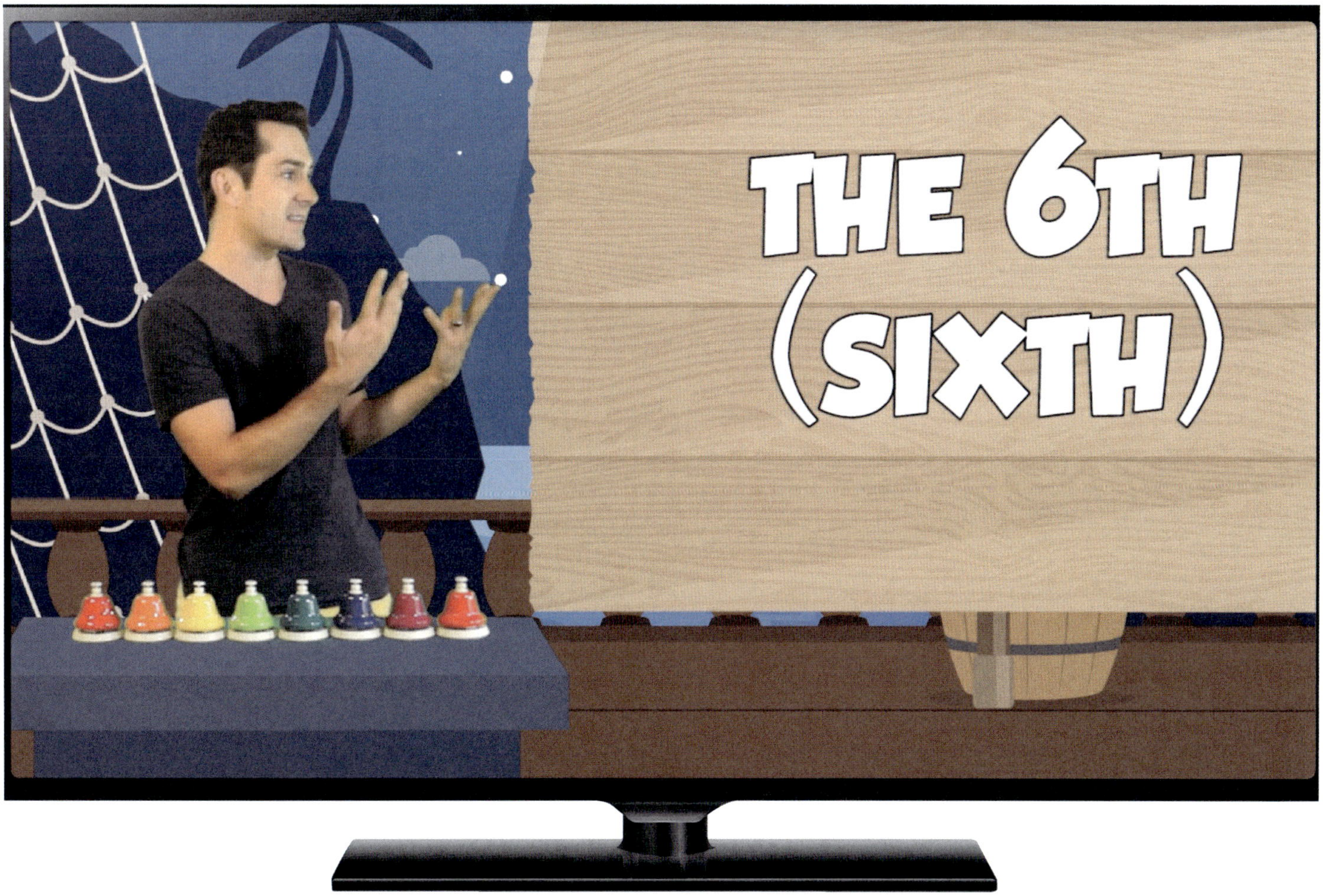

6THS WITH "MY BONNIE"

Section 2.6

My Bonnie Lies Over the Ocean

F Major - Verse 1

F F B♭ B♭
C F D G F
BRING BACK BRING BACK OH
do do do fa fa fa re re re sol sol fa
C C F F
E E E E D E F G A
BRING BACK MY BON - NIE TO ME TO ME
mi mi mi mi re mi fa fa sol la la la
F F B♭ B♭
C F D G F
BRING BACK BRING BACK OH
do do do fa fa fa re re re sol sol fa
C C F F
E E E E D E F C
BRING BACK MY BON - NIE TO ME OH THE
mi mi mi mi re mi fa fa fa do

My Bonnie Lies Over the Ocean

Verses 2 & 3 in Black & White

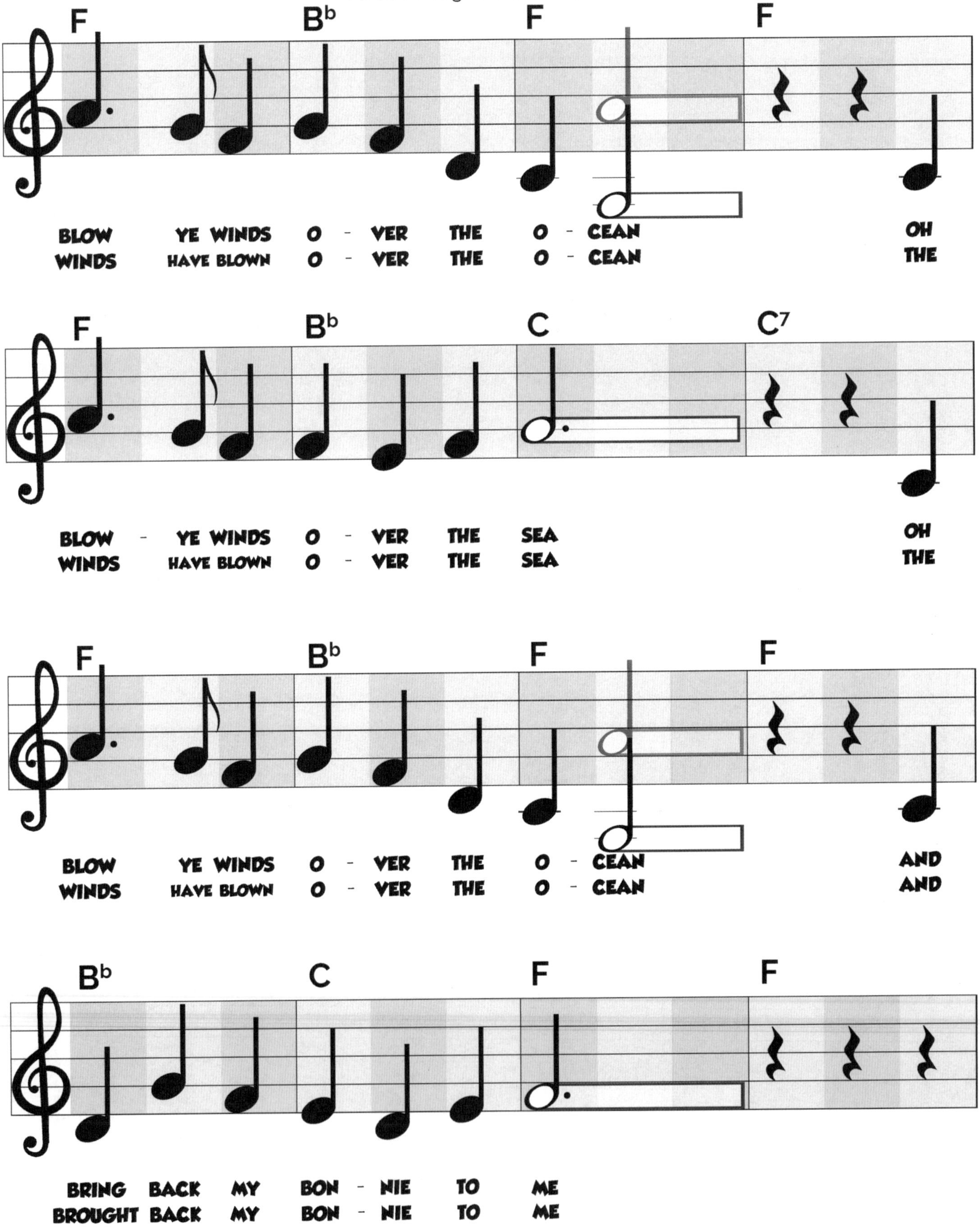

F Bb F F

BLOW YE WINDS O - VER THE O - CEAN OH
WINDS HAVE BLOWN O - VER THE O - CEAN THE

F Bb C C7

BLOW - YE WINDS O - VER THE SEA OH
WINDS HAVE BLOWN O - VER THE SEA THE

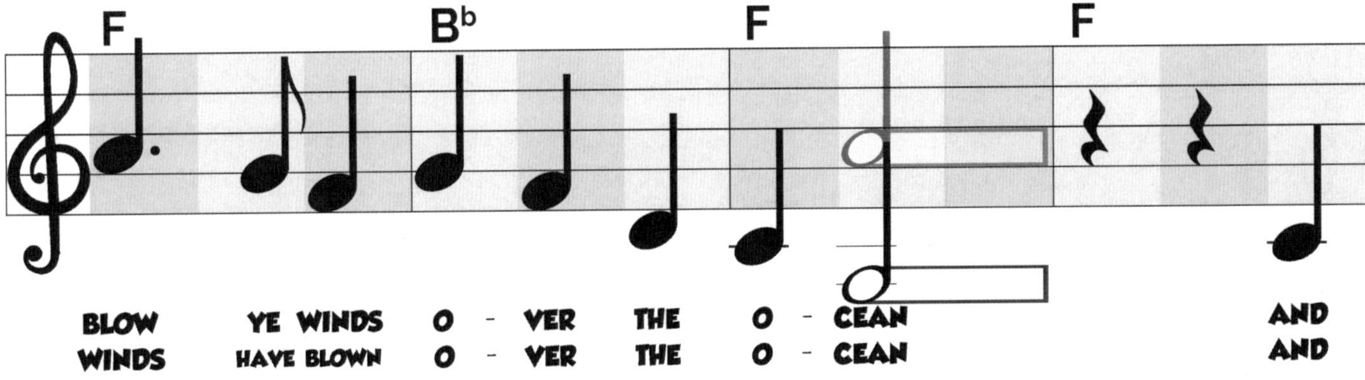

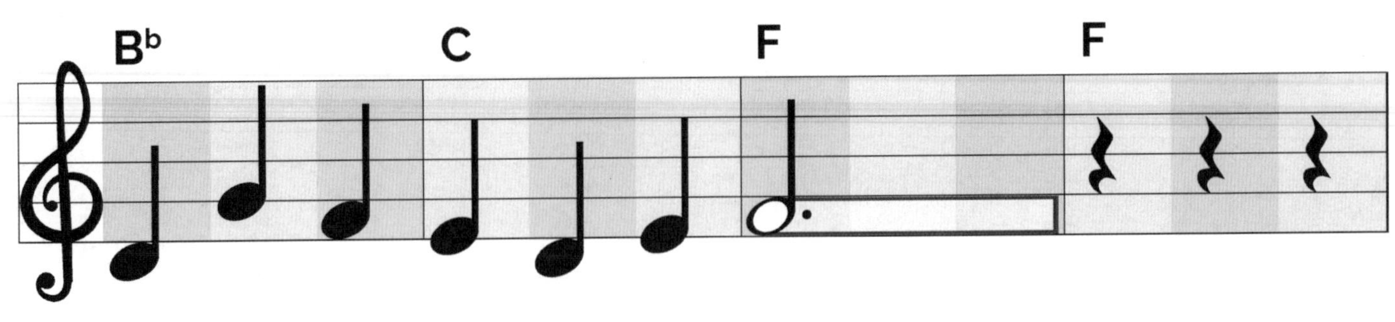

BRING BACK MY BON - NIE TO ME
BROUGHT BACK MY BON - NIE TO ME

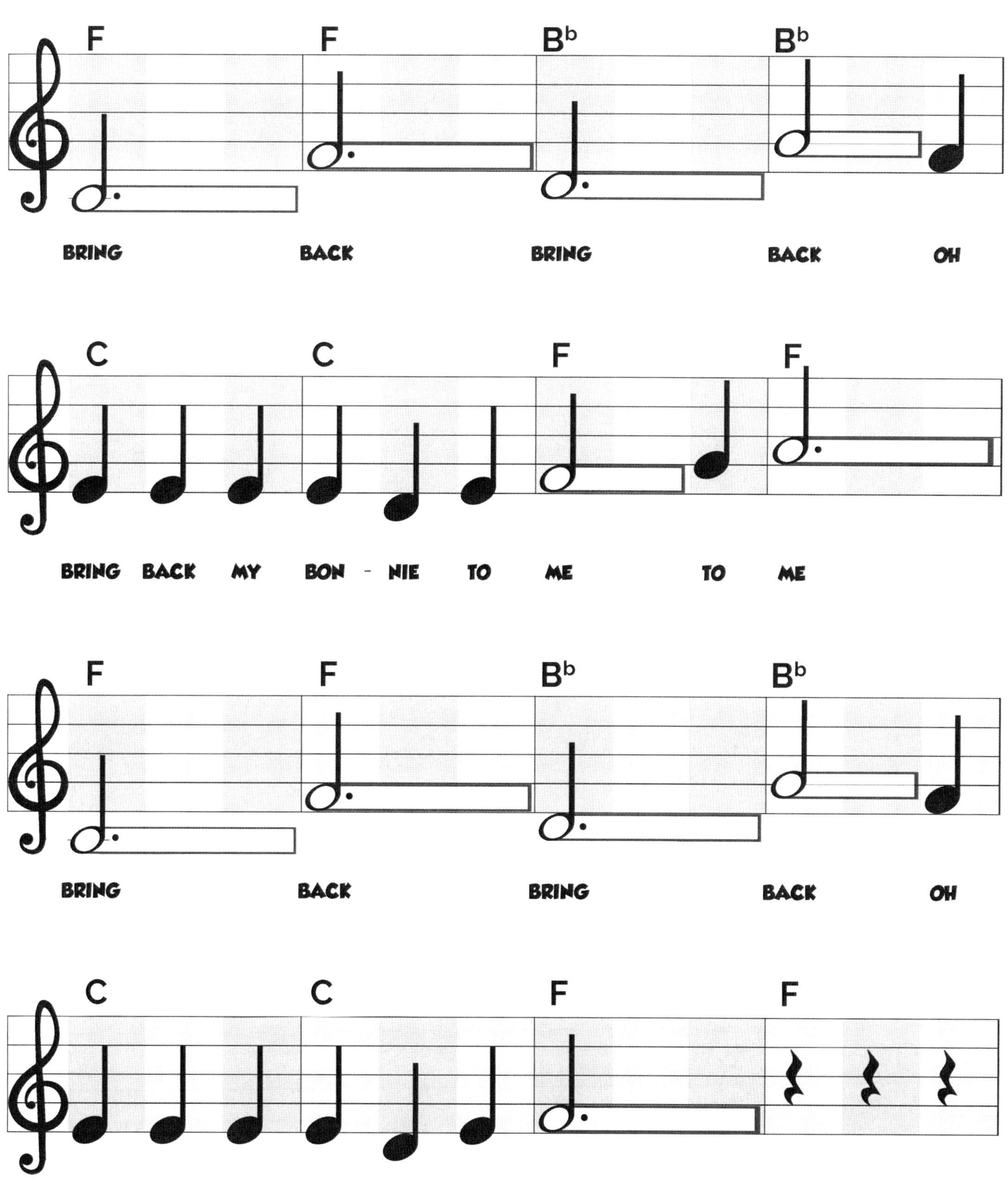
F F B♭ B♭
BRING BACK BRING BACK OH
C C F F
BRING BACK MY BON - NIE TO ME TO ME
F F B♭ B♭
BRING BACK BRING BACK OH
C C F F
BRING BACK MY BON - NIE TO ME

Sixths (6ths)

Sixths are the most whimsical of all the intervals. They can sound fanciful and sweet with major chords or they can add mystique and complexity with minor chords. Sixths are a team player. They know how to spice up a melody or dress up a chord without being too flashy.

Harmonically, they occur when we build any 1st or 2nd inversion major or minor triad. In a G Major chord, spelled GBD, if you move G above D, BDG, the distance from B to G is a minor 6th.

In a major key, 6ths will either be...

Minor 6th

8 Semitones

Melodically Sounds Like...

The Entertainer
Go Down Moses
"Waltz in C# Minor" Frédéric Chopin

Harmonically Sounds Like...

Spacious and stable
Combined with M6 harmonized riffs in Country, Jazz, and Blues

Major 6th

9 Semitones

Melodically Sounds Like...

NBC chimes
My Bonnie Lies Over the Ocean
Hush Little Baby

Harmonically Sounds Like...

Blues music
The Beatles "Across the Universe"

Minor 6ths in C Major

Major 6ths in C Major

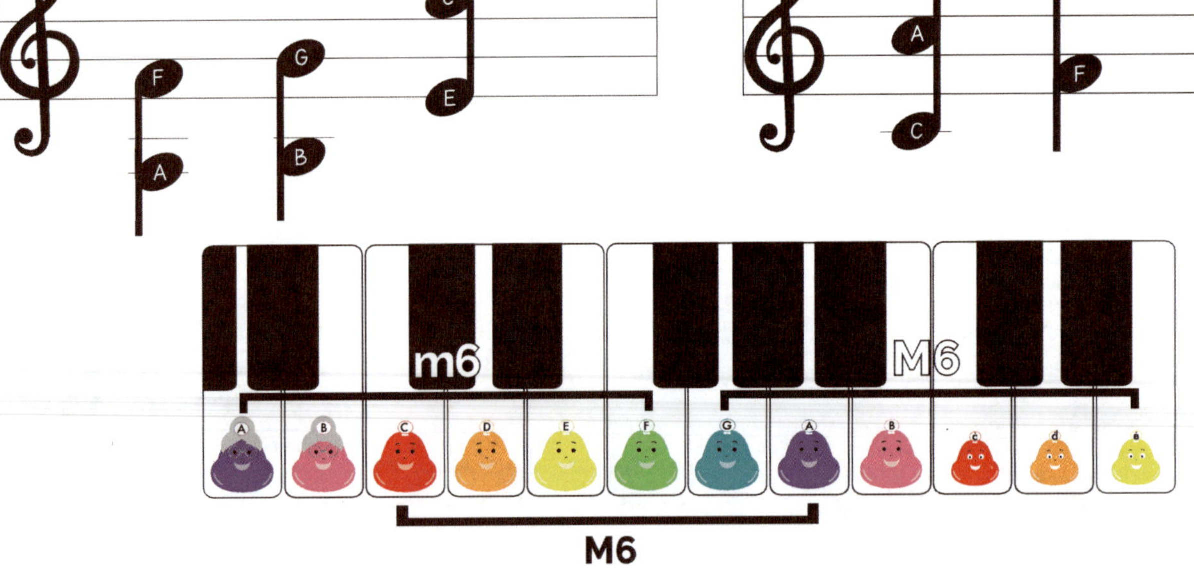

E to _____ is a minor 6th

B to _____ is a minor 6th

C to _____ is a Major 6th

D to _____ is a Major 6th

Piano Intervals - 2nds, 3rds, 4ths, 5ths, 6ths

On the keyboards below you'll see 2nds, 3rds, 4ths, 5ths, & 6ths.
Circle the correct answer below each piano.

Bonus: Play your instrument as you go to hear the sound of the interval.

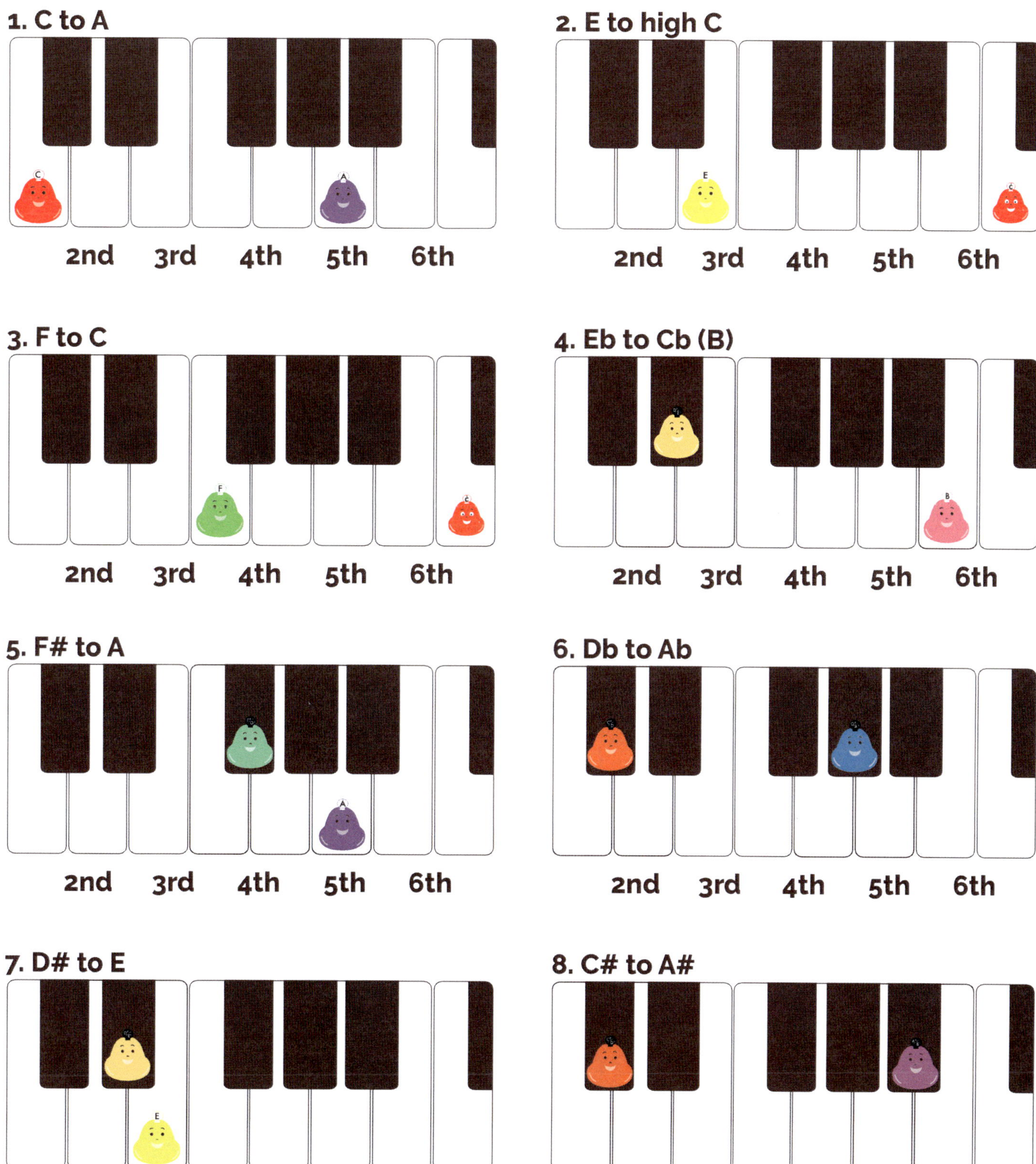

Notating Intervals - 2nds, 3rds, 4ths, 5ths, 6ths

Let's draw some HARMONIC Intervals. These intervals happen at the same time.
Then, write the name of the interval below

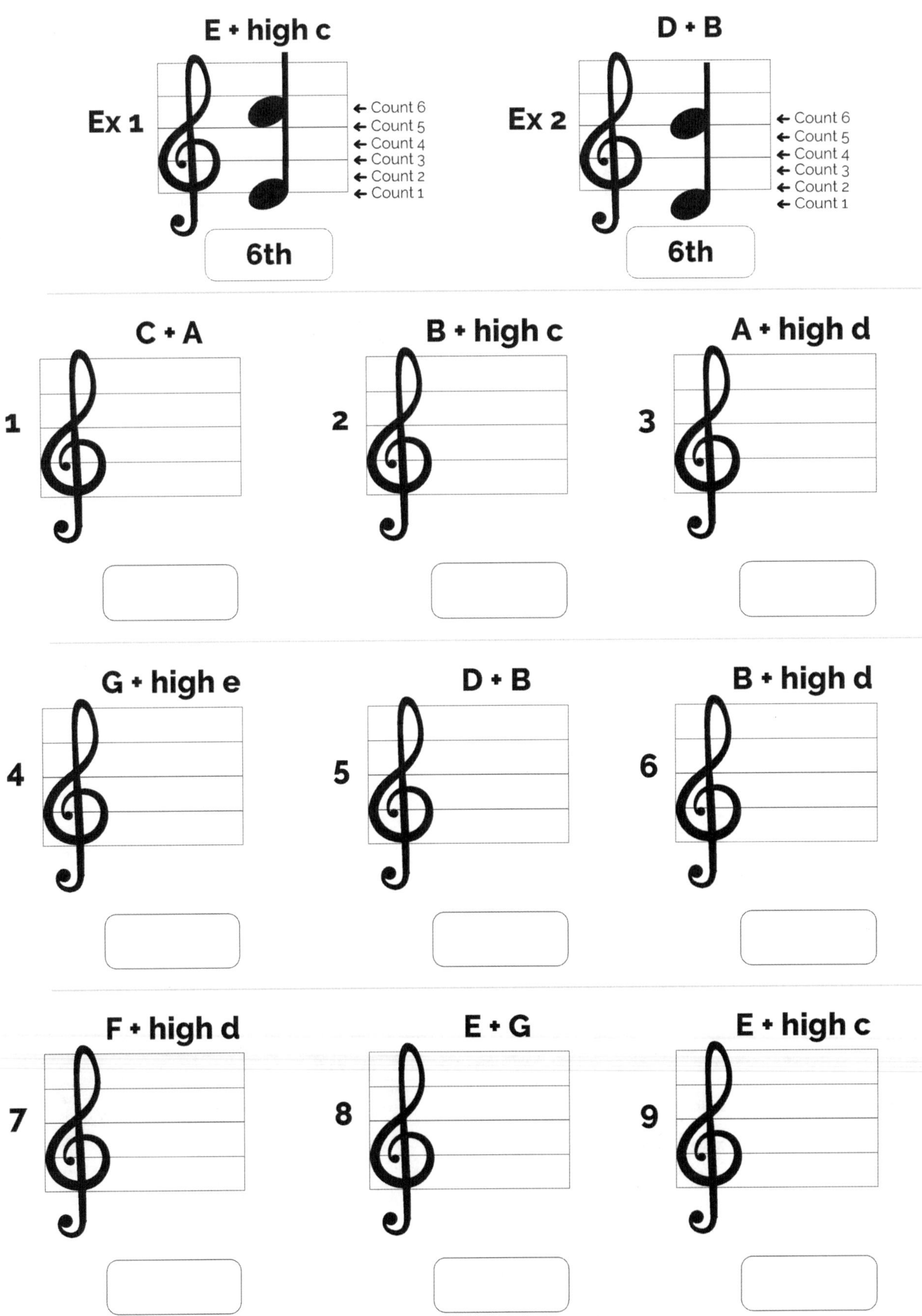

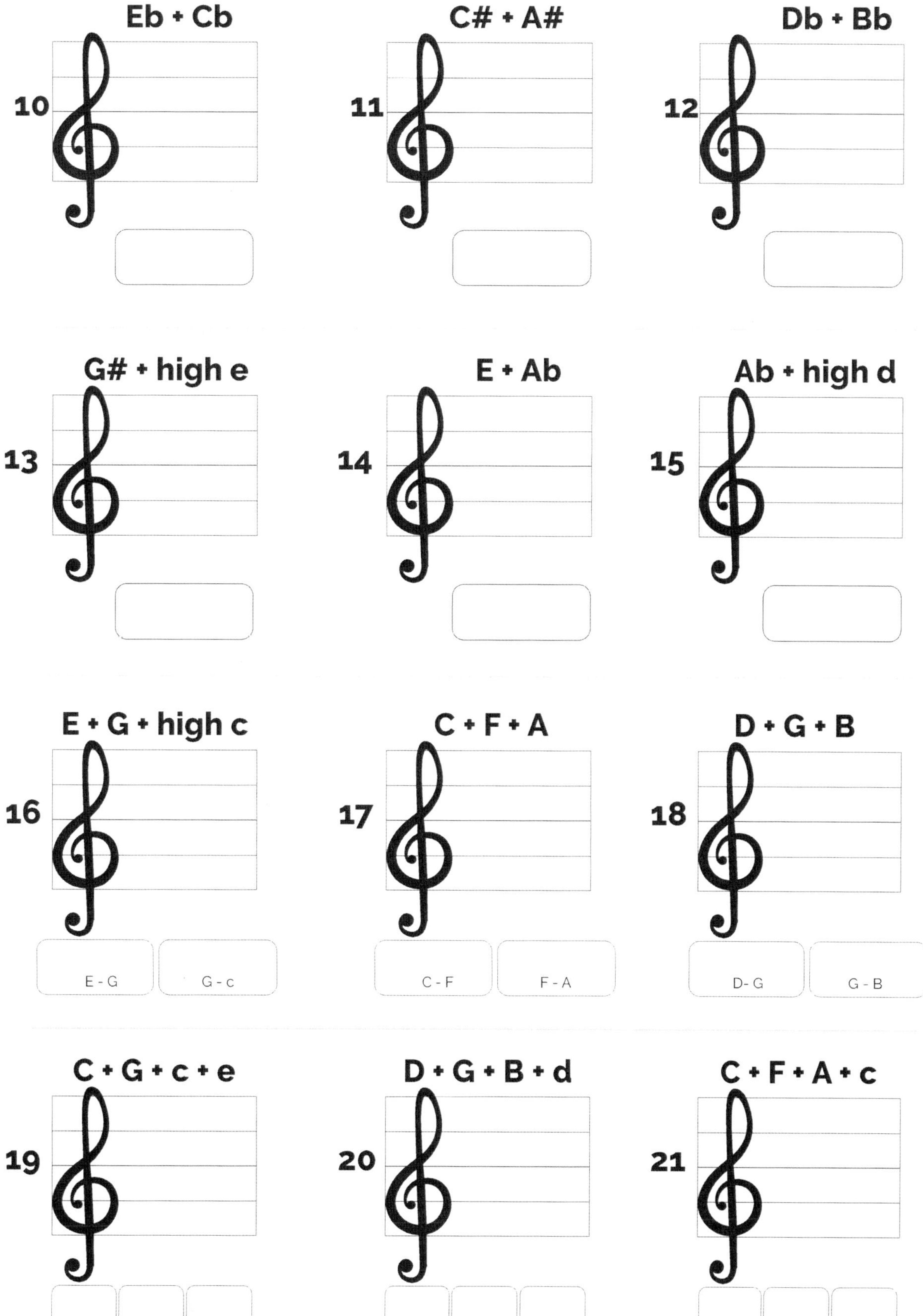
Eb + Cb
10
C# + A#
11
Db + Bb
12
G# + high e
13
E + Ab
14
Ab + high d
15
E + G + high c
16
E - G
G - c
C + F + A
17
C - F
F - A
D + G + B
18
D- G
G - B
C + G + c + e
19
C - G
G - c
c - e
D + G + B + d
20
D - G
G - B
B - d
C + F + A + c
21
C - F
F - A
A - c

Semitone Challenge with 6ths

Let's practice some more semitones. This time we'll use...
8 semitones (a Minor 6th) & 9 semitones (a Major 6th)

1. Circle C and the note 9 semitones above

Minor 6th **Major 6th**

2. Circle Ab and the note 8 semitones below

Minor 6th **Major 6th**

3. Circle B and the note 9 semitones below

Minor 6th **Major 6th**

4. Circle high c and the note 9 semitones below

Minor 6th **Major 6th**

5. Circle Bb and the note 8 semitones below

Minor 6th **Major 6th**

6. Circle D and the note 9 semitones above

Minor 6th **Major 6th**

7. Circle E and the note 8 semitones above

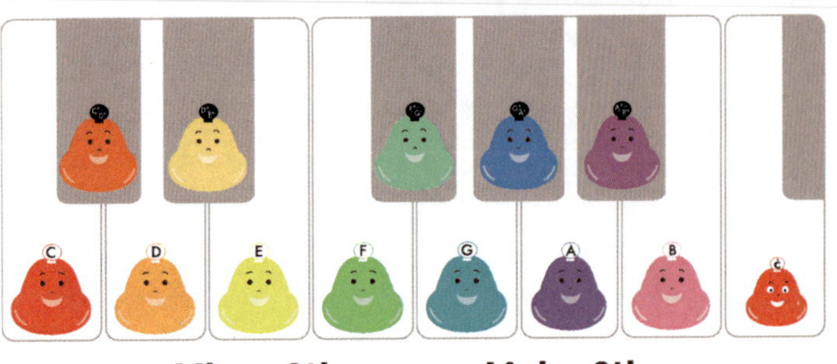

Minor 6th **Major 6th**

8. Circle C# and the note 9 semitones above

Minor 6th **Major 6th**

PRIMARY PRODIGIES

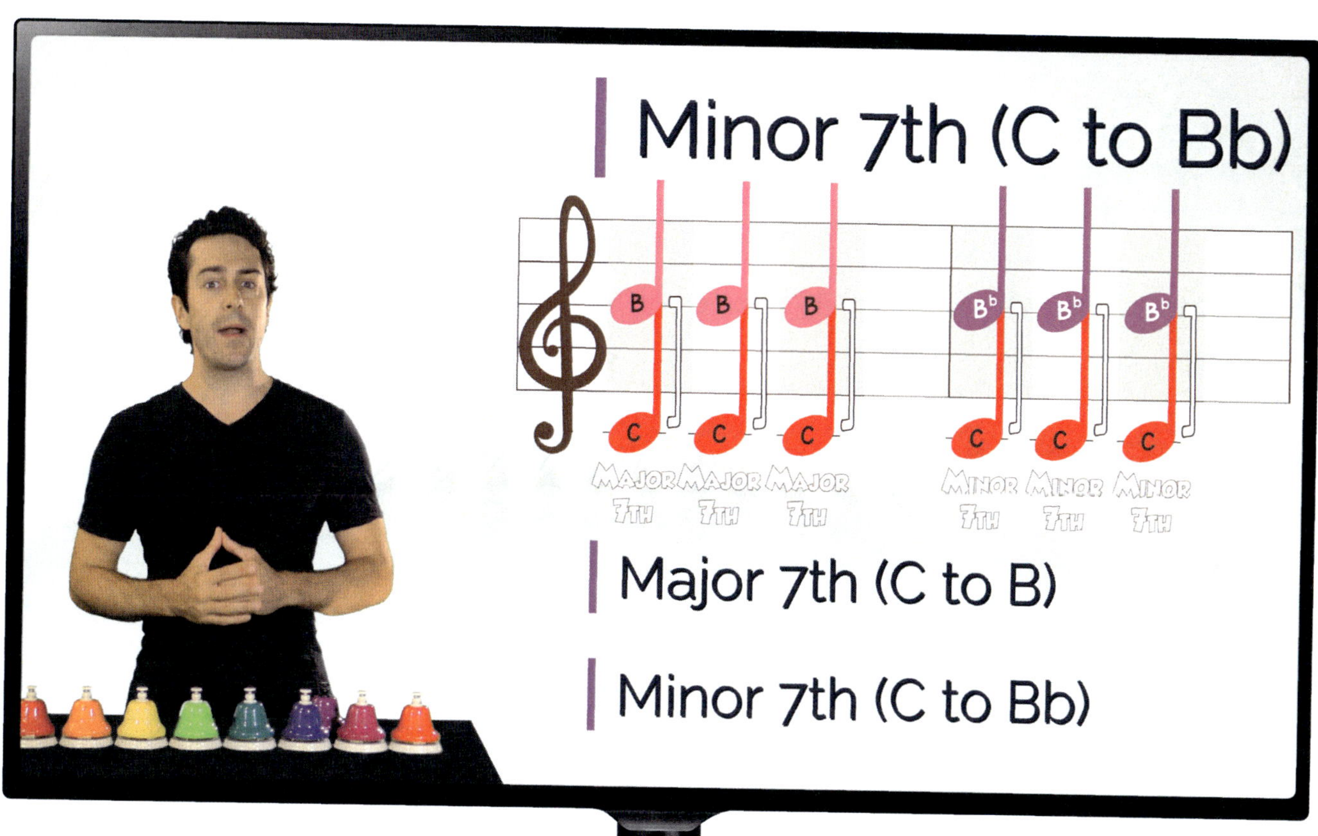

7THS & OCTAVES WITH "HOT CROSS HARMONIES"

Section 2.7

Notes Used:

Hot Cross Harmonies

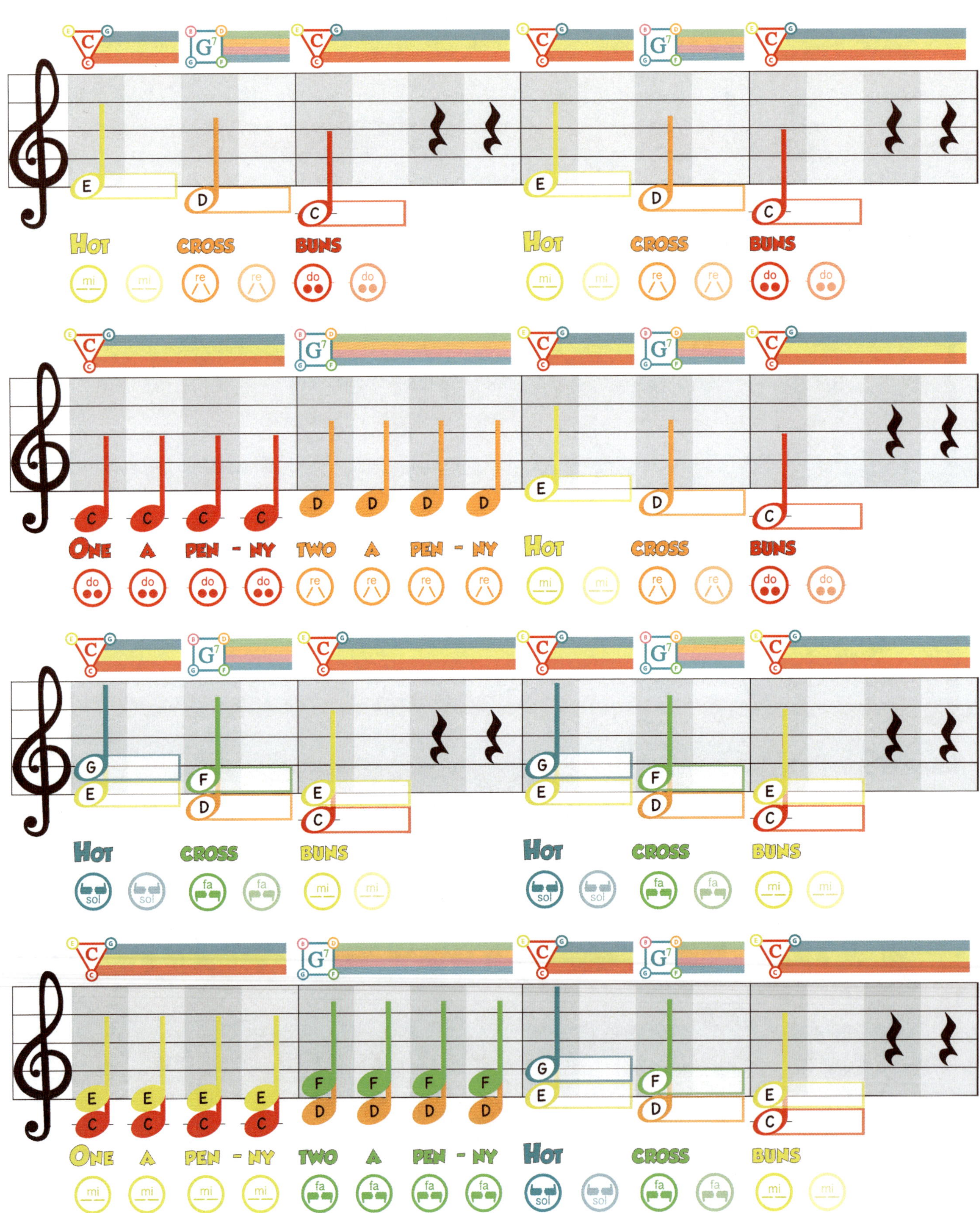

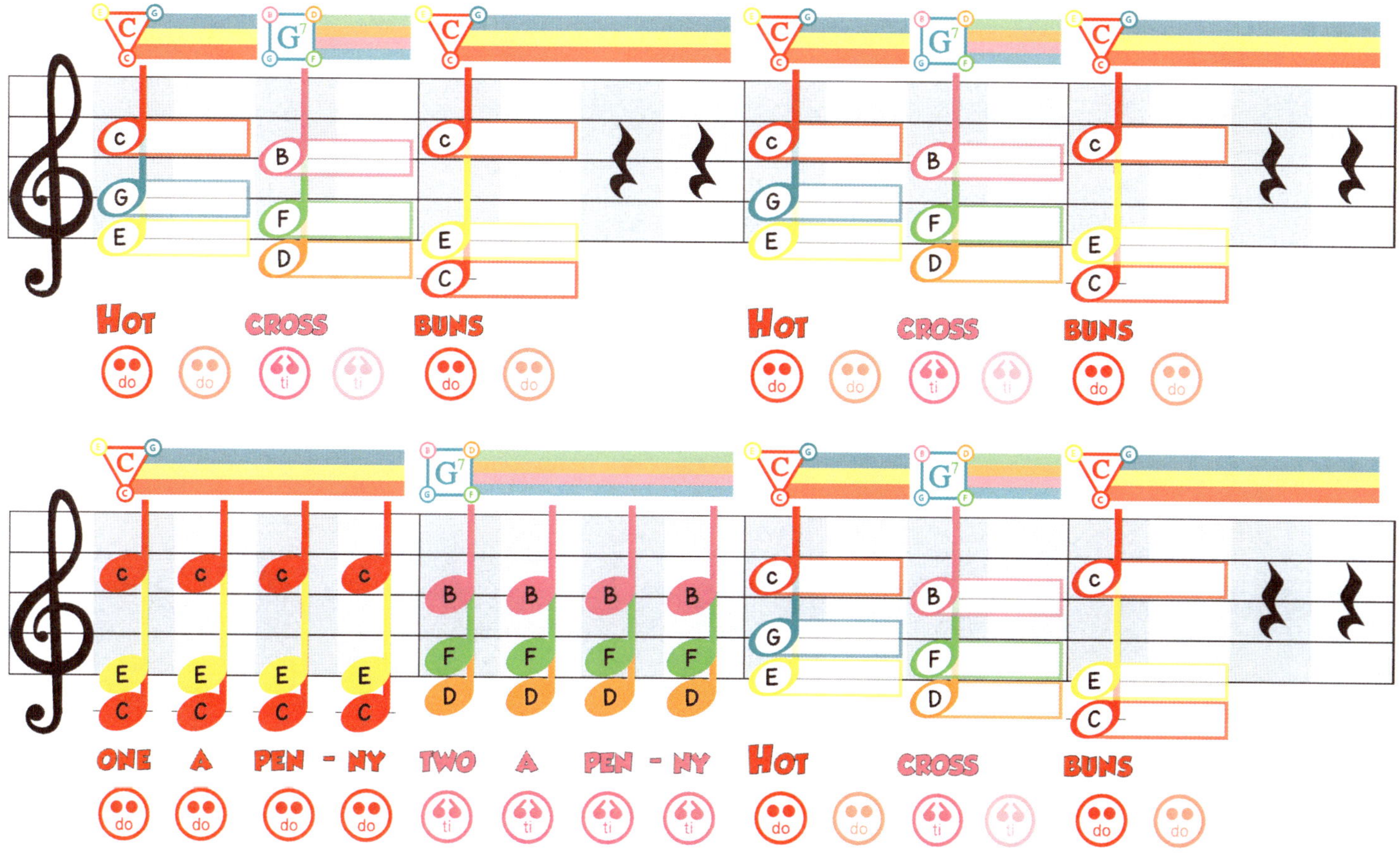

C G7 C C G7 C

C G E | B F D | C E C | C G E | B F D | C E C

HOT CROSS BUNS HOT CROSS BUNS

do do ti ti do do do do ti ti do do

C G7 C G7 C

C E C C E C C E C C E C | B F D B F D B F D B F D | C G E | B F D | C E C

ONE A PEN - NY TWO A PEN - NY HOT CROSS BUNS

do do do do ti ti ti ti do do ti ti do do

One more time in Black and White

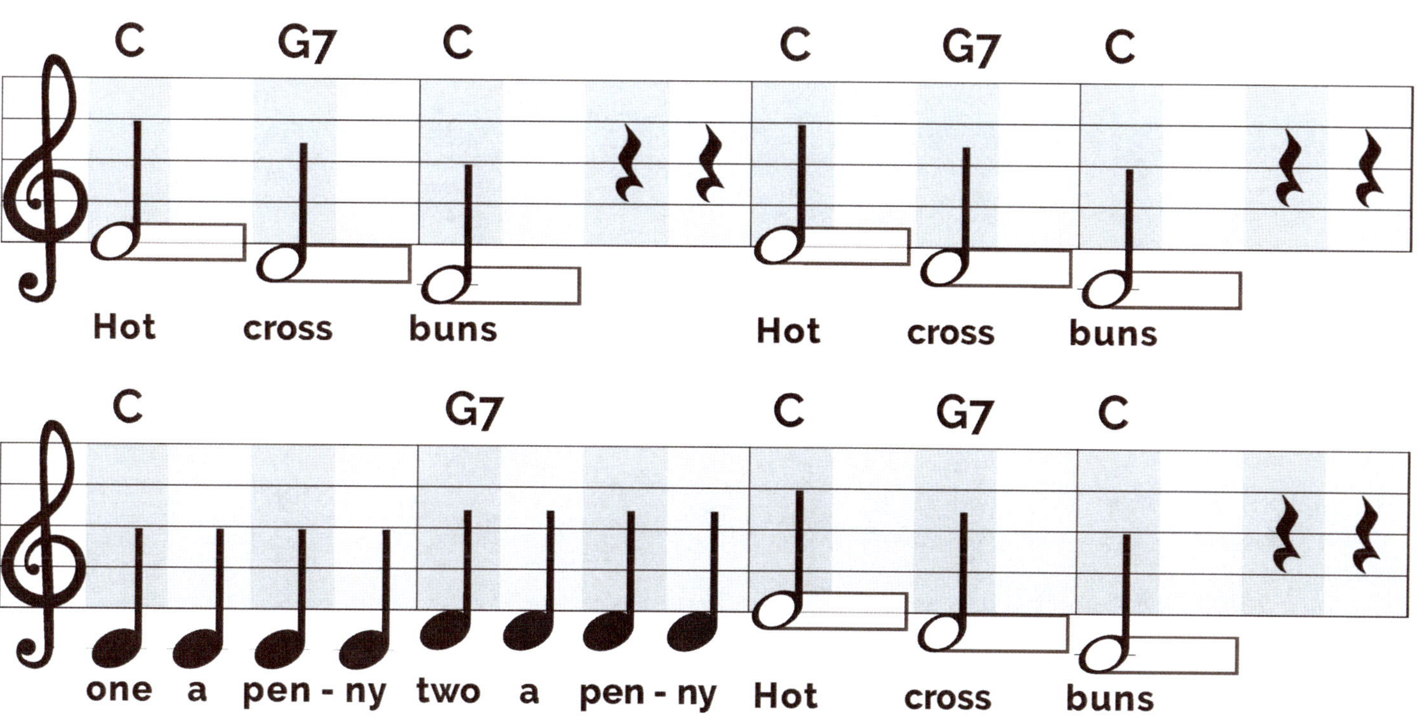

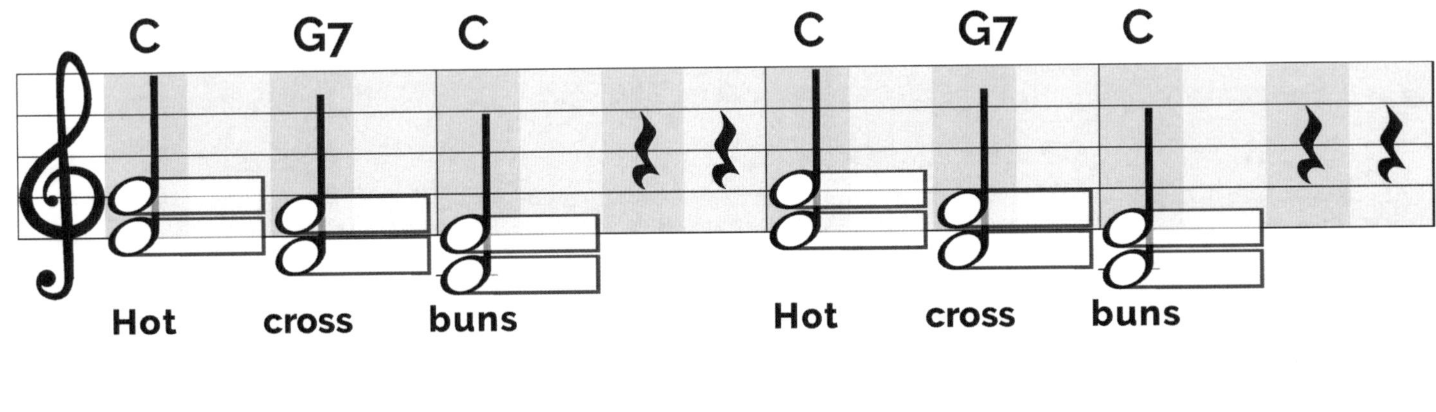
C G7 C C G7 C
Hot cross buns Hot cross buns

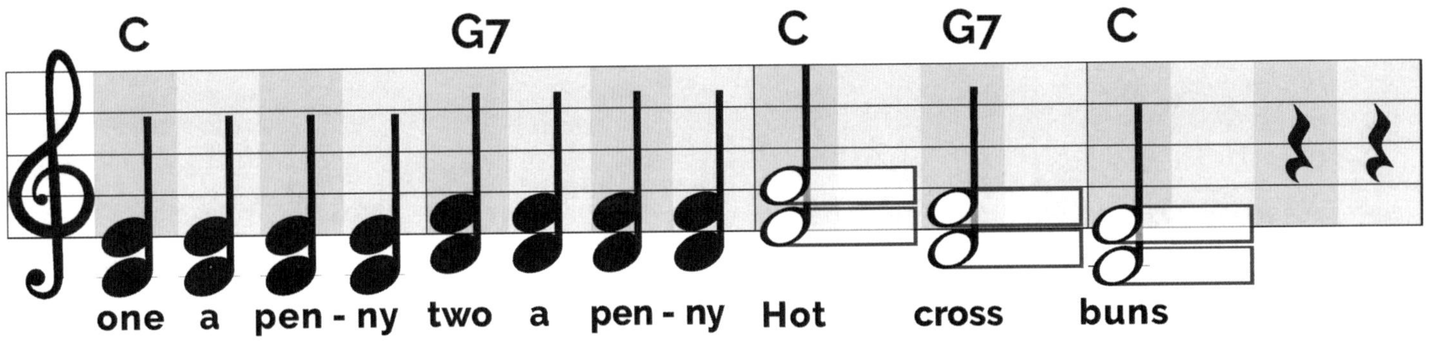
C G7 C G7 C
one a pen - ny two a pen - ny Hot cross buns

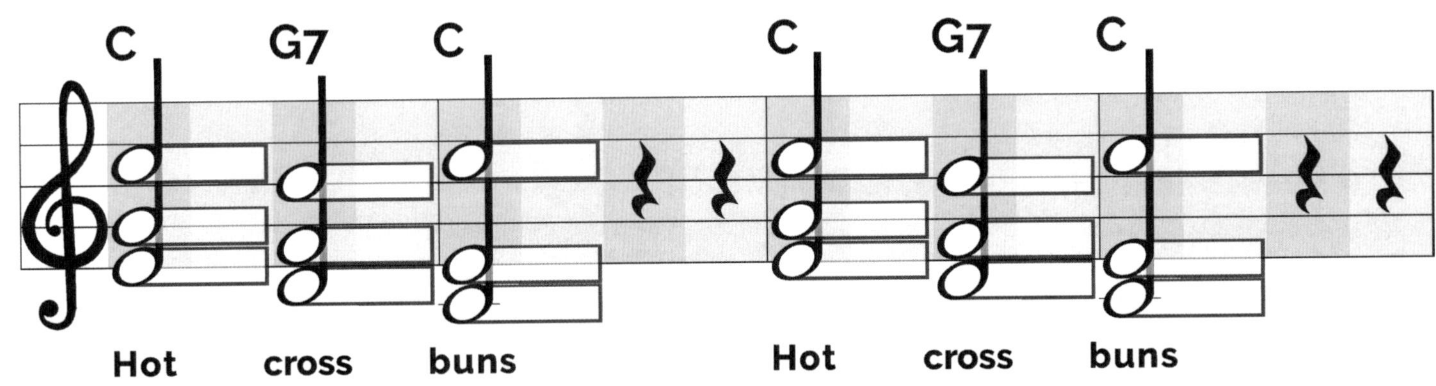
C G7 C C G7 C
Hot cross buns Hot cross buns

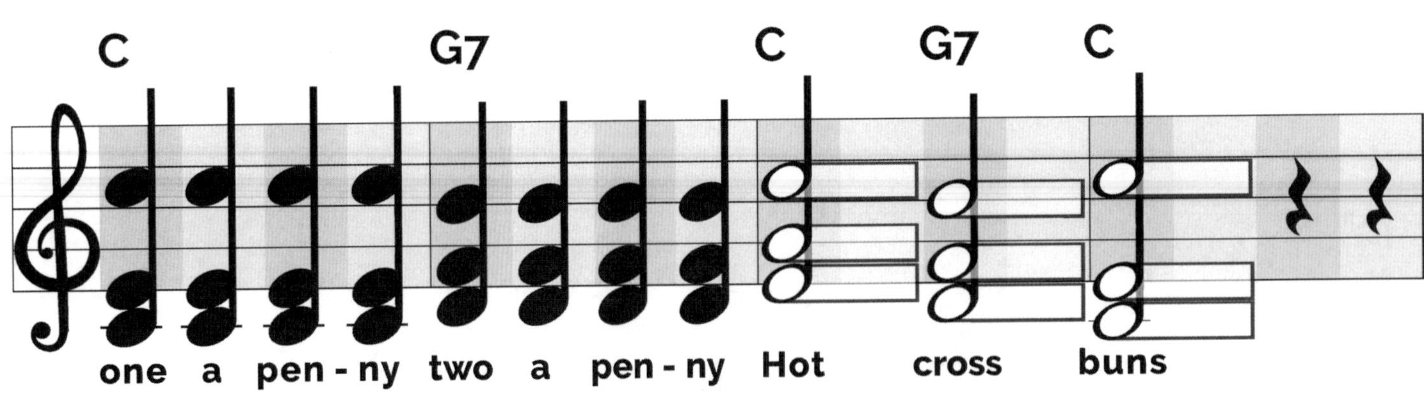
C G7 C G7 C
one a pen - ny two a pen - ny Hot cross buns

Sevenths (7ths)

Sevenths represent a certain level of sophistication in our interval studies. Performing a melody or ostinato that plays heavily with 7ths requires that we train our ears to be comfortable with the sound. When we harness it, the 7th is an incredible tool for playing advanced styles of music.

Harmonically, they add complexity and maturity to our basic triads. If we play a G major triad, GBD, and add an F note, G to F is a minor 7th interval. The new sound created with the 4 note chord is a game changer.

In a major key, 7ths will either be...

Minor 7th

10 Semitones

Melodically Sounds Like...

"Animals" chorus by Maroon 5
Star Trek: The Original Series theme
Funk and blues music

Harmonically Sounds Like...

Comping chords, used to support a soloist in a jazz setting

Major 7th

11 Semitones

Melodically Sounds Like...

"Take On Me" chorus by A-Ha
The first and third notes of "Somewhere Over the Rainbow"

Harmonically Sounds Like...

Sounds harsh and distant but can sound lush and spacey when paired with a major triad.

Minor 7ths in C Major

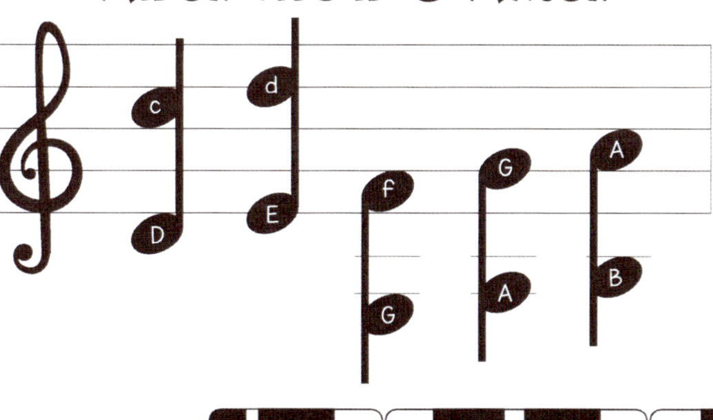

Major 7ths in C Major

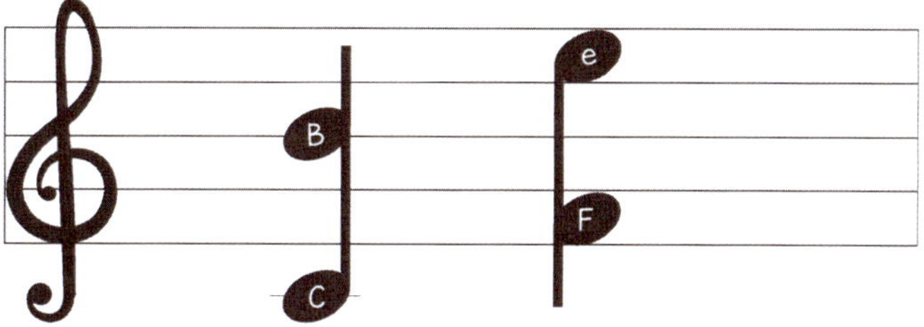

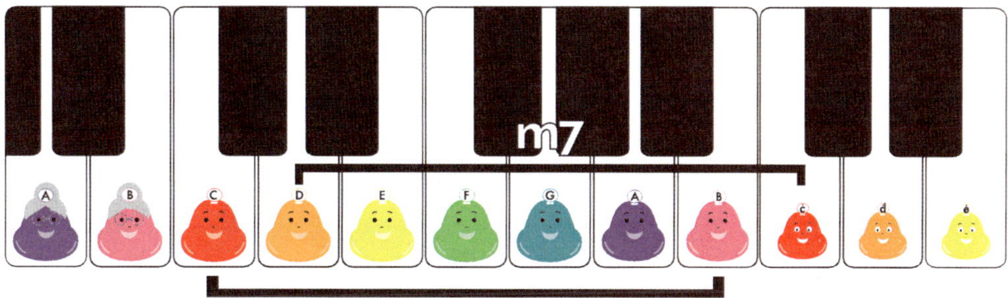

G to _____ is a minor 7th

D to _____ is a minor 7th

C to _____ is a Major 7th

F to _____ is a Major 7th

2.7 Resolutions

Every Song Tells a Story

A song can be a really fun analogy for telling a story. The instruments being played can act as characters. The harmony can depict a setting or convey a mood. The melody can describe the plot, even if there aren't any lyrics. Many emotions can be conjured with all of these musical elements, the same emotions we feel when reading a story. How do know when the musical story is over? **Resolutions!**

A **resolution** is a trick composers and song writers use to communicate to the listener that it is the end of a song or phrase. In this section, we'll use our knowledge of intervals to understand how resolutions function. There will be some fun new vocabulary along the way.

Dissonance is not my jam!

When we hear the word resolution, we might think that there is a problem that needs to be solved. That's true, and in music, we describe that problem as **dissonance** or musical tension. This means that some intervals sound harsher or less stable, like something needs to happen, immediately! Think about how a story might get more intense.

This is where a pleasant resolution can save the day. This idea is known as **consonance**. It gives us a sense of relief. These concepts remind us that music is very subjective and allows us to connect on a deeper level.

Cadences - Using Chords as Musical Punctuation

Consonance and dissonance describe the way certain sounds make us feel, but how do you create that feeling in your playing? The answer lies in the concept of cadences. **Cadences** are a type of resolution that act as punctuation. They give our "story" more structure. We'll use a series of chords like a period, to end a song.

For a cadence to be effective, we need to learn which chords are dissonant and which chords are consonant. The most dissonant chord that we've learned so far is the dominant. This is denoted with the Roman numeral **V** in a key. The most consonant chord we've learned so far is the tonic. This is denoted with the Roman numeral **I**. We mentioned earlier that an interval is how two notes communicate with each other. A cadence is how a group of notes communicates with another group of notes.

Let's break down these chords and understand the communication between the **V-I** chords. This is what teachers call an **authentic cadence**.

V - I Resolutions in the key of C

Below are two examples of a G chord resolving to a C chord. To understand how these chords are communicating, think about the notes individually. In the first measure, the B note moves down to G. In the second measure it moves up to high c. Which resolution sounds better? It feels like a stronger resolution when B moves up to high c. Let's look at a similar example below using the piano. We'll use a sound that's more dissonant, the G7 chord.

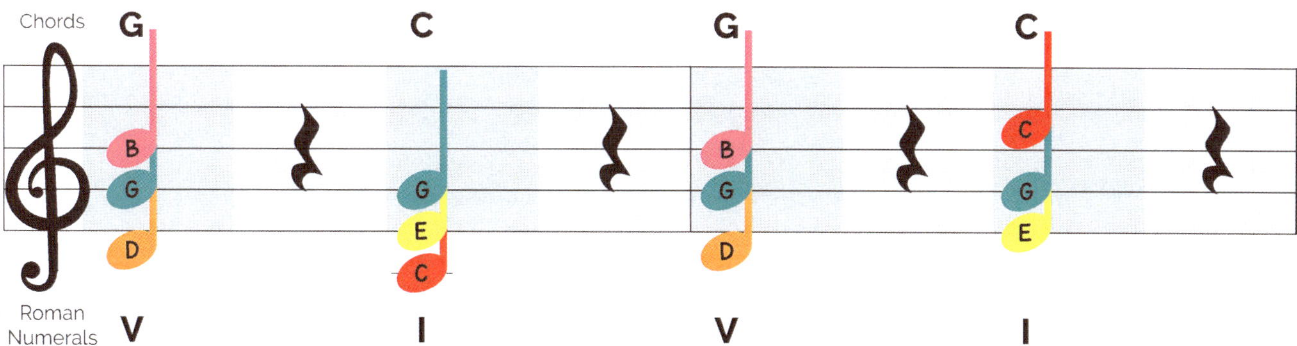

Voice Leading

From Bach to Brian Wilson, composers throughout the years have practiced good voice leading. **Voice leading** is making smooth transitions in our chord progressions. We need to be thoughtful about how the notes move, using mostly stepwise motion, and if possible, staying the same.

Let's look at the piano below using a G7 to C cadence.

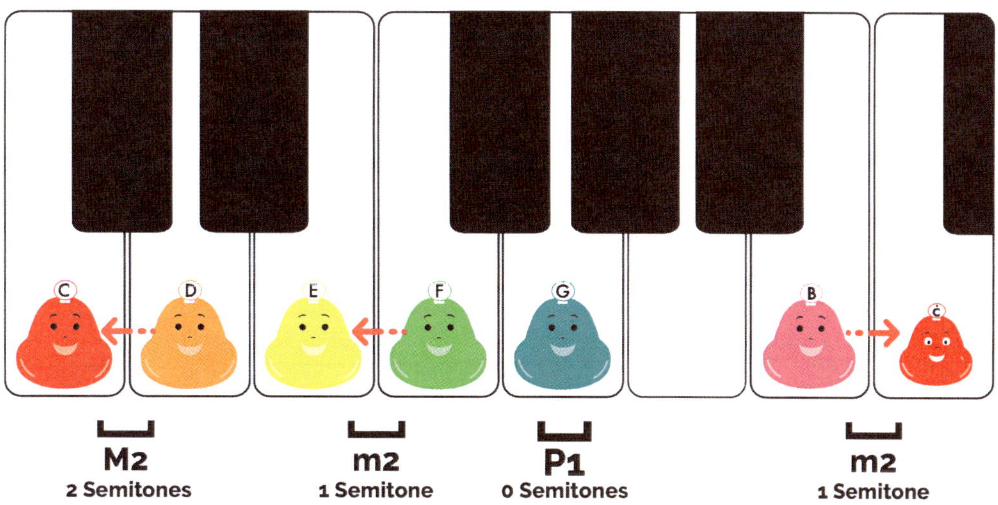

Notice how the notes move only in steps or skips, the G plays a perfect unison and B, the leading tone, resolves up to c, the tonic. That's so satisfying to hear, Ti Do!

Octaves

If you're playing a scale, once you begin, you have to navigate through the right pattern of notes. This can be confusing on chromatic instruments, but once you reach the octave, it's like you're home, only higher. Melodically, it's safe to take a large leap to the octave without seeming jarring to the listener, though it takes lots of practice to sing those notes.

Harmonically, octaves can enhance a melody or a background motif. When forming chords, you can add the octave of any note in that chord.

In a major key, octaves will be...

Perfect Octave

12 Semitones

Melodically Sounds Like...	**Harmonically Sounds Like...**
Somewhere Over the Rainbow	Wes Montgomery's guitar
"Salt Peanuts" Dizzy Gillespie	Bulkier than a single note
Funkytown	Lots of space in between
"Ow-ooh" Werewolves of London	

Perfect Octaves in C Major

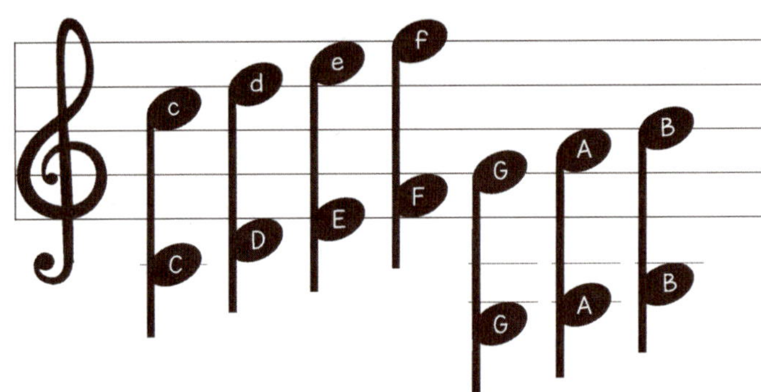

F to _____ is a Perfect octave

G to _____ is a Perfect octave

D to _____ is a Perfect octave

B to _____ is a Perfect octave

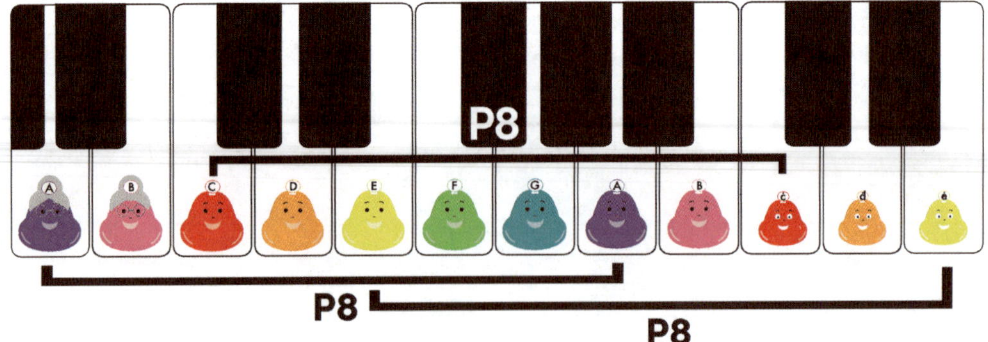

A to _____ is a Perfect octave

E to _____ is a Perfect octave

C to _____ is a Perfect octave

Piano Intervals - 2nds, 3rds, 4ths, 5ths, 6ths, 7ths

On the keyboards below you'll see 2nds, 3rds, 4ths, 5ths, & 6ths.
Circle the correct answer below each piano.

Bonus: Play your instrument as you go to hear the sound of the interval.

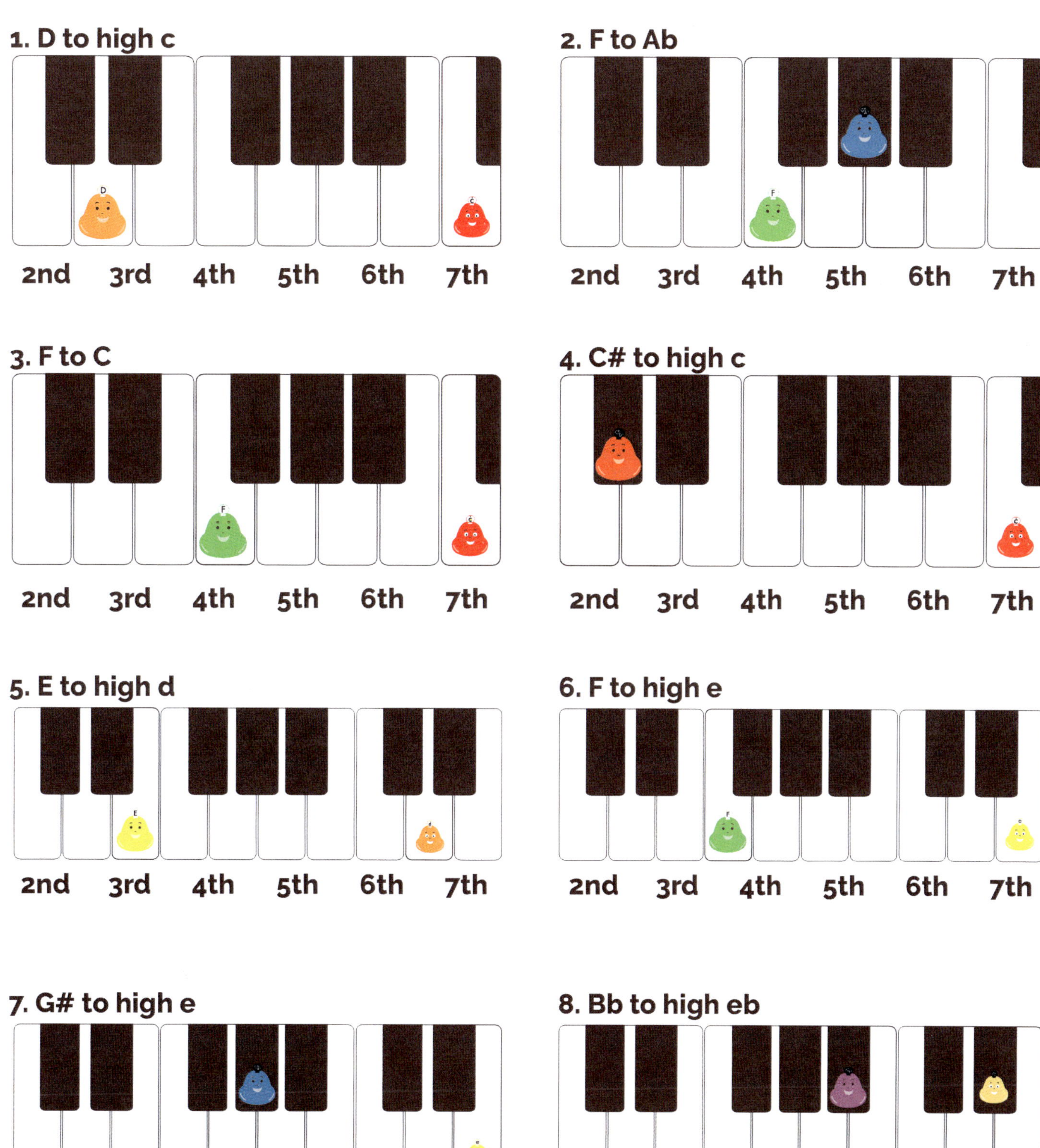

2nd 3rd 4th 5th 6th 7th

2nd 3rd 4th 5th 6th 7th

Notating Intervals - 2nds, 3rds, 4ths, 5ths, 6ths, 7ths, Octaves

Let's draw some HARMONIC Intervals. These intervals happen at the same time.
Then, write the name of the interval below

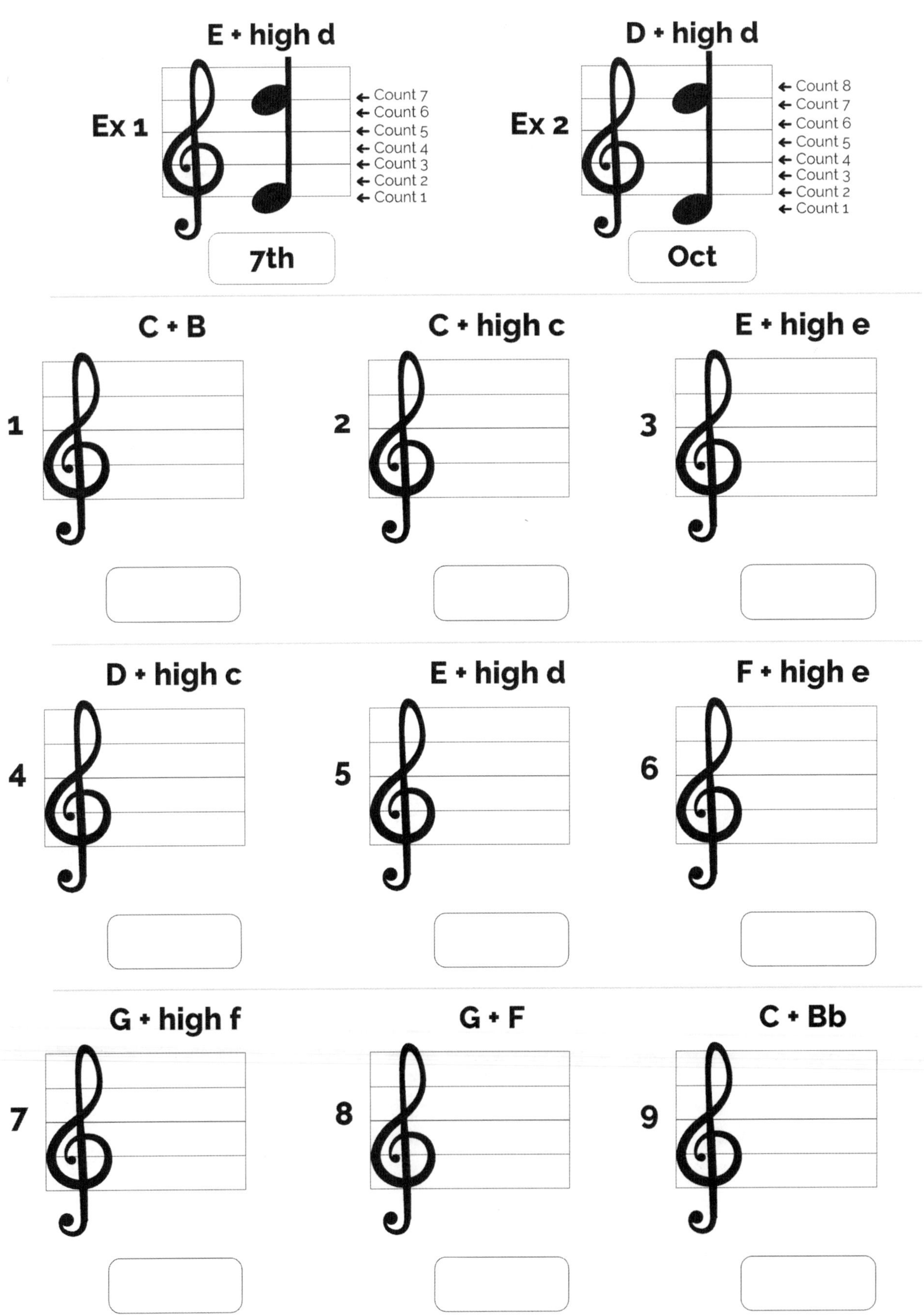

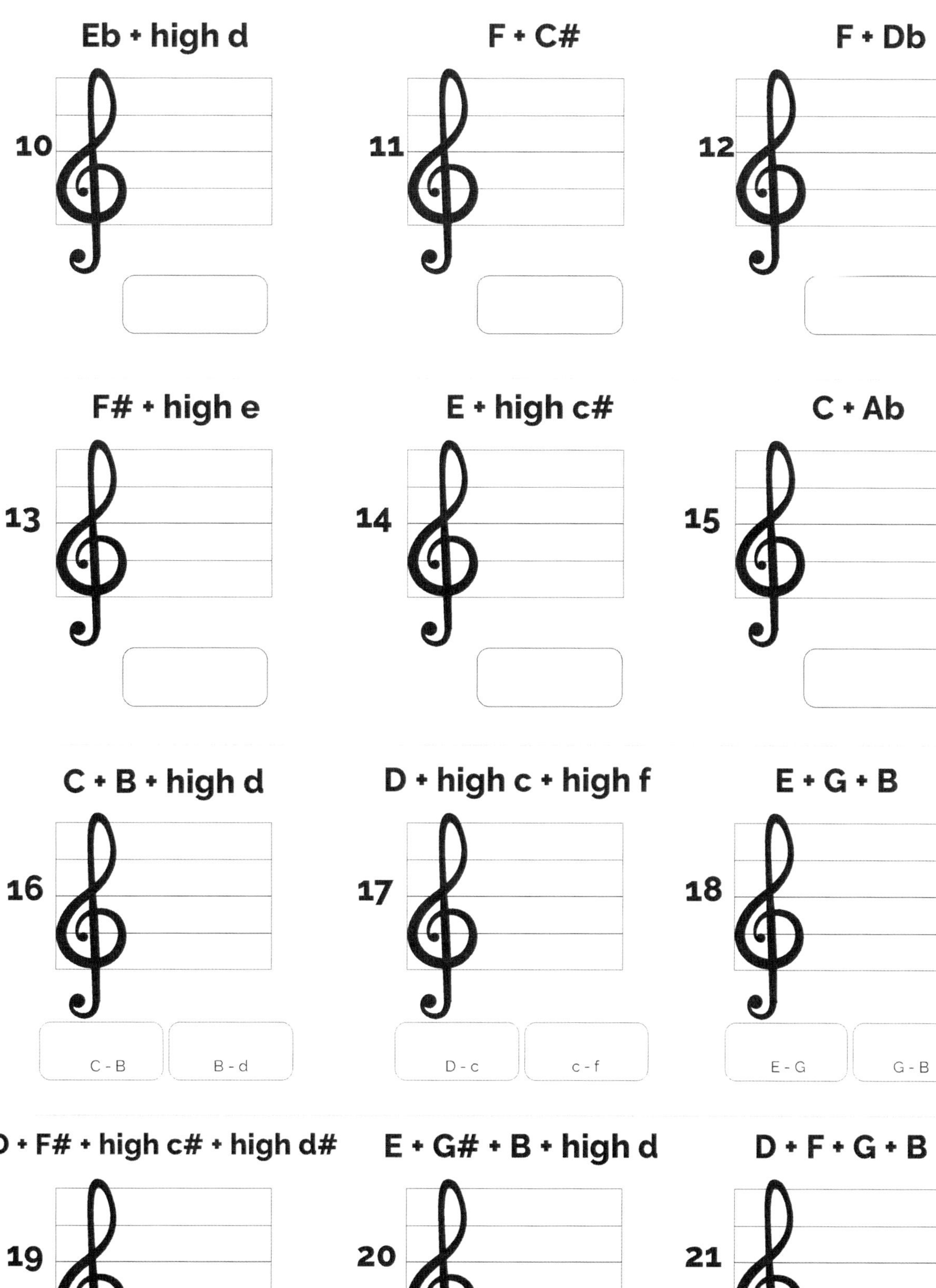

D - F# | F# - c# | c# - d#

E - G# | G# - B | B - d

D - F | F - G | G - B

SEMITONE CHALLENGE WITH 7THS & OCTAVES

Let's practice some more semitones. This time we'll use...

10 semitones (a Minor 7th), 11 semitones (a Major 7th), & 12 Semitones (an Octave)

1. Circle C and the note 12 semitones above

Minor 7 **Major 7** **Octave**

2. Circle high c and the note 10 semitones below

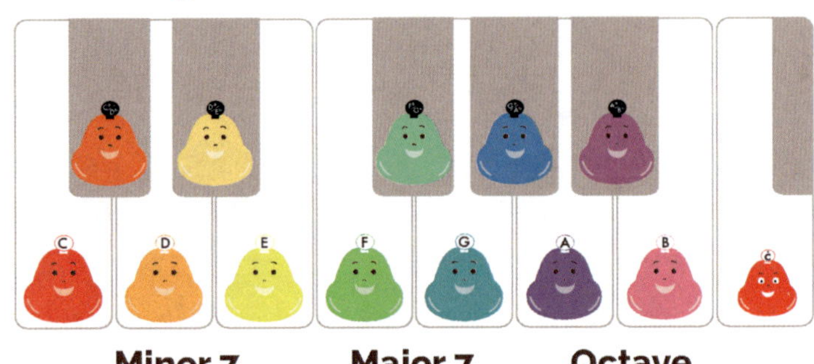

Minor 7 **Major 7** **Octave**

3. Circle C and the note 11 semitones above

Minor 7 **Major 7** **Octave**

4. Circle D and the note 10 semitones above

Minor 7 **Major 7** **Octave**

5. Circle high c and the note 11 semitones below

Minor 7 **Major 7** **Octave**

6. Circle D and the note 9 semitones above

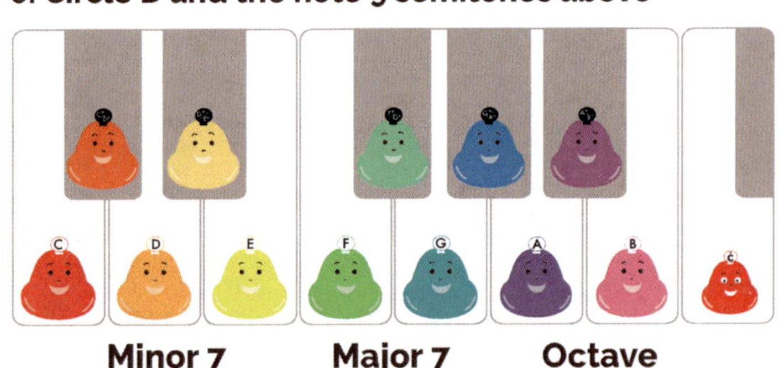

Minor 7 **Major 7** **Octave**

7. Circle B and the note 9 semitones below

Minor 7 **Major 7** **Octave**

8. Circle Bb and the note 10 semitones below

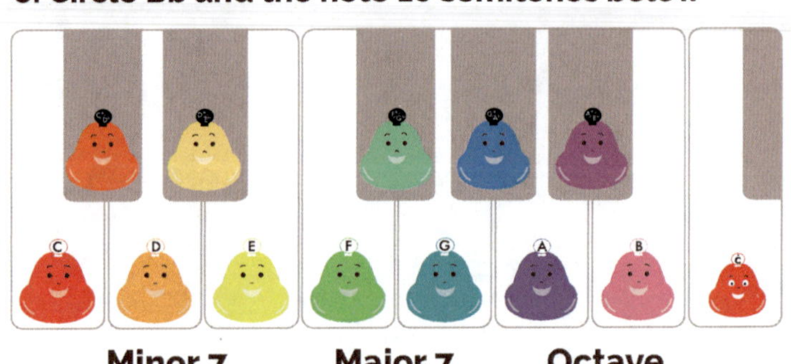

Minor 7 **Major 7** **Octave**

PRIMARY PRODIGIES

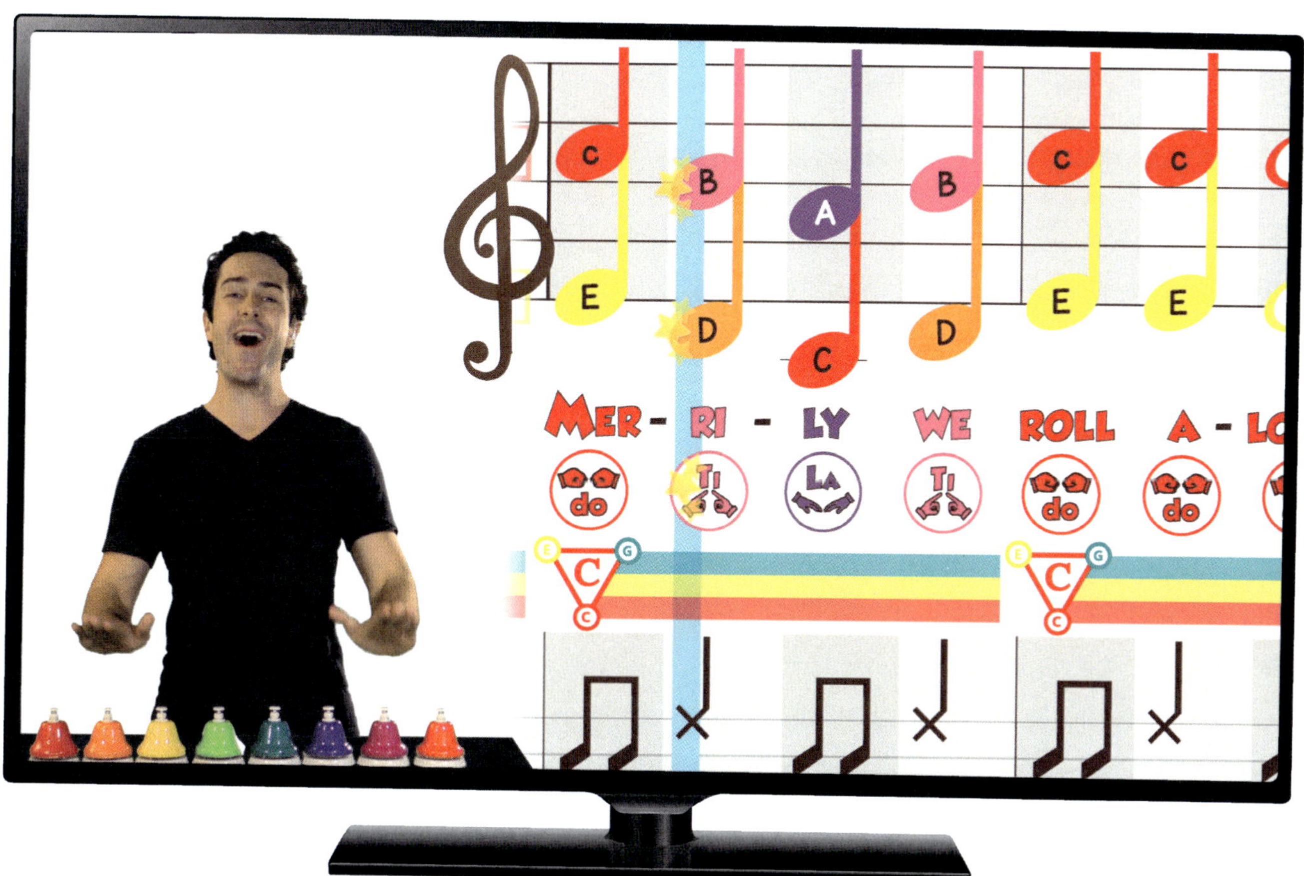

PARALLEL HARMONIES WITH "MERRILY WE HARMONIZE"

Section 2.8

Notes Used:

Merrily We Harmonize

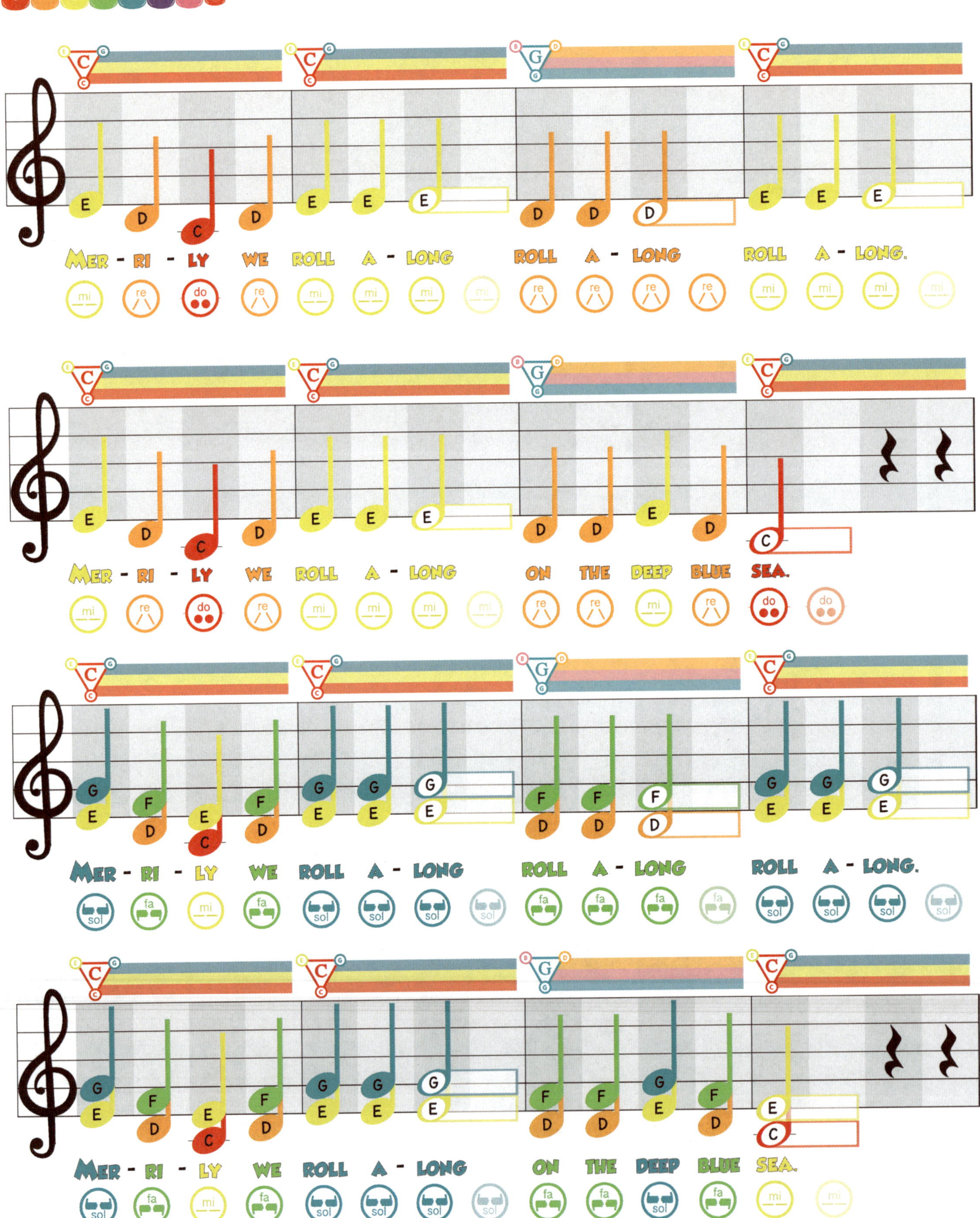

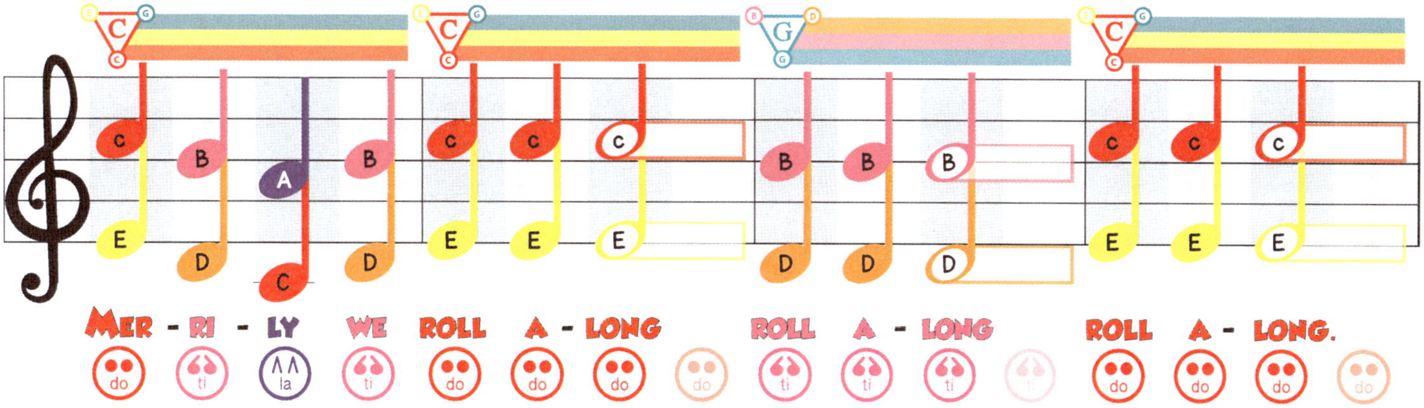

C C G C

C B A B C C C B B B C C C

E D C D E E E D D D E E E

MER - RI - LY WE ROLL A - LONG ROLL A - LONG ROLL A - LONG.

do ti la ti do do do do ti ti ti ti do do do do

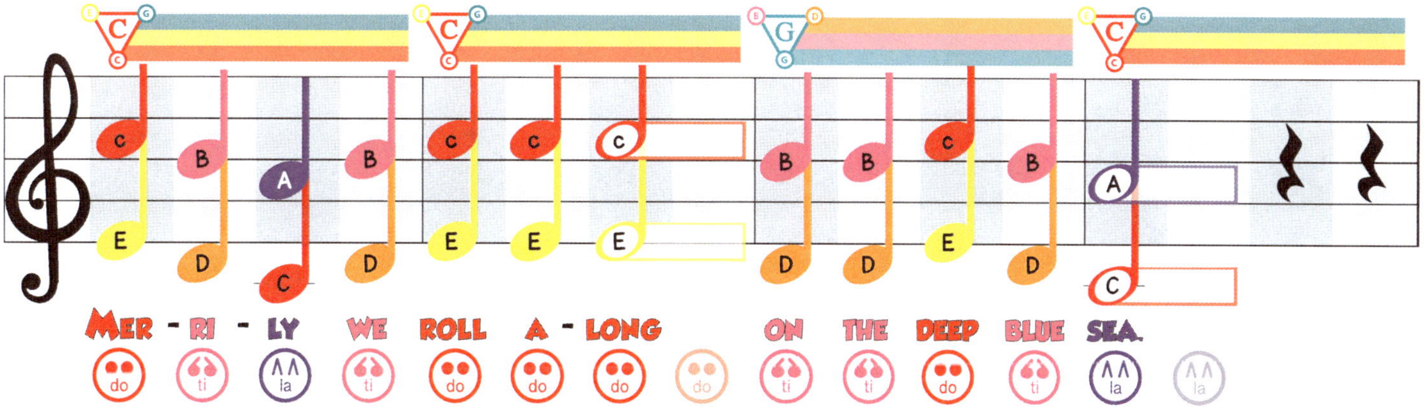

C C G C

C B A B C C C B B C B A

E D C D E E E D D E D C

MER - RI - LY WE ROLL A - LONG ON THE DEEP BLUE SEA.

do ti la ti do do do do ti ti do ti la la

One more time in Black and White

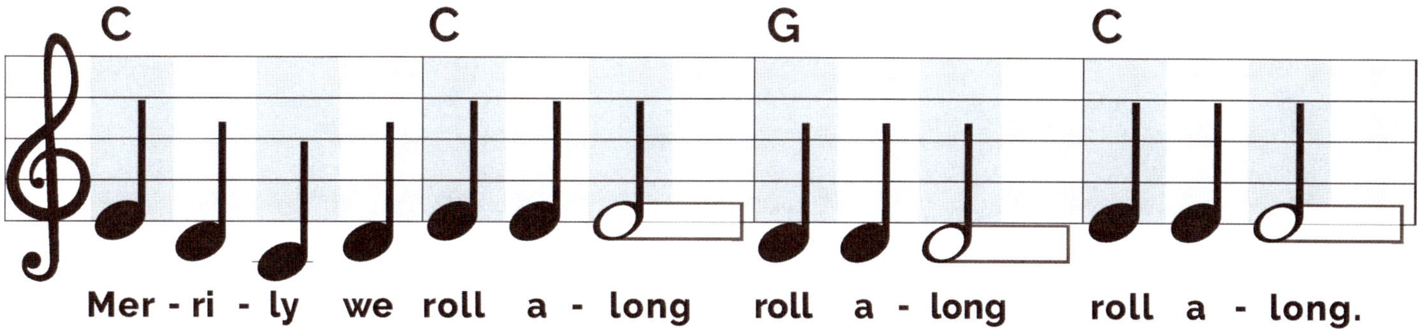

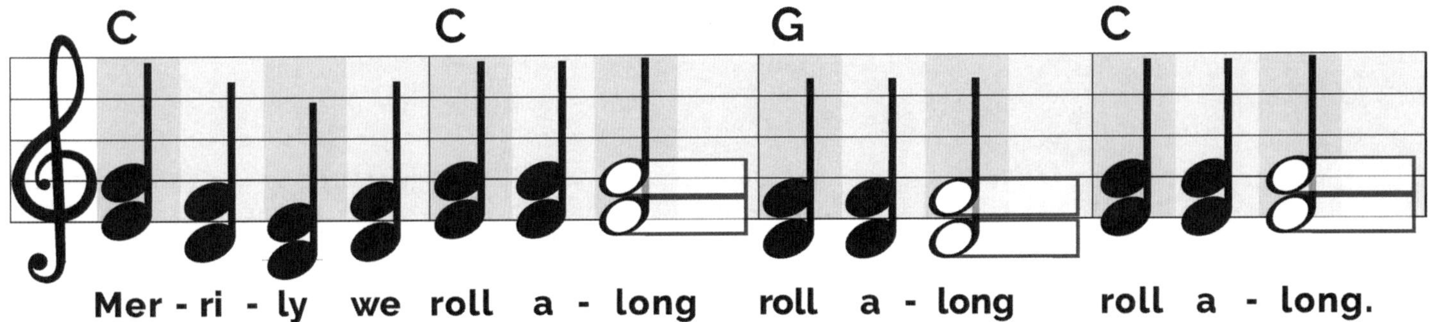
C
C
G
C
Mer - ri - ly we roll a - long roll a - long roll a - long.

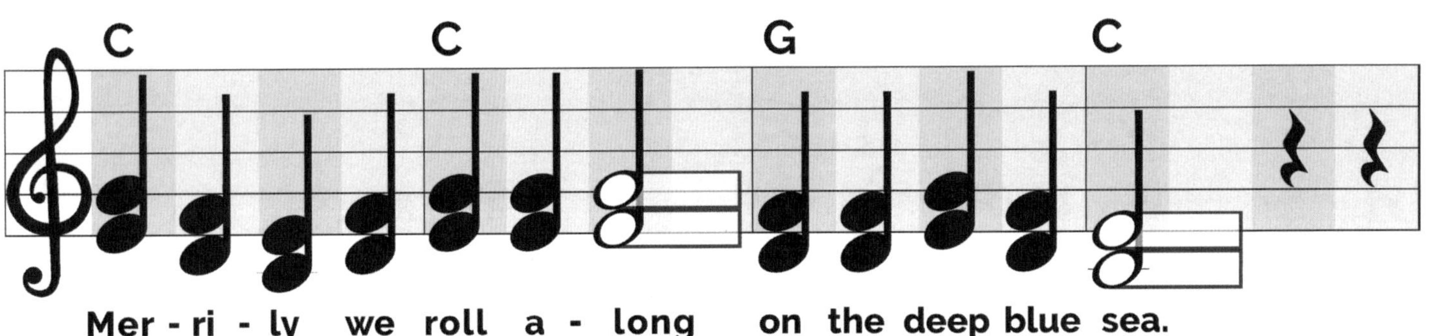
C
C
G
C
Mer - ri - ly we roll a - long on the deep blue sea.

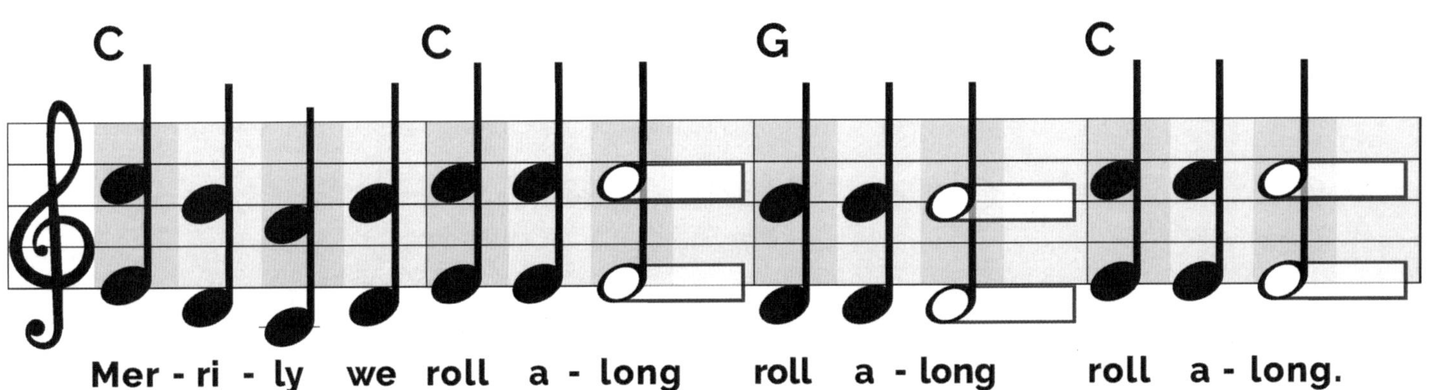
C
C
G
C
Mer - ri - ly we roll a - long roll a - long roll a - long.

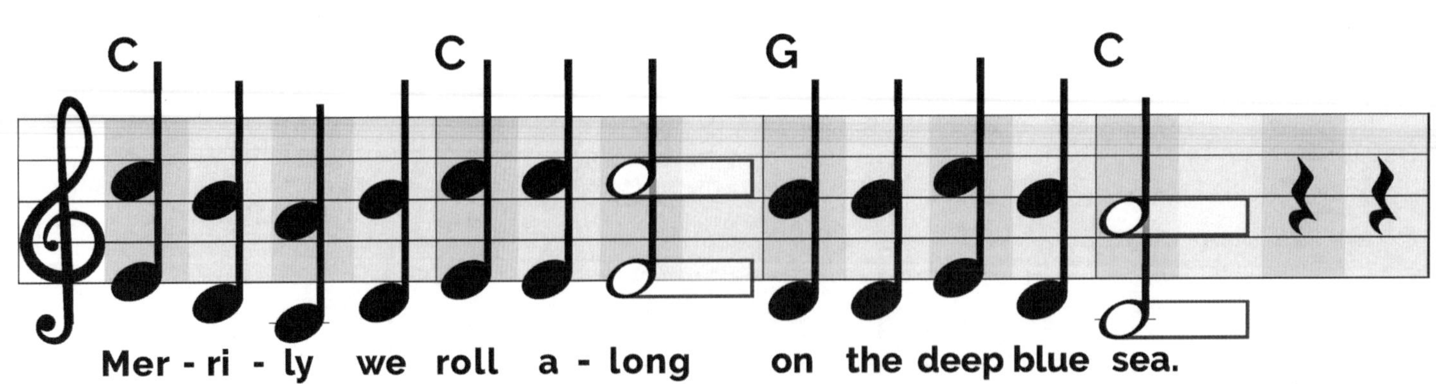
C
C
G
C
Mer - ri - ly we roll a - long on the deep blue sea.

2.8 Parallel Harmonies

We've learned about so many types of intervals by now, but what do we do with that information? If we're jamming with our friends and someone plays a melody, we can use our knowledge of intervals to harmonize.

We can add notes that are a certain interval apart, moving up or down with the melody, keeping a relative distance. It's important to know in which key we're playing and how to play or sing an interval of a note, which we've learned to do in this book! From there, a few basic guidelines will result in the most pleasant sound.

It's most common to harmonize in 3rds. Their inverse intervals, 6ths, also work well. Stay away from parallel 4ths and 5ths for entire melodies. They're most effective when used sparingly. Parallel 2nds and 7ths are also to be used in moderation, like if you're trying to create timbre or texture, like the sound of things falling. Our ears will tell us which intervals sound the best.

If we follow these rules at first, it's easier to break those rules when we're writing our masterpiece. As a rule of thumb, write or play what suits the music or your instrument the best. Let's look below to see how parallel 3rds were used to harmonize two measures of the Prodigies Theme Song!

Prodigies Theme Song

Interval Guided Composition

It is said that Mozart wrote his first composition at the age of five, that's incredible! The Prodigies Team wants our students to know how it feels to write an advanced piece of music following our instructions. This exercise will show how important it is to pay attention to our new music vocabulary carefully as we guide you through the composition process.

This may be a little tricky, but we'll provide lots of hints along the way. Read carefully, and take your time. We'll add some notes to keep you on the right track.

The first measure will be all 8th notes **The first 4 notes will be 8th notes**

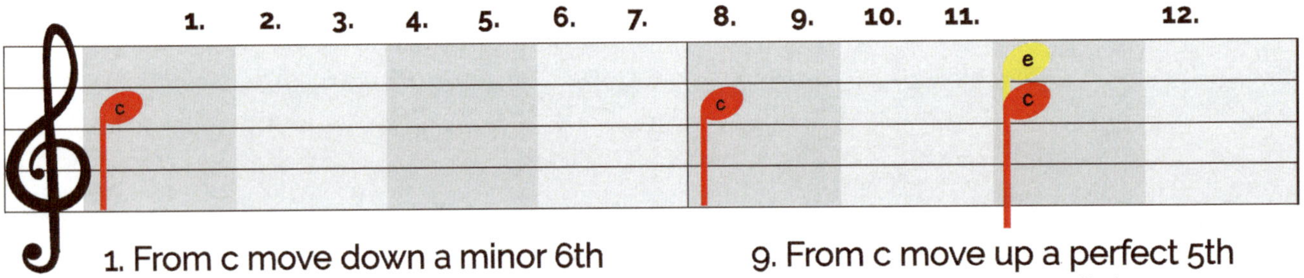

1. 2. 3. 4. 5. 6. 7. 8. 9. 10. 11. 12.

c c e c

1. From c move down a minor 6th
Count backwards from c and you'll find Mi
c down to ____ is a m6

2. Up a minor 2nd
Mr. Rob plays Jaws with these two notes
____ up to ____ is a m2

3. Up an augmented unison
I'm the new note in Baby Shark, I have a #
____ up to ____ is an A1

4. Up a minor 2nd
To reach your goal, search your Sol
____ up to ____ is a m2

5. Up a major 2nd
Daydreaming? Are you in La La Land?
____ up to ____ is a M2

6. Up a minor 2nd
Happy Birthday, here's a special note!
____ up to ____ is a m2

7. Up an augmented unison
You'll need a natural symbol to find me
____ up to ____ is an A1

8. Up a minor 2nd
If you composed correctly, you should have Ti Do
____ up to high c is a m2

9. From c move up a perfect 5th
Twinkle, Twinkle you little star
c up to ____ is a P5

10. Down a minor 3rd
Are you calling me yellow?
____ down to ____ is a m3

11. Up a minor 2nd
Better ask Mr. Rob to play Jaws again
____ up to ____ is a m2

The 4 notes in the first two beats will be the same as "All dressed in white" from Here Comes the Bride.

12. Down an octave
Move the notes C and E down an octave
high c & e down to ____ & ____ is a P8

Answer Key on p.119

Write The Intervals

Each piano below has 3 or 4 notes. Name the intervals between each and write them in the boxes below the piano.

1. C - E - G

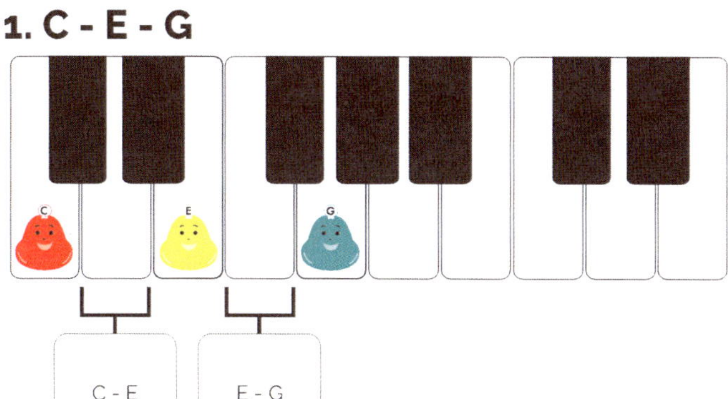

2. D - A - d

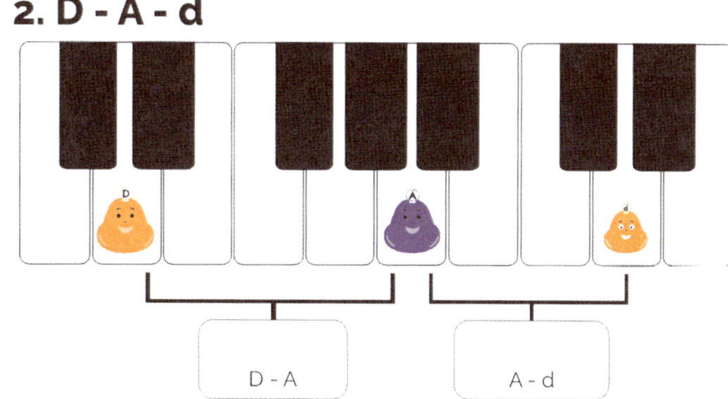

3. F - Bb - d

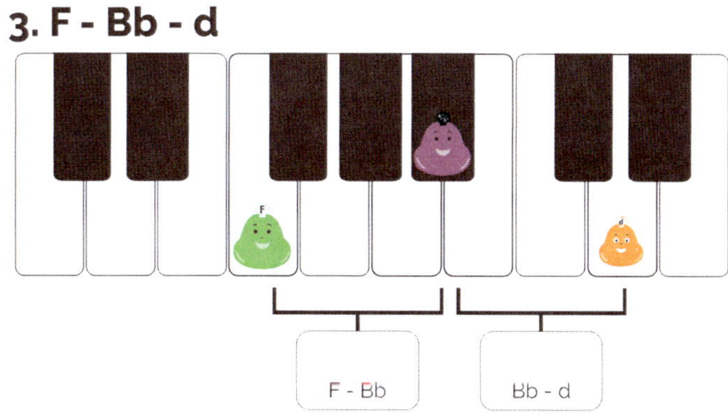

4. D - G - B - d

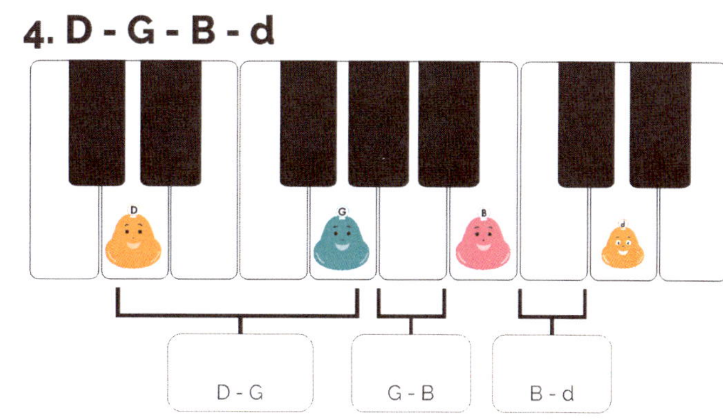

5. E - c - e

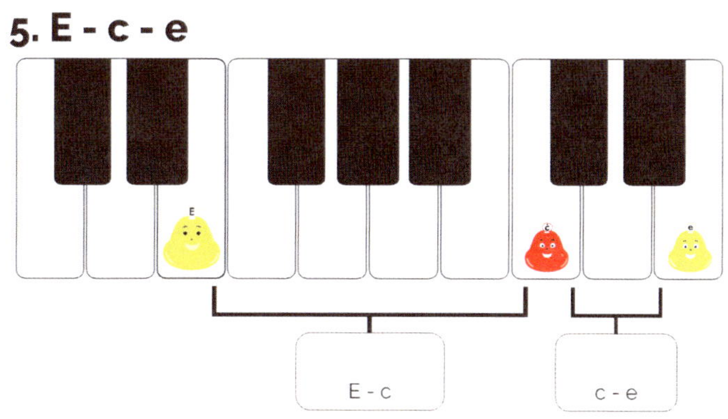

6. D - F - G - B

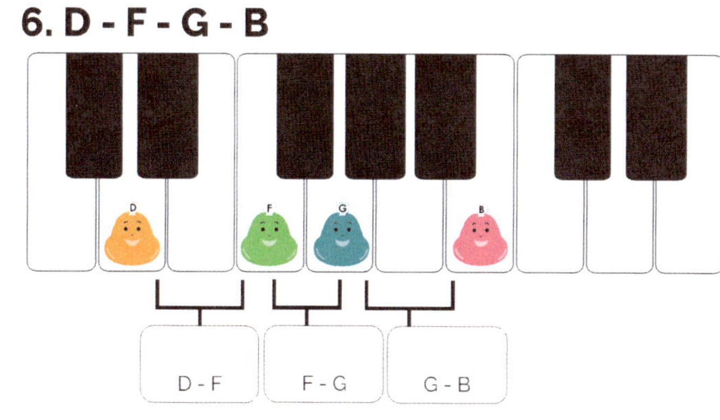

7. E - G# - B - e

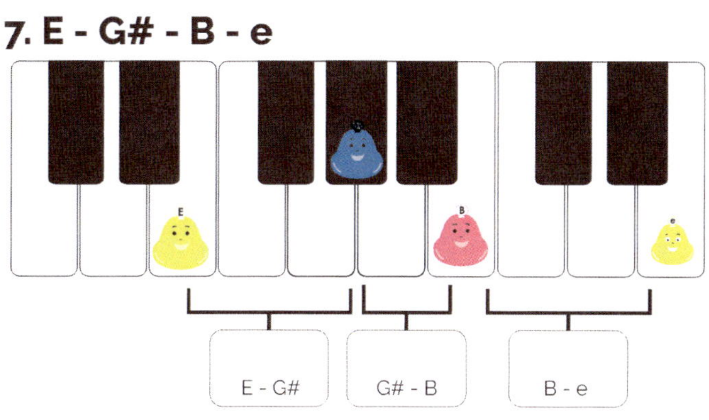

8. E - A - c

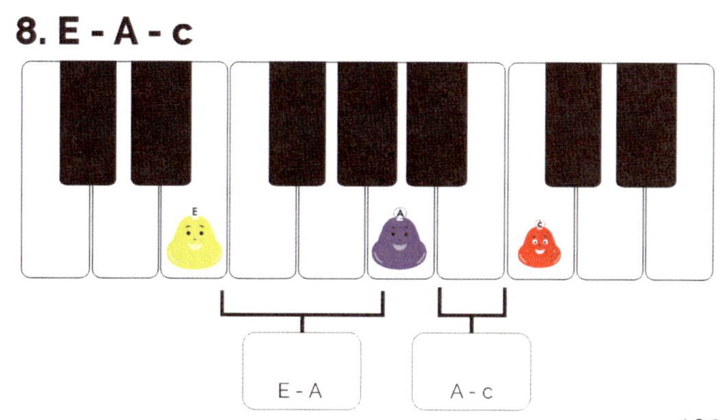

Naming Intervals - 2nds, 3rds, 4ths, 5ths, 6ths, 7ths, Octaves

Let's draw some HARMONIC Intervals. These intervals happen at the same time.
Then, write the name of the interval below

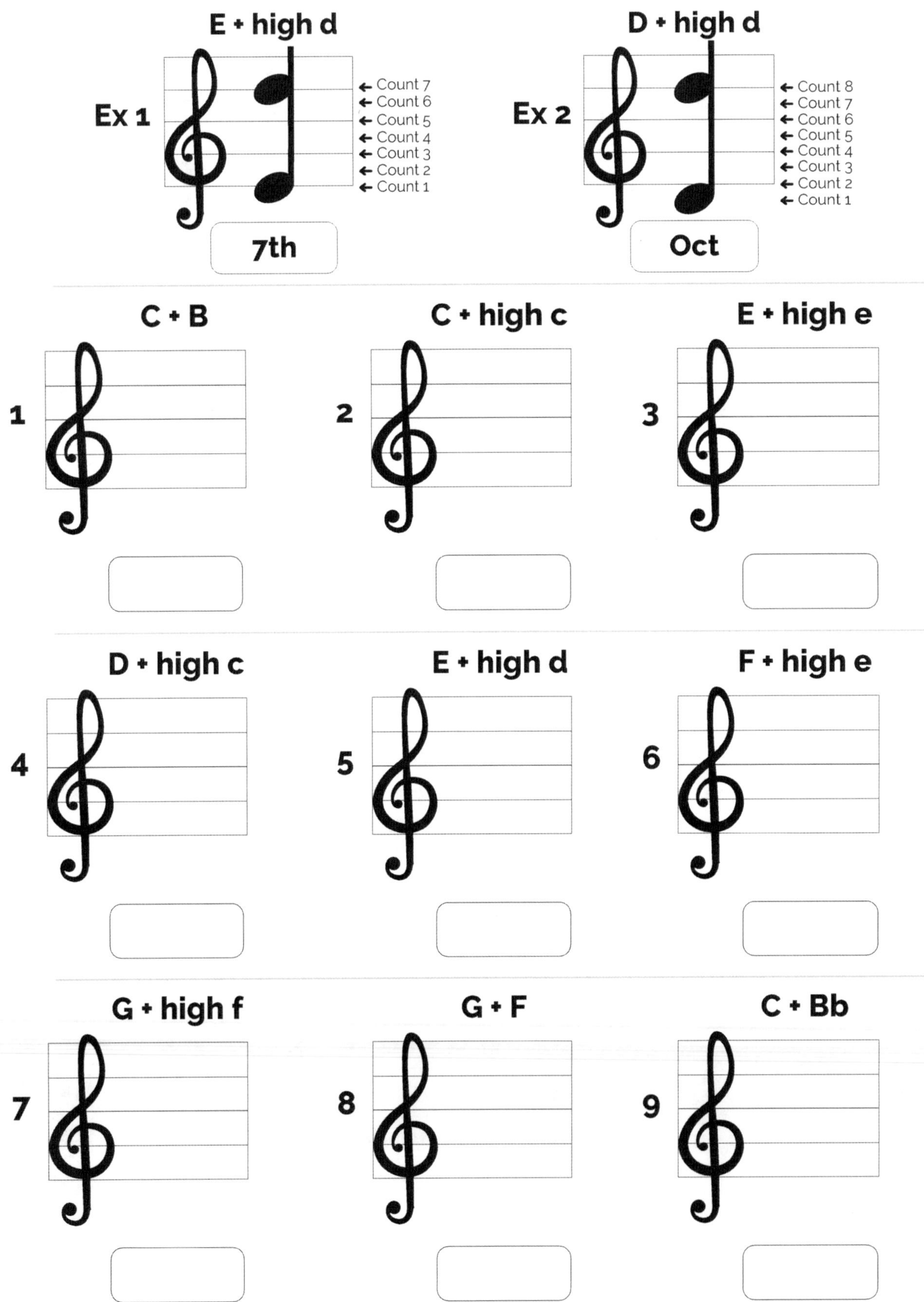

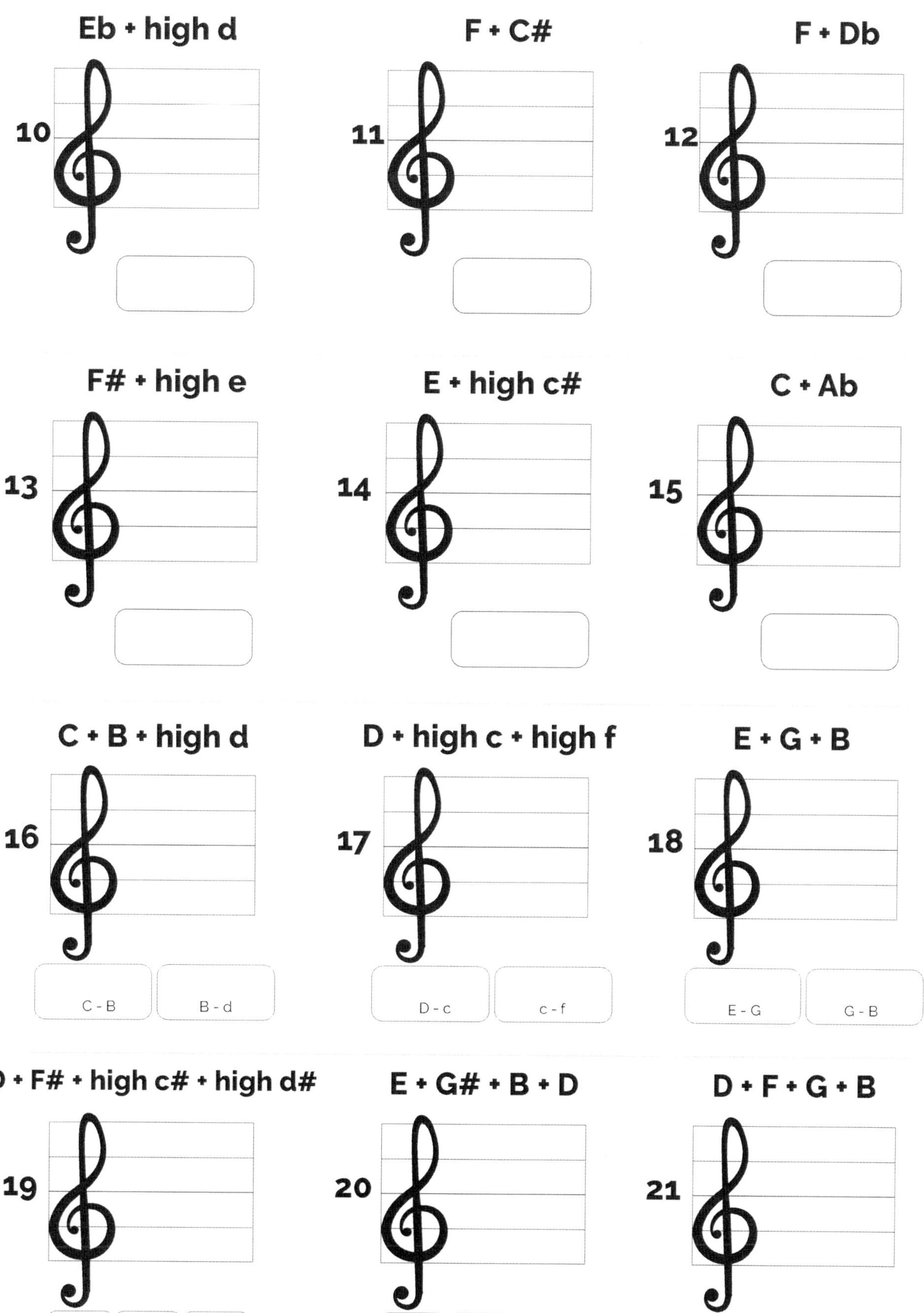
Eb + high d
10
F + C#
11
F + Db
12
F# + high e
13
E + high c#
14
C + Ab
15
C + B + high d
16
C - B
B - d
D + high c + high f
17
D - c
c - f
E + G + B
18
E - G
G - B
D + F# + high c# + high d#
19
D - F#
F# - c#
c# - d#
E + G# + B + D
20
E - G#
G# - B
B - d
D + F + G + B
21
D - F
F - G
G - B

Semitone Challenge - All Intervals

Let's practice some more semitones. This time, we'll use **all the semitones.**
Challenge: write the interval name (i.e. Perfect 5th) in the box below the bells

1. Circle E and the note 7 semitones above

2. Circle high d and the note 3 semitones below

3. Circle F and the note 5 semitones below

4. Circle B and the note 9 semitones below

5. Circle F# and the note 6 semitones above

6. Circle F# and the note 6 semitones below

7. Circle A and the note 4 semitones below

8. Circle Bb and the note 10 semitones below

9. Circle high e and the note 16 semitones below

10. Circle E and the note 3 semitones above

Primary Prodigies

Semitones & More Intervals with "Baby Shark" in G

Section 2.9

Baby Shark

Notes Used: D E F# G A

G C Em D

G D E G E G A D E

sol sol re re mi mi sol sol mi mi sol sol la re mi

Ba - by

G C

G G G G G G G G D E G G G G G G G G D E

Shark doo doo doo doo doo doo Ba - by Shark doo doo doo doo doo doo Ba - by

sol sol sol sol sol sol sol sol re mi sol sol sol sol sol sol sol sol re mi

Em D

G G G G G G G G G G #F D E

Shark doo doo doo doo doo doo Ba - by Shark Mom - my

sol sol sol sol sol sol sol sol sol sol fi re mi

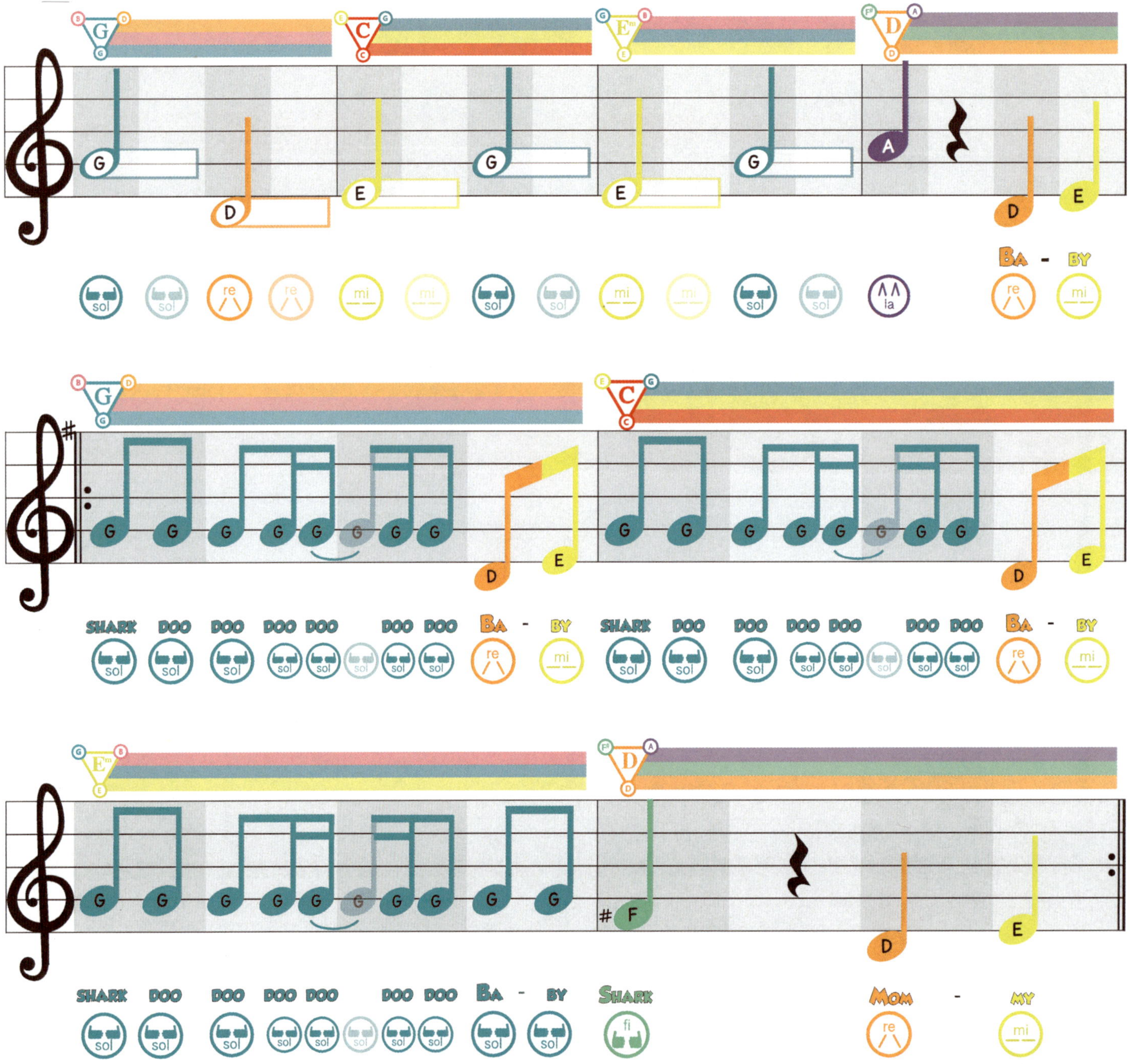

Additional Lyrics:

2. Mommy shark, etc.
3. Daddy shark, etc.
4. Grandma shark, etc.
5. Grandpa shark, etc.
6. Let's go hunt, etc.
7. Run away, etc.
8. Safe at last, etc.
9. It's the end, etc.

Baby Shark

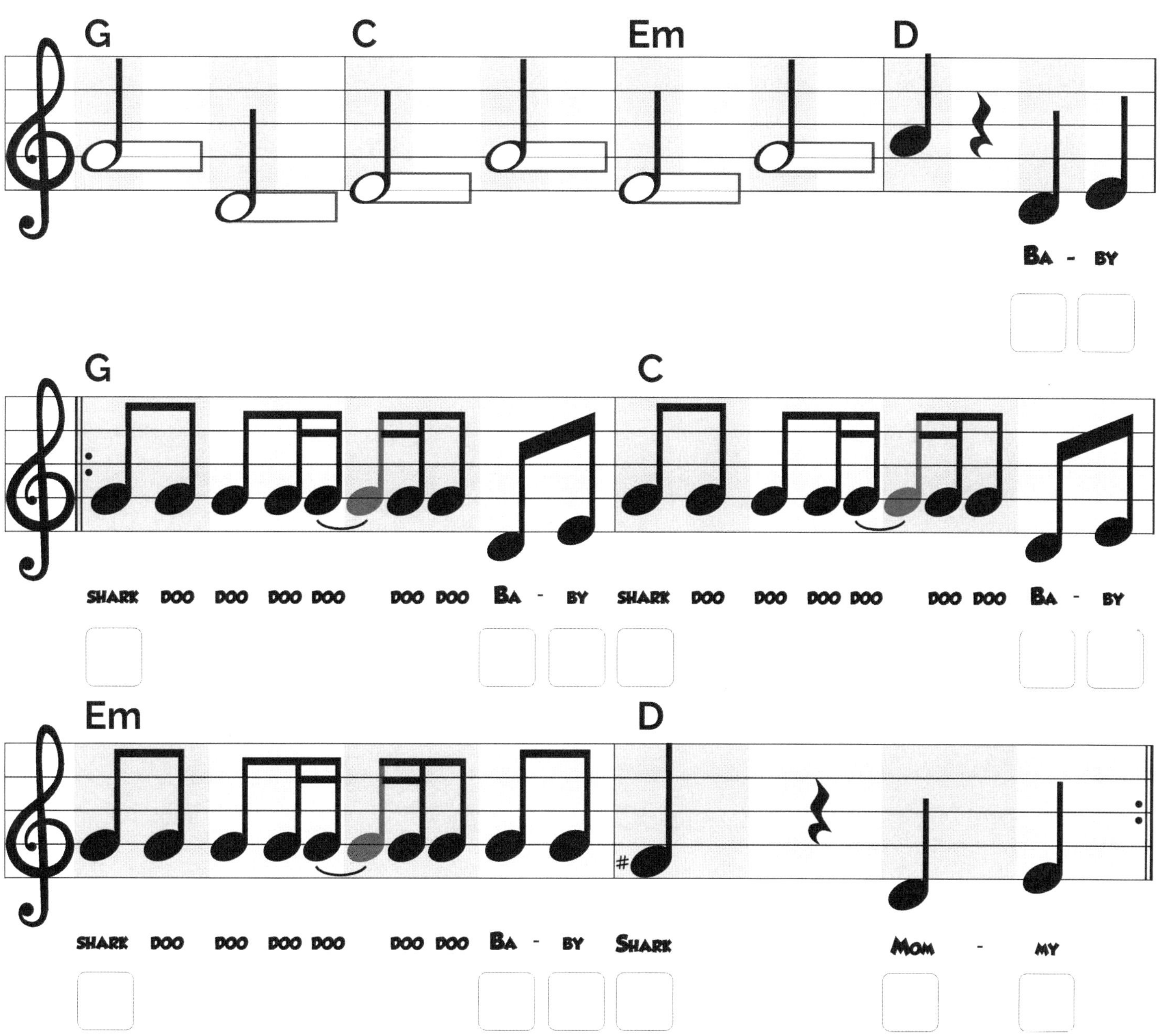

Additional Lyrics:

2. Mommy shark, etc.
3. Daddy shark, etc.
4. Grandma shark, etc.
5. Grandpa shark, etc.
6. Let's go hunt, etc.
7. Run away, etc.
8. Safe at last, etc.
9. It's the end, etc.

2.9 Chromatic Semitones

You've learned so much about intervals so far. Let's take it one step further. In the major scale, the notes are already in place. We can go back and analyze them, discovering which intervals exist. But wait! We can also create those intervals chromatically, without having to think about any scale at all.

If we want to create a minor 6th above C, we can use our knowledge of interval number and interval quality to spell it out. Before we begin, let's note that we have three minor 6th intervals in the key of C but not one starting on the C note. This is a big hint that our answer will include a note NOT in the key of C.

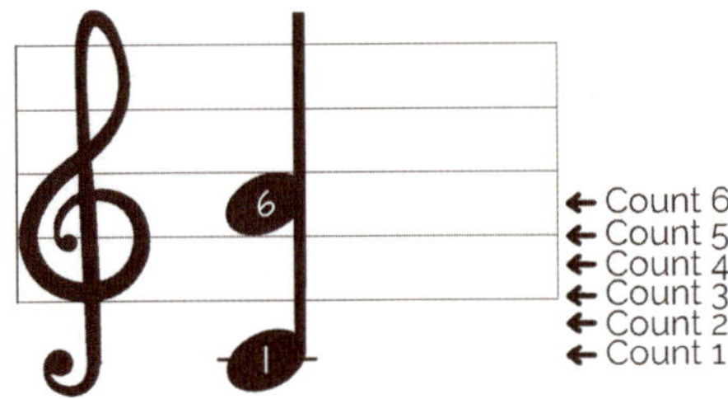

Ok, first we find the interval number. Starting on C, count up 6 letters, C (1) D (2) E (3) F (4) G (5) A (6). It must be an A note, but is A a minor 6th above C? Let's count the number of semitones to determine the interval quality.

Refer back to the section on 6ths to check that minor 6th is 8 semitones from our starting note. Remember, when counting semitones, we don't include our starting note. We've landed on the blue bell, it must be Ab. This matches our interval number and the correct number of semitones.

How do we check our work? We can play the notes. Do they sound like a minor 6th? You'll learn many ways to get the same answer along your musical journey.

Chromatic Intervals

Use the semitone number line above to help with learning chromatic intervals from C. If all these interval combinations seem intimidating, just remember, there are only 7 letters (ABCDEFG), and we use accidentals (flat, sharp) to modify that note up or down. If you know your major intervals, the minor will be one semitone below. C to A is a **MAJOR 6TH**. C to Ab is a **MINOR 6TH**. Try some others and as always, practice makes perfect... intervals!

Interval Qualities Vocab

Match the interval qualities on the left to the abbreviation on the right

Interval	Abbreviation
Perfect Unison	m7
Augmented Unison	M2
Minor Second	M7
Major Second	P1
Minor Third	P5
Major Third	P8
Perfect Fourth	d5
Augmented Fourth	m2
Tritone	M3
Diminished Fifth	A1
Perfect Fifth	M6
Minor Sixth	m3
Major Sixth	m6
Minor Seventh	P4
Major Seventh	TT
Perfect Octave	A4

CHANGING INTERVAL QUALITY

You can find an example of every interval quality we've discussed in the key of C. However there are lots of chromatic intervals outside the range of that scale. Learning these intervals is essential in theory, forever furthering our quest for musical knowledge!

Using sharps, flats, and natural symbols, we can raise or lower a note by one semitone. This allows us to keep the **interval number** the same while changing the **interval quality**. Follow these flow charts when modifying intervals.

C to A is a major 6th. We can make it a minor 6th by adding a flat to Ab. C to Ab is a minor 6th. Similarly, if you started with a minor 6th, C to Ab, you could add a natural symbol to A, giving you C to A natural, a major 6th.

Major and minor intervals can be augmented and diminished, respectively, but no matter how hard they try, they'll never be perfect. *Ba dum, tiss!*

CHANGING PERFECT INTERVALS

Perfect intervals can never be major or minor. If we increase the interval quality by one semitone, it's **augmented.** If we decrease the interval quality by one semitone, it's **diminished.**

In the key of C, you could play C to G, a **perfect 5th**. If you raise G by one semitone using a sharp symbol to G#, you've created an **augmented 5th.** If you lower G by one semitone using a flat symbol to Gb, you've created a **diminished 5th.**

The intervals we learn in the key of C make an excellent reference for all other intervals in the musical universe, especially when it's uncharted territory. Start with what you know, and use the tools you have learned to guide you through this new frontier.

Interval Qualities Vocab

Match the abbreviation on the left to the interval qualities on the right

Abbreviation	Interval
m7	Major Seventh
m6	Major Second
P4	Perfect Fifth
P1	Minor Sixth
TT	Perfect Fourth
M2	Augmented Unison
M7	Major Third
m2	Diminished Fifth
M3	Perfect Unison
m3	Minor Seventh
P5	Major Sixth
P8	Perfect Octave
d5	Minor Second
A4	Augmented Fourth
M6	Tritone
A1	Minor Third

Chapter 2 Review

You've talked the talk, let's walk the walk.

The lessons in this book help provide a foundation to a lifetime of music. Your knowledge of intervals will make you a better performer. You'll hear music more clearly and listen more intently. This vocabulary allows you to analyze and discuss music like never before. Use these new words to voice your thoughts about music with great confidence because you are a well-educated Prodigies student!

Hypothetically speaking...

We hope that everyone who enjoyed this book had the opportunity to sing and play along. If you found any examples of intervals that don't have corresponding bells, don't worry! As you progress in your studies, you'll have the opportunity to explore other instruments with greater range. It's important to see music as an academic subject. We should understand the concepts as much as possible, even if they are outside the range of your current instrument.

On the road ahead

In the upcoming chapters, you'll be spelling chords with intervals "stacked" on the staff. You'll play new sequences of consecutive intervals that form exotic sounding scales. With lots of practice, you'll develop a strong grasp of the relationship between melody and harmony. Begin questioning what you hear. Learn to translate what you hear into words. Let your words become the music.

We really wanted to end on a motivational note but there's one more quick lesson before you go.

Descending Melodic Intervals

In the following exercises, you'll be asked to notate and name melodic intervals that move downward. Here's some helpful tips before you get started.

If you're asked to form the interval high c down to F, you may think, "C (1) D (2) E (3) F (4), down a Perfect 4th." This would be correct if the interval were ascending, but we need to count backwards, C (1) B (2) A (3) G (4) F (5), down a 5th. We'd then use the piano or the semitone number line to get the quality, Perfect 5th.

HIGH C DOWN
A P5 TO F

Similarly, you could analyze the interval from the low note up to the high note, F to high c is a Perfect 5th.

Notating Descending Intervals

Solve each problem using the piano and the semitone number line from earlier in this chapter. Check your work. Write the note in the box, and then notate the interval melodically.

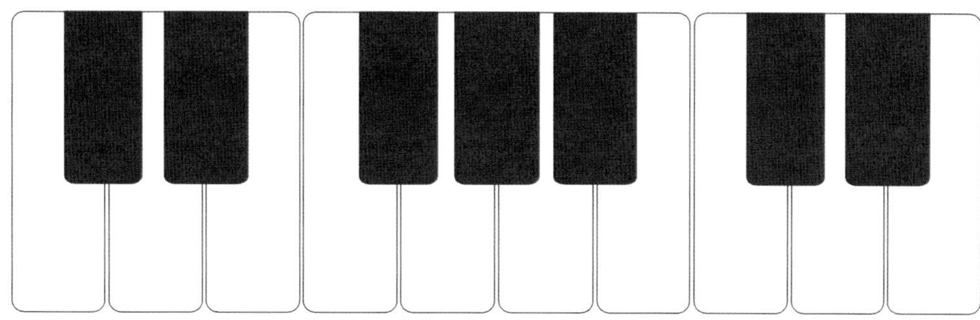

Ex 1

Notate Ab
+ a m3 lower

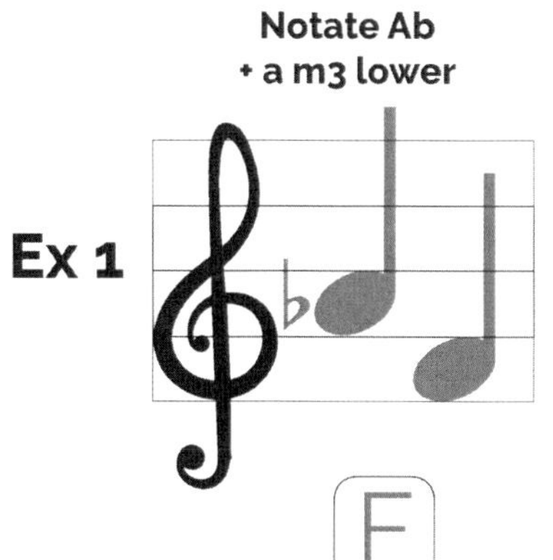

Hint: Find the **Interval Number** first. Ab(3) G(2) F(1). Must be an F note. Is it F#? Let's count the semitones.

Hint: Find the **Interval Quality**. A m3 is 3 semitones. Count away from Ab 3 piano keys. It's F natural.

Ex 2

Notate high c#
+ a M3 below

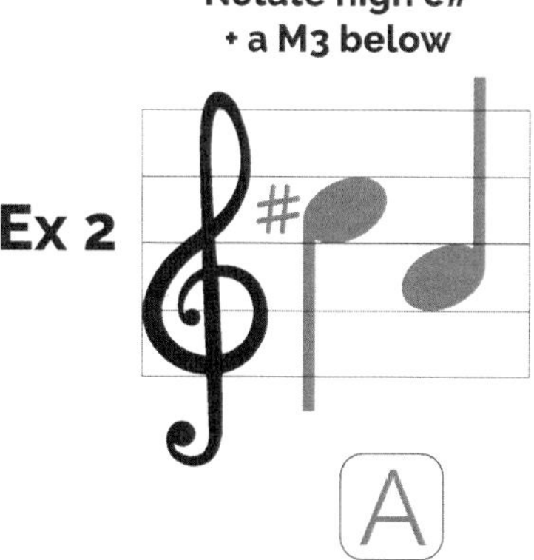

1

Notate high d
+ a M6 below

2

Notate F#
+ a M3 below

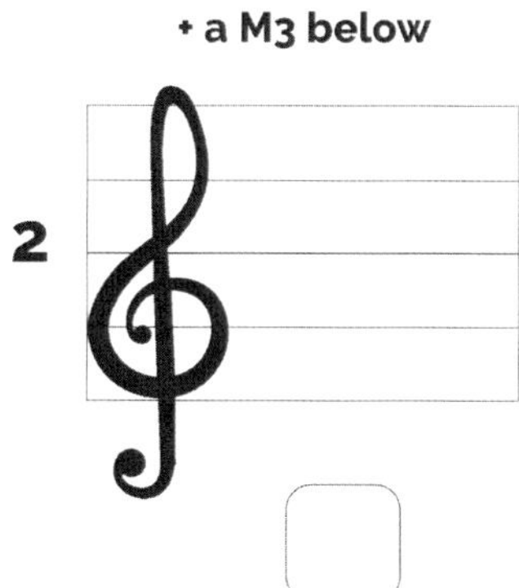

3

Notate Gb
+ a P5 below

4

Notate Bb
+ a M3 below

5

Notate high f
+ a d5 below

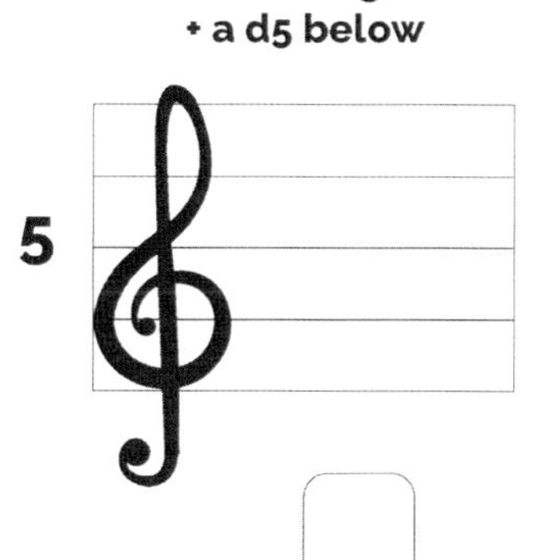

6

Notate high e
+ a m6 below

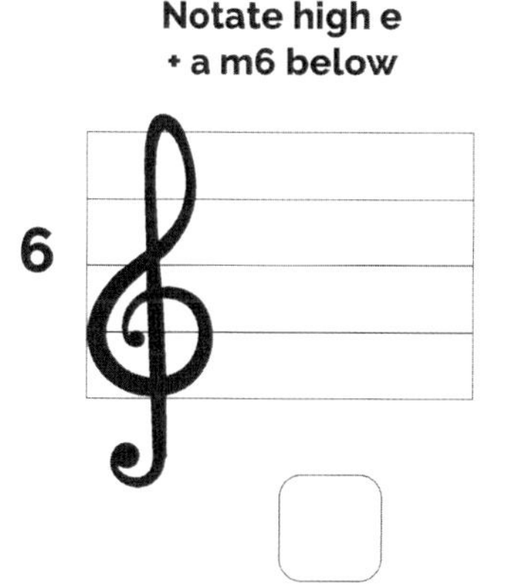

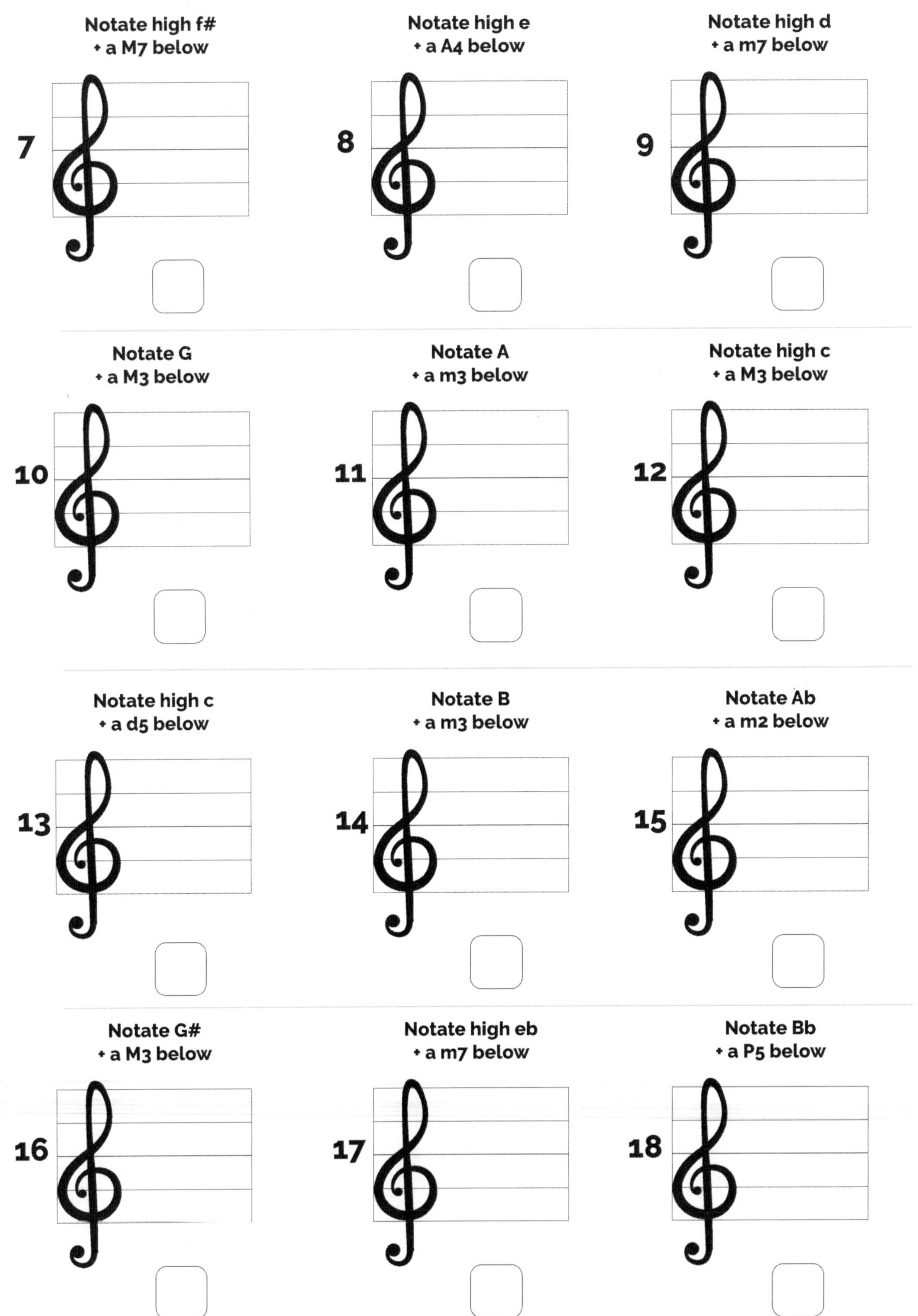
Notate high f#
+ a M7 below
7
Notate high e
+ a A4 below
8
Notate high d
+ a m7 below
9
Notate G
+ a M3 below
10
Notate A
+ a m3 below
11
Notate high c
+ a M3 below
12
Notate high c
+ a d5 below
13
Notate B
+ a m3 below
14
Notate Ab
+ a m2 below
15
Notate G#
+ a M3 below
16
Notate high eb
+ a m7 below
17
Notate Bb
+ a P5 below
18

Final Semitone Challenge - All Intervals, No Bells

For this final challenge, we'll give you the starting note and an interval up or down. You'll have to use your knowledge of intervals to know how many semitones to travel. To show your answer, write the note names on the piano keys.

1. Find F and the note a perfect 4th above

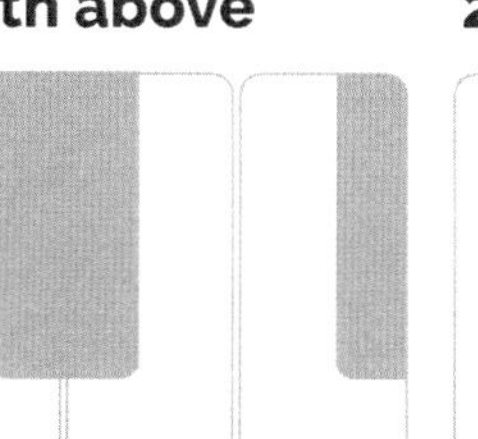

2. Find Eb and the note a major 2nd below

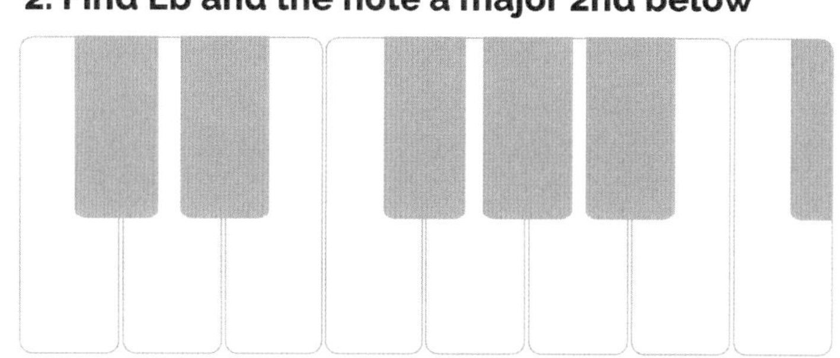

3. Find D and the note a minor 6th above

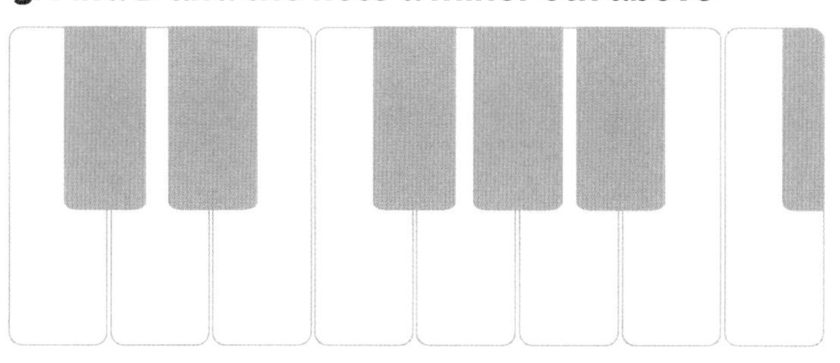

4. Find C# and the note a minor 3rd above

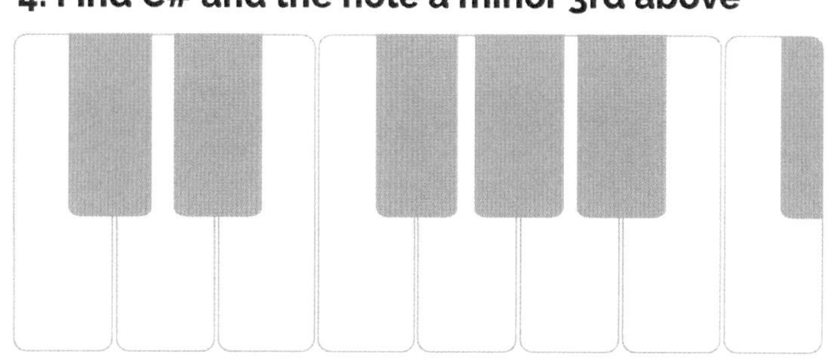

5. Find A and the note a major 3rd below

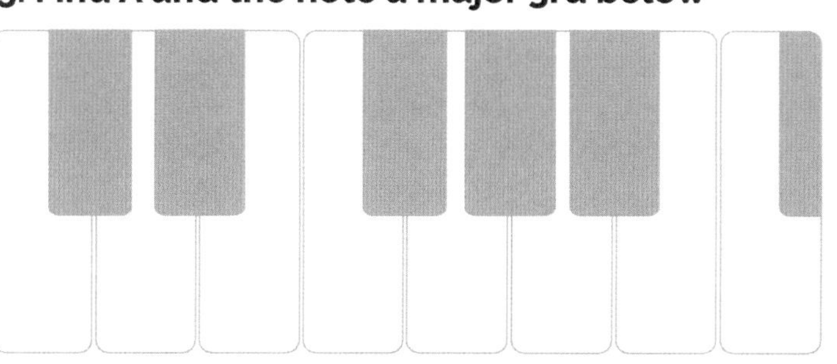

6. Find B and the note a major 6th below

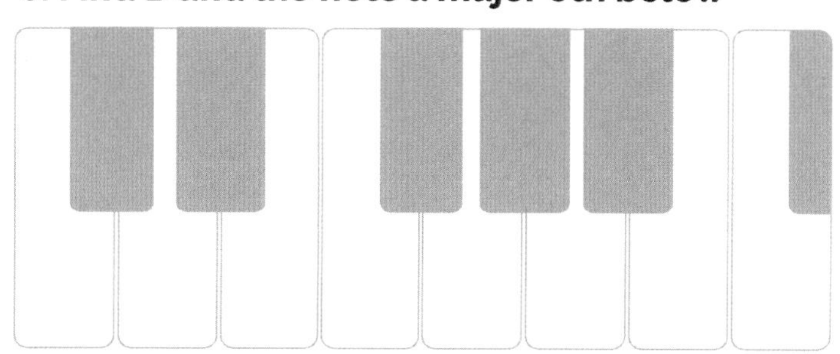

7. Find C and the note an augmented 4th above

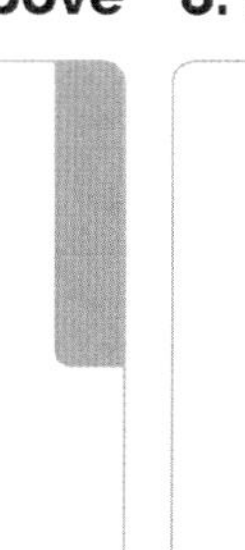

8. Find D# and the note a minor 7th above

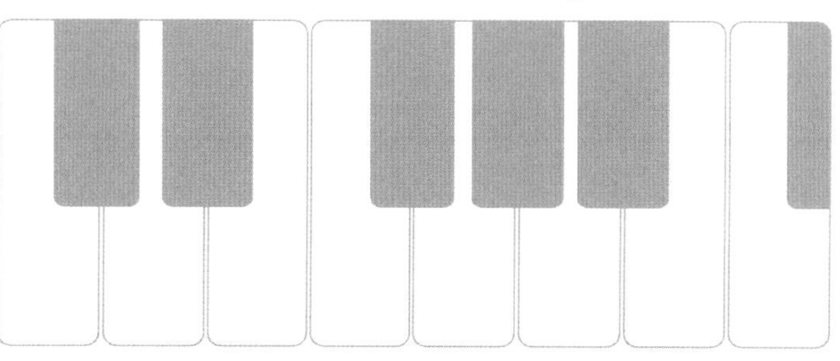

More Intervals in C Major

In section 2.1, you will find sheet music with all of the intervals starting on C. If you look closely, you will notice they are all **major** or **perfect** intervals.

This is an expanded list of intervals referenced throughout the book. Flip back to the sections covering specific intervals for a closer look.

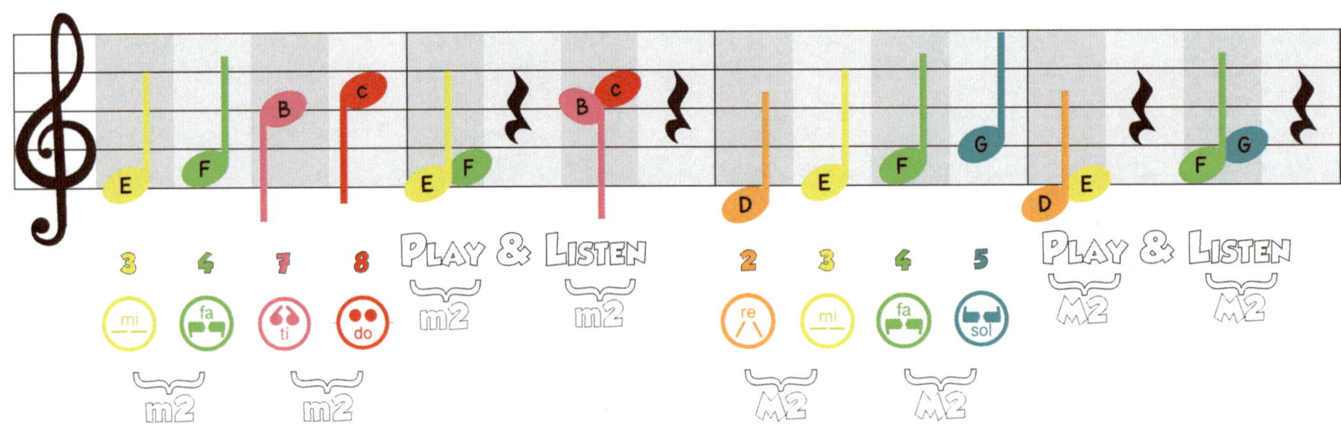

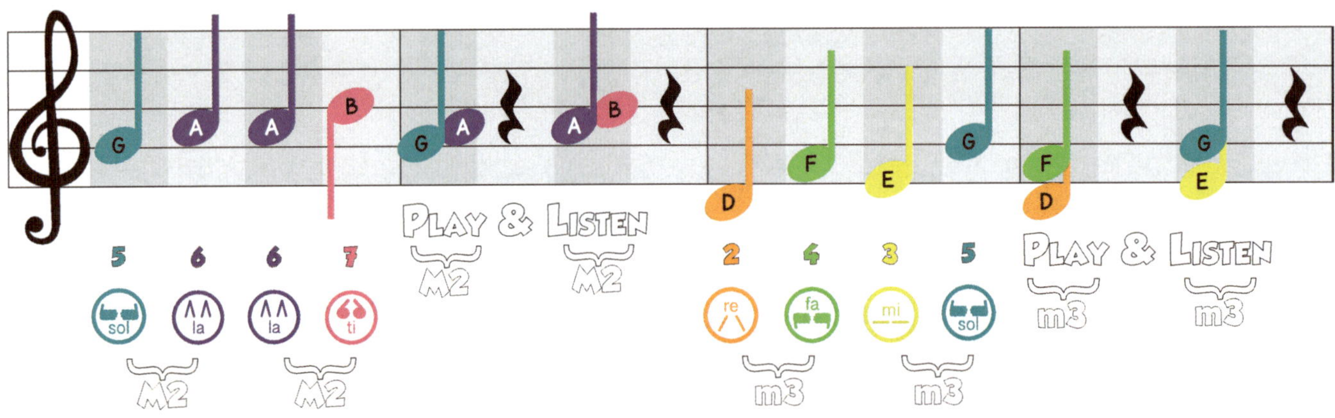

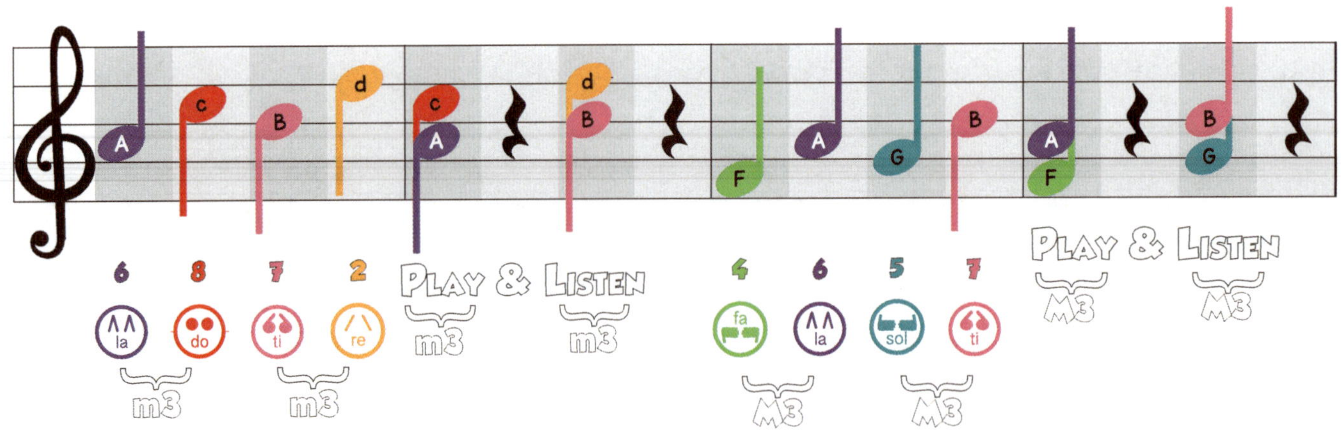

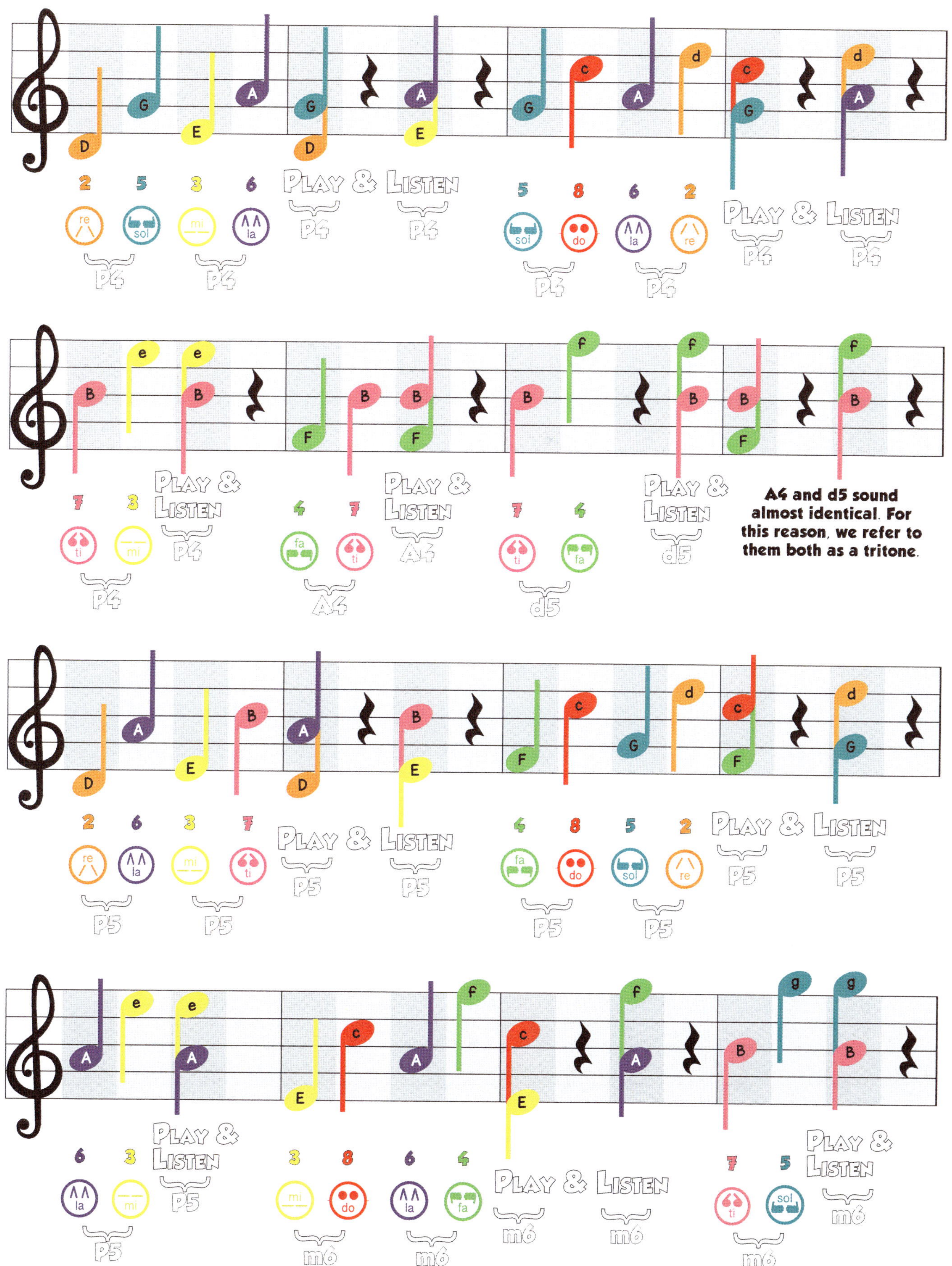

D G E A
2 5 3 6
re sol mi la
P4 P4
G D A E
PLAY & LISTEN
P4 P4
G c A d
5 8 6 2
sol do la re
P4 P4
c G d A
PLAY & LISTEN
P4 P4
B e e B
7 3
ti mi
P4
PLAY & LISTEN
P4
F B B F
4 7
fa ti
A4
PLAY & LISTEN
A4
B f f B
7 4
ti fa
d5
PLAY & LISTEN
d5
B F f B
A4 and d5 sound almost identical. For this reason, we refer to them both as a tritone.
D A E B
2 6 3 7
re la mi ti
P5 P5
A D B E
PLAY & LISTEN
P5 P5
F c G d
4 8 5 2
fa do sol re
P5 P5
c F d G
PLAY & LISTEN
P5 P5
A e e A
6 3
la mi
P5
PLAY & LISTEN
P5
E c A f
3 8 6 4
mi do la fa
m6 m6
c E f A
PLAY & LISTEN
m6 m6
B g g B
7 5
ti sol
m6
PLAY & LISTEN
m6

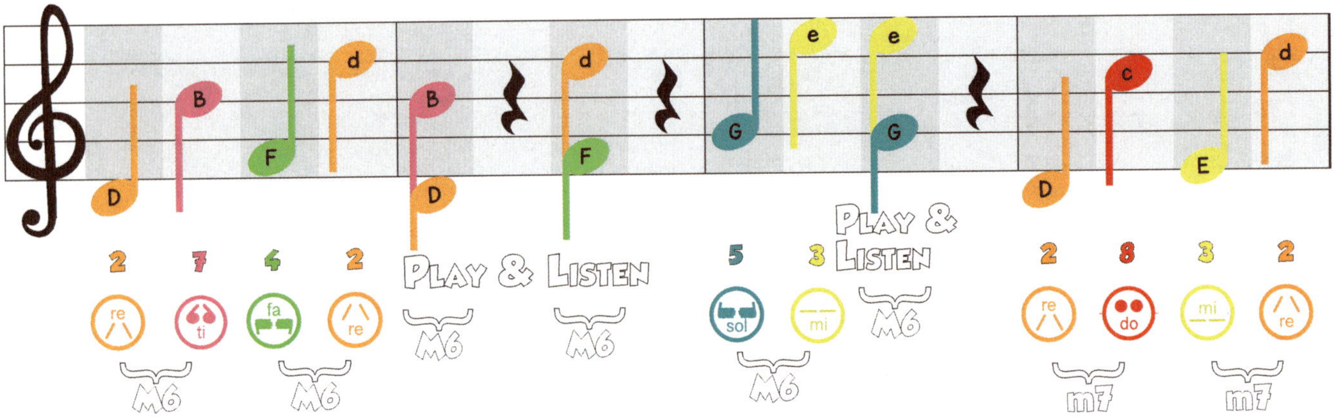

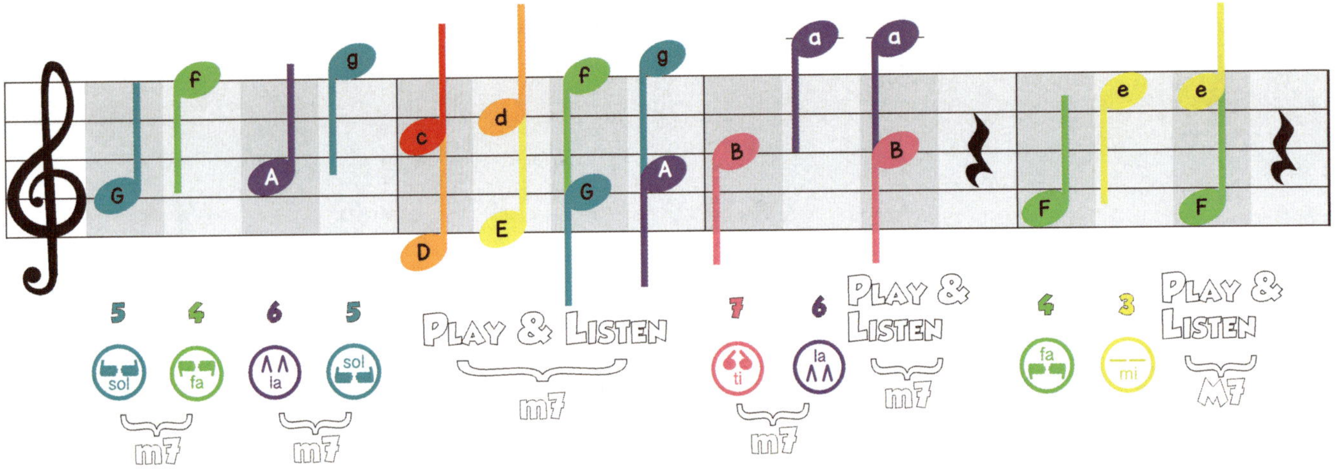

D B F d B D d F G e e G D c E d

2 7 4 2

re ti fa re

M6 M6

Play & Listen

M6 M6

5 3

sol mi

Play & Listen

M6

M6

2 8 3 2

re do mi re

m7 m7

G f A g c D d E f G g A B a a B F e e F

5 4 6 5

sol fa la sol

m7 m7

Play & Listen

m7

7 6

ti la

m7

Play & Listen

m7

4 3

fa mi

Play & Listen

M7

Answer Key

Congratulations on completing the **Interval Guided Composition** on **p.101**. Hopefully you made it without peeking! However you got to the end result, you'll enjoy playing this melody. These two measures would make a great **cadence** at the end of a song in the key of C.

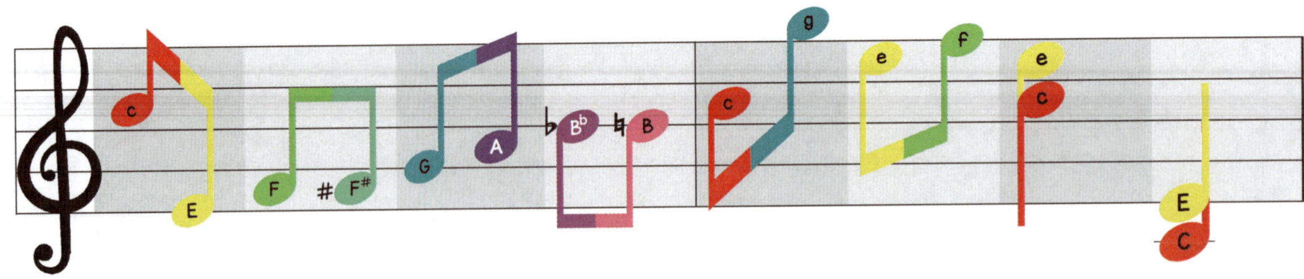

Made in the USA
Middletown, DE
17 July 2021

43882777R00069